Cooperative Learning through a Reflective Lens

Reflective Practice in Language Education
Series Editor: Thomas S. C. Farrell, Brock University

This series covers different issues related to reflective practice in language education and includes an introductory book which introduces these areas. The other books in the series clarify the different approaches that have been taken within reflective practice and outline current themes that have emerged in the research on various topics and methods of reflection that have occurred.

Published:

Reflective Practice in ELT
Thomas S. C. Farrell

Micro-Reflection on Classroom Communication: A FAB Framework
Hansun Zhang Waring and Sarah Chepkirui Creider

Reflecting on Leadership in Language Education
Edited by Andy Curtis

Forthcoming:

English Language Teacher Beliefs
Farahnaz Faez and Michael Karas

Exploring the Principles of Reflective Practice in ELT: Research and Perspectives from Turkey
Edited by Bahar Gün and Evrim Üstünlüoğlu

Language Teacher Identity and Reflective Practice
Zia Tajeddin

Reflective Practice in TESOL Service-Learning
Cynthia Macknish

Surviving the Induction Years of Language Teaching: The Importance of Reflective Practice
Thomas S. C. Farrell

Teachers Reflecting on Boredom in the Language Classroom
Mirosław Pawlak, Mariusz Kruk, and Joanna Zawodniak

The Reflective Cycle of the Teaching Practicum
Fiona Farr and Angela Farrell

Using Video to Support Teacher Reflection and Development in ELT
Laura Baecher, Steve Mann, and Cecilia Nobre

Cooperative Learning through a Reflective Lens

George M. Jacobs, Anita Lie, and Siti Mina Tamah

SHEFFIELD UK   BRISTOL CT

Published by Equinox Publishing Ltd.

UK: Office 415, The Workstation, 15 Paternoster Row, Sheffield, South Yorkshire S1 2BX
USA: ISD, 70 Enterprise Drive, Bristol, CT 06010

www.equinoxpub.com

First published 2022
© George M. Jacobs, Anita Lie, and Siti Mina Tamah 2022

British Library Cataloguing-in-Publication Data
A catalogue record for this book is available from the British Library.

ISBN-13 978 1 80050 225 3   (hardback)
         978 1 80050 226 0   (paperback)
         978 1 80050 227 7   (ePDF)
         978 1 80050 262 8   (ePub)

Library of Congress Cataloging-in-Publication Data

Names: Jacobs, George M., author. | Lie, Anita, author. | Tamah, Siti Mina,
    author.
Title: Cooperative learning through a reflective lens / George M. Jacobs,
    Anita Lie and Siti Mina Tamah.
Description: Bristol, CT : Equinox Publishing Ltd., 2022. | Series:
    Reflective Practice in Language Education / series editor, Thomas S. C.
    Farrell, Brock University | Includes bibliographical references and
    index. | Summary: "This book explores cooperative learning (CL) through
    the lens of reflective language teaching, delving into a wide range of
    issues on which teachers will want to reflect and suggesting ways that
    they could do that reflection. Example lessons bring to life the
    principles and practicalities discussed"-- Provided by publisher.
Identifiers: LCCN 2022014446 (print) | LCCN 2022014447 (ebook) | ISBN
    9781800502253 (Hardback) | ISBN 9781800502260 (Paperback) | ISBN
    9781800502277 (pdf) | ISBN 9781800502628 (epub)
Subjects: LCSH: Group work in education. | Reflective teaching. | Team
    learning approach in education. | Language and languages--Study and
    teaching.
Classification: LCC LB1032 .J36 2022 (print) | LCC LB1032 (ebook) | DDC
    371.3/6--dc23/eng/20220707
LC record available at https://lccn.loc.gov/2022014446
LC ebook record available at https://lccn.loc.gov/2022014447

Typeset by S.J.I. Services, New Delhi, India

Contents

Series Editor's Preface

The very first chapter of *Cooperative Learning through a Reflective Lens* by George M. Jacobs, Anita Lie, and Siti Mina Tamah asks: 'Is this book about language teaching or social studies teaching?' And, further: 'Will talking about rising ocean levels and starving children upset students who already face the anxiety of trying to learn a new language?' Indeed, the authors suggest that these questions go beyond the scope of their book, but posit that cooperative learning can help in at least two ways. First, it provides a forum for students to learn from and discuss with peers and teachers whether to take any action. Second, if students decide to take action, there is power in numbers. The 'Hurray for Cooperation' with which their Introduction begins shows the authors' true joy in writing this book; all three cooperated in different ways to produce a wonderful book that provides relevant details about cooperative learning that language teachers and students can reflect on.

The background on cooperative learning, including history, roots in cultural traditions, supporting theories, and research, is provided in Chapter 1. Chapter 2 outlines the eight principles that underlie cooperative learning: Positive interdependence; Individual accountability; Equal opportunity to participate; Maximum peer interactions; Group autonomy; Heterogeneous grouping; Teaching cooperative skills; Cooperation as a value. Chapter 3 details the nuts and bolts of cooperative learning with lots of practical advice on how students and teachers can implement cooperative learning, followed by the difficult issue in Chapter 4 of how to assess cooperative learning. The authors then link cooperative learning and teaching to reflective teaching as in the context of a student-centered paradigm in Chapter 5. Chapter 6 logically proceeds to outline and discuss how teachers can cooperate and reflect together as they facilitate cooperation among students in their lessons. Chapter 7 outlines five language lessons in which teachers encourage students to cooperate with their peers, and discusses how these lessons make use of the eight principles outlined in Chapter 2. The authors conclude their book with another 'Hurray for Cooperative Learning' but this time add the rest of the book's title: 'through a Reflective Lens,' which is very appropriate given the wealth of details readers will have read up to the conclusion.

Throughout *Cooperative Learning through a Reflective Lens* the reader gets a real sense of the vast knowledge and skills of each of these authors who have already written, as they say, at least seven other books on cooperative learning; however, they note that this book is 'the one we have enjoyed writing the most.' One of the main reasons they say they enjoyed writing their book was the reflective breaks that they put in each chapter; they hope, and I know, that you the reader will also enjoy reflecting on the excellent, short questions they pose at important junctures within each chapter. As they remark: 'For ourselves, we just can't survive without regular doses of Vitamin R (reflection).' This of course is the heart beat of the *Reflective Practice in Language Education* series in which the book is located.

Pre-service and in-service language teachers, language teacher educators, and teachers and teacher educators beyond language education will find the details about cooperative learning outlined and discussed in this book a very useful, engaging, and enlightening window into cooperation not only in the field of language education but in all walks of life. The authors end their book by urging readers to make cooperation and reflection foundations upon which to build both their teaching and their life. As the book concludes, 'Cooperation brings strength and kindness, and reflection brings insight and wisdom. Now, more than ever, teachers and everyone else can never have enough of those qualities.' *Cooperative Learning through a Reflective Lens* will certainly benefit all teachers and other education stakeholders to become (more) cooperative and reflective practitioners throughout their lives.

Thomas S. C. Farrell
Series Editor, *Reflective Practice in Language Education*

Introduction

Hurray for Cooperation!

In 1987, National Geographic produced a lesson plan titled *The world in a candy bar* (National Geographic Society Geography Education Program, 1987). In the lesson, students discovered all the different countries from which the candy bar's ingredients came – chocolate from Africa, coconut from Asia and the Pacific, and paper and milk (for the milk chocolate) from Canada and the US. This knowledge facilitated students' realization of how connected the world is, of how much cooperation takes place, even for something as seemingly simple and unnecessary as a candy bar. The number of geographic connections which contribute to the candy bar is dwarfed by the number of occupations involved in growing, harvesting, transporting, and processing the raw materials in the candy bar, not to mention the accountants, insurance providers, and food companies involved in manufacturing the bars and bringing them to stores. Plus, let us not forget the dentists who fix the teeth of those who eat too many candy bars, and the staff of the NGOs who campaign for the rights of the agricultural workers and the cows.

Candy bars provide just one of the myriad examples of cooperation's vital role in almost everything we do and everything else that touches our lives. Of course, teachers offer a fantastic example of how cooperation pervades our lives. Years ago, a bumper sticker read, 'If you can read this bumper sticker, thank a teacher.' We language teachers lay the foundation for so much that our students do in the years they are studying with us and afterward.

Reflective Break
1. Think of any activity, place, or product in your life, now or in the past. List at least ten occupations or individuals (including family or friends) who were involved in making it possible.
2. What about you? Are you part of any of the chains of cooperation that make things possible for others?
3. Can you think of anything in your life for which fewer than ten occupations or individuals were necessary?

All this cooperation in our lives does not always proceed smoothly. Cooperation stumbles for small and large reasons. Miscommunication may seem small, but it can lead to major problems. For example, someone can propose a meeting on Tuesday, but the people with whom they want to meet might hear Thursday or might think it is Tuesday of the following week. Cooperation can also fail when people put competition above cooperation and fairness. This occurs, for instance, when someone cheats in order to win in a sporting event instead of playing fair.

Other times, people want to cooperate, but they do not know how. An example would be when someone tries to teach someone else to use a piece of software, but their teaching only confuses the person they are trying to help. Cooperation can also fail when people lack the resources they need to cooperate, such as when more fortunate people want to help those without enough money to buy food and other vital materials, but the more fortunate ones lack the money to help more than a few times, and the less fortunate people cannot find work to sustain themselves and their families on an ongoing basis.

Two other causes of failure to cooperate are lack of trust and lack of awareness of commonality. Lack of trust can arise when people have had negative past experiences and cannot leave those experiences in the past and start with a clean slate. For example, someone promised to help you with a project, but did not appear at the appointed time. Lack of awareness of commonality takes place when people focus on differences they have with each other – different nationality, religion, ethnicity, etc. – and overlook their common interests, such as that people everywhere in the world being vaccinated against a virus makes it more likely that the virus's impact anywhere in the world will be lessened.

> **Reflective Break**
> 1. What is your experience with situations in which cooperation would help everyone, but for some reason people did not cooperate effectively? What were the causes of this failure to cooperate?
> 2. In such situations, what did you do or what could you have done to help cooperation succeed?

COOPERATIVE LEARNING

Cooperative learning constitutes a methodology in education that seeks to maximize the benefits of cooperation among teachers and others and to overcome the obstacles that impede cooperation. Many other education methodologies share characteristics with cooperative learning, including collaborative learning, problem-based learning, project-based learning, peer learning, peer-assisted learning, and peer instruction. The book you are currently reading seeks to examine how, when cooperative learning interacts with teacher reflection, the whole is greater than the sum of the parts.

This book's first chapter provides background on cooperative learning, including a brief history, as well as philosophical, theoretical, and research support. Chapter 2 explains eight principles that can underpin implementation of cooperative learning, while Chapter 3 discusses the nuts and bolts in the day-to-day implementation of cooperative learning. One implementation matter – assessment – receives special attention in Chapter 4. Chapter 5 does a deep dive into the paradigm shift to student-centered learning of which cooperative learning and reflection form significant parts. Chapter 6 examines reflection among teachers generally, as well as in regard to cooperative learning. Chapter 7 provides examples of language learning lessons using cooperative learning and reflection.

Reflective Break

1. What attracted you to read this book?
2. Had you heard of cooperative learning previously? If so, what are some of the things you heard?
3. When you were a student, at whatever level, did you learn in groups of two or more, in or out of class? Now, as a teacher, do you encourage your students to learn in groups?

Chapter 1

Background on Cooperative Learning

INTRODUCTION

The opening book in this series on teacher reflection by Farrell, *Reflective Practice in ELT*, provides readers with a detailed and up-to-date background on reflection by language teachers. Chapter 1 in the current book aims to provide readers with useful background on cooperative learning. The chapter begins with a history of cooperative learning, highlighting pioneers from the 1970s onwards, while acknowledging their predecessors from earlier in the same century and the 1800s, as well as much further in the past. Cooperative learning also has roots in cultural traditions, as is discussed next. One outstanding feature of cooperative learning is its support from a wide array of theories in both general education and language education. These theories are profiled next, followed by a brief review of some of the extensive research on cooperative learning that has been done and continues to be done.

A BRIEF HISTORY OF COOPERATIVE LEARNING

David and Roger Johnson, two brothers, are perhaps the best-known names in cooperative learning, together with Robert Slavin, and Yael and Shlomo Sharan. These scholars and their many collaborators have produced thousands of publications and done countless presentations, workshops, courses, and studies, which have enriched the literature on cooperative learning. Most importantly, millions of teachers have taken ideas from cooperative learning and, together with their students, fellow educators, and others, they have made the ideas their own and implemented them around the world in a plethora of subject areas including language learning. Johnson & Johnson (1989) prepared a concise, although Western-centric, history of cooperative learning which is paraphrased below.

Before referring to the Johnsons' history, which goes back to the ideas of Confucius and Socrates, it is the experience of the authors of this book that cooperative learning ideas are just common sense and resonate with many cultures. Thus, we often witness cases of 'great minds think alike.' For instance, we have introduced cooperative learning techniques such as Jigsaw (see Chapter 2) to teachers, only to have them tell us, 'I was already doing that; I just didn't know the name for it.' Thus, no doubt, we believe that cooperative learning has long had many unsung practitioners, including those students to whom it just seemed natural to help their peers.

Let's begin a more formal history of cooperative learning with Seneca, a Roman philosopher and writer in the 1st century AD. He advocated education practices which promoted friendship, humility, and helping others. His emphasis on interdependence, a concept to be discussed later in this chapter, is foundational to cooperative learning. In particular, the belief that 'When you teach, you learn twice' is attributed to Seneca and often repeated 2,000 years later by teachers who want to encourage higher-proficiency students to assist their lower-proficiency peers.

Jumping ahead from the 1st century AD to the middle of the next millennium and the Renaissance in Europe, Johan Amos Comenius, considered one of the parents of modern education, advocated many ideas still seen as progressive today, half a millennium later. These ideas for education include lifelong learning, equal opportunity for students regardless of sex and social class, avoidance of rote learning, the use of practical tasks, education as enjoyment not drudgery, and students learning together.

Great minds thinking alike but in different places seems to have occurred with Joseph Lancaster and Andrew Bell in the late 18th and early 19th centuries (Bell, 1823/2019). The story goes that Bell was acting as a chaplain for British soldiers in India and also as superintendent of a children's home. He witnessed some of the older children on a beach writing in the sand to teach language to younger children. From there was born a teaching method in which more advanced students taught their less advanced peers. Lancaster was doing something similar in the UK. However, as too often happens among humans, Lancaster and Bell found something to disagree about; as a result, their cooperation did not blossom. Later in the 19th century, Colonel Francis Parker trumpeted a form of cooperative learning as part of education for idealism, practicality, freedom, and democracy (Henson, 2003). Following Parker, John Dewey and William Heard Kilpatrick also emphasized democracy and service to society in their Project Method (Kilpatrick, 1918; Pecore, 2015) and overall philosophy of education (Dewey, 1916).

The Johnsons view the period from the 1930s to 1970s as a rather quiet one for cooperative learning, as it was a period dominated by teacher-centered instruction and extrinsic motivation. That began to change with an overall paradigm shift away from Behaviorist Psychology and toward Constructivist Psychology and related perspectives, including Information Processing Theory, Social Cognitivism, and Sociocultural Theory (Farrell & Jacobs, 2020). These will be discussed in more depth below, but for now suffice it to say that they all shared an emphasis on students being active and having more control, so that their intrinsic interests became more central to learning.

A key year in the history of cooperative learning was 1979 when the International Association for the Study of Cooperation in Education (IASCE) – https://jasce. jp/2130AboutIASCE.html – was founded. IASCE, a non-profit organization, went on to initiate a great deal of work on cooperative learning, including many publications, conferences with cooperative features (such as discussion among audience members during and after presentations), studies, and workshops, as well as helping to start national and regional affiliates, such as the Japan Association for the Study of Cooperation in Education. Cooperative learning has gone on to become a foundational part of education, such as in programs for pre-service and in-service teachers, in journals in a very wide range of areas of education, in mission statements of ministries of education and schools worldwide, and in the teachers' guides and similar addendums to textbooks and other education materials. Perhaps partly due to this success, in the 2010s, membership in IASCE started to dwindle, and the organization decided to dissolve itself in 2019.

Reflective Break
1. What year was the first time you heard of cooperative learning or related terms?
2. What was your first impression? It will be interesting to see if your current impression changes as you read and reflect on the contents of this book.

CULTURAL TRADITIONS AND COOPERATION

Before we examine the support cooperative learning receives from various theories and thousands of studies in education, let us look at the major role of cooperation in traditions from all over the world, starting with Indonesia, the home of two of the authors of this book. A key concept in the lives of many Indonesians is *gotong royong*. This can be translated as 'cooperation in a community,' 'communal helping of one another,' and 'mutual aid.' In nearby Singapore, home of the book's first author, people speak of the 'kampung spirit,' with a *kampung* being a village, where in the spirit of neighborliness, people share both their successes, such as a good harvest, and their burdens, such as when a child faces difficulties. The first author volunteers with an organization in Singapore known as Kampung Senang Charity and Education Foundation, *senang* meaning harmony, and *kampung senang* denoting a harmonious village in which people look out for and aid one another. Other languages express similar sentiments: *talkoot* (Finnish), *bayanihan* (Filipino), *harambee* (Kenyan), *imece* (Turkish), and *meitheal* (Irish).

On the other hand, in many cultures, some views push against cooperation. One of these views states that collaboration leads to weakness, to overdependence on others, and that the antidote for this weakness lies in promoting 'rugged individualism' (Bazzi, Fiszbein, & Gebresilasse, 2021). Some see individualism as a masculine quality, with collaboration being a feminine quality (Lamb, Pagán-Ortiz, & Bonilla, 2021). Another view that might decrease students' willingness to cooperate sees human nature as innately selfish (Debate.org, 2021). In other words, in this view, most people only want to receive help, but will not reciprocate that assistance. A third anti-cooperation perspective contradicts Dewey's belief that school should operate on democratic principles to help students learn the democratic arts. Instead, this anti-cooperation perspective argues that democracy weakens society (Forrest, 2019).

Reflective Break

1. What about your own culture and the cultures of your students? How do they promote cooperation?
2. What aspects in those same cultures might make students less accepting of cooperation? What might you do to increase students' acceptance of cooperation?

THEORIES SUPPORTING COOPERATIVE LEARNING

Many theories in both General Education as well as Second Language Education seem to support and inform the use of cooperative learning. Some of these theories are discussed below. Furthermore, as we educators in language education learn from our colleagues in other areas of education and in other areas of life, theories will overlap. For instance, in the opening volume of the present series on reflection in language education, Farrell (2019) notes that his view of reflection has been informed by the work of Kuhn (1970), who studied the history of science. The following two subsections examine some of these theories.

Theories from General Education

Sociocultural Theory

Sociocultural Theory sees learning as a process of people taking from the outside, internalizing it, and making it their own. What Vygotsky, the theory's founder, explained for children, is equally applicable regardless of people's age:

> Any function in the child's cultural development appears twice, or on two planes. First it appears on the social plane, and then on the psychological [i.e., the internal] plane. First it appears between people, as an interpsychological category, and then within the child as an intrapsychological category. (Vygotsky, 1981, p. 163)

Newman & Holzman (1993, p. 77) believed that, 'Vygotsky's strategy was essentially a cooperative learning strategy. He created heterogeneous groups of ... children (he called them a collective), providing them not only with the opportunity but the need for cooperation and joint activity by giving them tasks that were beyond the developmental level of some, if not all, of them.'

Two key concepts in Sociocultural Theory are the *Zone of Proximal Development (ZPD)* and *scaffolding*. The ZPD is one of three zones. To use layperson terms, the first zone is the Easy Peasy Zone. There, students can do tasks without assistance from teachers or peers, e.g., asking toddlers to crawl. On the other end of the spectrum of difficulty lies the Panic Zone, where, even with the assistance of teachers and peers, students are not ready to master tasks, e.g., asking toddlers to run. The ZPD lies in the middle as the Challenge Zone: not too easy, not too difficult, e.g., asking toddlers to walk while someone holds their hands. In the ZPD, through collaboration with teachers and/or peers, along with their own effort, students can learn to do tasks.

The second key concept in Sociocultural Theory is scaffolding (Wood, Bruner, & Ross, 1976). Scaffolding represents the help students receive from peers and teachers, such as holding toddlers' hands so they can walk, while they also use their own internal resources as they engage with tasks in the ZPD. Scaffolding gradually decreases as students' competence in a particular task increases, e.g., only holding one of a toddler's hands, or letting toddlers walk by themselves on playgrounds with rubbery surfaces. The end goal is that students become able to do tasks on their own. Scaffolding methods include dividing a task into smaller parts, demonstrating how to do a task while thinking aloud about what one is doing (Karlsson et al., 2018) or using visuals to illustrate, coaching someone while they do a task (not doing it for them), and asking questions that guide others to discover for themselves.

In typical teacher-fronted learning, teachers serve as the main, or even the only scaffolders. In contrast, with student-centered learning, students also scaffold for each other. As a result, cooperative learning provides a huge increase in the number of potential scaffolders, from one teacher scaffolding alone to many students doing scaffolding along with the teacher. Today, teaching benefits from many electronic devices that scaffold for students, including smart phones, tablets, projectors, and laptops. However, these pieces of scaffolding equipment all cost money, and the more we use them, the sooner they wear out and need to be replaced, not to mention the cost of the electricity to run the devices. In contrast, one piece of scaffolding 'equipment' does not wear out; in fact, the more use it receives, the stronger it becomes. That piece of equipment is the students' minds. Thus, Sociocultural Theory promotes cooperative learning (Lantolf, 2000; McCafferty, 2016), because in cooperative learning, students scaffold for each other, and learn in either case, whether they receive or provide scaffolding.

Reflective Break

1. Do you ever feel that an administrator where you teach has given you a task in your Panic Zone?
2. What are some ways that you scaffold for your students?
3. Are your students capable of scaffolding for each other? What could you do to increase their capability for scaffolding?

Humanistic Psychology

Maslow's (1970) Hierarchy of Needs is well known. It states that we humans have certain needs and, to be happy and to fulfil our potential, these needs should be met. We usually see the hierarchy presented as a pyramid, wide at the base and narrow at the top. Physiological needs, such as food and shelter, lie at the pyramid's base. Peers might be able to assist here. For instance, 'cooperative learning base groups are long-term, heterogeneous cooperative learning groups with stable membership whose primary responsibilities are to provide support, encouragement, and assistance to make academic progress and develop cognitively and socially in healthy ways as well as holding each other accountable for striving to learn' (Johnson & Johnson, 2009, p. 276). Base groups are less about what happens in the classroom and more about each member's life generally.

Then come Safety needs, including physical protection, such as protection from beatings, as well as psychological safety, including protection from cyber bullying. One of the authors of this book had a cyber bullying incident in a class he was teaching. A fake email was sent, supposedly from female students, accusing a male, who was a top student, of pathetically showing interest in them although they had no interest in him. Yes, the teacher intervened, but even better was intervention from peers. When students feel positively interdependent with each other, no one is alone; their groupmates have their back.

This peer support is also valuable in terms of the next set of needs: Belonging. Feeling alone, feeling that no one cares about you as a person or as a student, as in the case of a student who has no one to sit with in the school canteen, can be poisonous to learning. Cooperative learning provides a foundation for meeting students' belonging needs. For example, if someone misses class due to illness or a family emergency, group members notice and can help the affected person catch up. Even students who may be different from their classmates have a place of belonging in their group. For instance, one of the authors of this book had a student whom no one wanted as a partner. What the teacher did was to approach two of the more mature students in the class and ask them to be his partners.

Fourth from the base of the pyramid in Maslow's Hierarchy of Needs come Esteem needs which fall into two interrelated types: self-esteem and the esteem of others. Cooperative learning can assist in meeting these needs in at least two ways. First, students' levels of success increase when they collaborate; as the saying goes, 'Two heads are better than one.' Thus, students' chances of doing well academically increase, thereby raising their self-esteem. Second, when students learn and use cooperative skills, those skills include praising each other for what they do well, both in terms of helping their group succeed at the assigned tasks, as well as helping their group function more effectively, e.g., encouraging everyone to participate.

Self-actualization sits at the top of the hierarchy. This can be defined as students reaching their full potential, also known as, 'Be the best you' (Standage, Cumming, & Gillison, 2013). The other four levels in the pyramid provide the support that makes it much more likely that students will indeed develop their potential. Furthermore, when potential develops in a cooperative context, the goal lies not in individual fame and fortune, but as Dewey believed, in benefiting the wider society, i.e., in the spirit of positive interdependence. For instance, one ophthalmologist (eye doctor) we know did very well academically, went to medical school, has a successful practice, but also volunteers to travel a few times a year (in non-pandemic times) to poor countries to do eye surgery. In a similar vein, the 19th-century poet Ralph Waldo Emerson (as cited in Siu, 2021) wrote: 'The purpose of life is not to be happy. It is to be useful, to be honorable, to be compassionate, to have it make some difference that you have lived and lived well.'

Discussion of Humanistic Psychology in this book on language teaching should mention two other influences. Moskowitz's (1978) book, *Caring and sharing in the foreign language class* inspired many teachers to make learning a new language about much more than grammar and vocabulary, but also to connect to students' lives and emotions. Rogers (1979) worked as a psychologist and developed the 'client-centered approach.' Later, he translated that into education with 'person-centered education,' now more typically called student-centered or learner-centered, and cooperative learning features prominently in this approach to education.

Reflective Break

1. How did you first hear of Maslow's Hierarchy of Needs? What was your reaction?
2. How can teachers and peers help meet the esteem needs of students who do poorly in language learning?
3. Do you feel that you are meeting your own self-actualization needs? If so, how? What can you do to more fully meet those needs?

Behaviorism

Behaviorist Psychology is a very influential view in education and often associated with teacher-centered classrooms. In second language teaching, the Audiolingual Method, involving heavy use of speaking drills, was one that applied Behaviorism (Richards & Rodgers, 1986). Perhaps the most famous Behaviorist was Skinner (1953). He talked about universal laws of learning, i.e., that children, even babies, learn in the same ways as adults, and humans learn in the same ways as other animals. For instance, Skinner used principles of Behaviorism to teach pigeons to play a form of table tennis with their beaks.

Sutherland (2019) described how she applied the same Behaviorist principles to train her husband that she used to train captive animals for the amusement of humans. The key principle in Behaviorism is positive reinforcement, i.e., when the trainees do something the trainers want, they receive a reward. Sutherland recounted, 'I began thanking Scott [her husband] if he threw one dirty shirt into the hamper. If he threw in two, I'd kiss him.'

Another principle of Behaviorism that Sutherland used involves attempting to ignore behaviors which trainers do not want: 'Meanwhile, I would step over any soiled clothes on the floor without one sharp word, ... But as he basked in my appreciation, the piles became smaller.' In other words, Sutherland used the slogan, 'Catch them being good,' i.e., she ignored negative behaviors but was quick to praise positive behaviors. Not only does Behaviorism tell us to reward good behaviors, we should even reward approximations of good behaviors: 'I began to praise every small act every time: if he drove just a mile an hour slower, ...'

As can be seen, with Behaviorism, motivation comes from outside individuals: students are motivated by rewards from teachers: praise, better grades, stars. Although punishment can also be used, according to Behaviorism, incorrect actions are best ignored, as we saw in Sutherland's case. This is extrinsic motivation. A variant of extrinsic motivation uses a different form of positive reinforcement, known as vicarious reinforcement (Bandura, Ross, & Ross, 1963). Here, trainers publicly reward one trainee. The other trainees witness this (that is why it is called a 'public' reward), and the goal is that the witnesses will copy the rewarded trainee's behavior in hopes of also being rewarded.

One way that Behaviorism links with cooperative learning can be in the fact that in teacher-fronted contexts, teachers are the main people who have opportunities to reward students, as teachers talk most of the time, and even when students talk, they are usually addressing their teachers, not their peers. In contrast, when students learn in small groups of two or more, they play many more roles in addition to responding to teachers.

Thus, they have many more opportunities to give each other positive reinforcement for contributing to the group. Collins et al. (2020) conducted a meta-analysis of studies of positive reinforcement by peers and found it to have a beneficial impact on student behavior. This positive reinforcement can be even more powerful if it is not confined to simple praise, such as, 'Well done' and 'Good job.' Instead, praise should be specific and detailed, so that the people being praised know what exactly they did that was well done, thereby making it easier for them to repeat their positive behavior, e.g., 'I really like the way that you gave examples, because they helped me understand.'

A factor that makes education or, indeed, any activity involving humans, complex is that the same action can be understood from many perspectives. For example, praising students can be seen as an extrinsic motivator, as an instrument of external control, from a Behaviorist perspective. At the same time, positive reinforcement can be welcomed from other perspectives including Humanistic Psychology (see the relevant subsection), where praise can be seen as meeting people's need for respect from others. As is often observed, 'Life is complicated!'

Reflective Break

1. Like Sutherland, do you use Behaviorism-inspired tactics with your family members? If so, give an example.
2. Do you teach your students to use specific praise with their peers (and maybe even with you)?
3. Do you think that your students could use Behaviorist principles to train you to do what they want?

Social Interdependence Theory

Social Interdependence Theory (Johnson & Johnson, 2009) has its roots in social psychology, specifically in Field Theory (Lewin, 1951). In Field Theory, Lewin likened human behavior to that of magnets in a magnetic field, with three options for how the magnets could interact: (1) they could attract each other; (2) they could repel each other; or (3) they could have no impact on each other. The same, Lewin thought, applies to the interaction of humans, and to create a harmonious society, a harmonious world, we need to create conditions in which humans want to work together for the common good. Deutsch (1949) wrote about cooperation (equivalent to magnets attracting each other) versus competition (equivalent to magnets repelling each other).

Johnson & Johnson (2009) applied these ideas to education, changing the magnets into students, with three possible ways the students might view each other. But first, here is a quick refresher on correlation: positive, negative, and no correlation. When two things are positively correlated, they move in the same direction. When one increases, the other increases, and when one decreases, the other decreases. An example would be the amount of exercise and the number of calories burned. When we exercise more, we burn more calories (both the amount of exercise done and the number of calories burned go up), and when we exercise less, we burn fewer calories (exercise done goes down as does the number of calories burned). If students see their outcomes as positively correlated with those of their groupmates, they are said to feel positively interdependent with each other. For example, if groupmates help a member increase their understanding, all group members benefit.

Negative correlation works in the opposite way from positive correlation. When one increases, the other decreases, and vice versa. An example would be the speed at which someone walks and the amount of time it takes them to reach their destination. When our walking speed goes up, our time to destination goes down, and when our walking speed decreases, our time to destination increases. If students see their outcomes as negatively correlated with those of their groupmates, they are said to feel negatively interdependent with each other. For example, students might worry that helping their groupmates might lead their groupmates to outscore them on exams, e.g., Student A feels that if Student B's score goes up, Student A's class rank or esteem in the eyes of teachers or parents will go down.

Last but not least, no correlation describes the situation in which people's outcomes are uncorrelated. Whether or not one person's outcome improves or worsens has no impact on whether another's outcome improves or worsens. For example, how much water someone drinks is unlikely to impact how many games their favorite professional sports team wins. If students feel their outcomes are uncorrelated with those of their groupmates, they are said to feel no interdependence with each other. For example, if three groupmates (students #1, #2, and #3) have a fourth group member (#4) who is struggling with a reading task, and the three believe that they neither benefit nor suffer based on how well #4 does with the task, they may feel no desire to help. Similarly, if #1, #2, and #3 feel negatively interdependent with #4, they may even welcome #4's reading struggles and ignore #4's requests for help or their teacher's requests to help #4. In contrast, if the other three feel positively interdependent with #4, they are likely to assist their groupmate, and to rejoice if #4 makes improvement in reading skill and language proficiency.

Please note, the terms positive, negative, and no interdependence do not describe objective reality. Instead, the three terms describe students' subjective beliefs. In reality, the research on cooperative learning, to be reported later in this chapter, describes a world in which students objectively do benefit from cooperation with peers. Thus, a key goal for teachers in facilitating cooperative learning involves creating conditions in which students can see for themselves the benefits of student–student interaction, and they can become proficient at learning together.

As noted in the final paragraph of the subsection on Behaviorism, humans can be complex. Another example of this complexity can be seen with interdependence. People can feel more than one type of interdependence toward the same person. For example, Paul has a very successful sibling, Iris. Paul feels positively interdependent with Iris and is happy about Iris's successes and happy to help Iris to continue to succeed, as Iris's success benefits the entire family. At the same time, Paul might feel negatively interdependent toward Iris and might envy his sibling, because everyone is talking about Iris and ignoring Paul. Thus, Paul may feel that as Iris's success and the amount of attention she receives go up, the amount of attention he receives goes down.

Reflective Break
1. Can you give your own example of people feeling positively interdependent with others, such as the members of an orchestra?
2. Can you give your own example of people feeling negatively interdependent with others, such as competing businesses?
3. What do you feel is the dominant feeling among your students? Do they feel they are positively interdependent, negatively interdependent, or not interdependent with their fellow students? What is your evidence?

Constructivism

Constructivism, also known as Cognitivism, can best be understood by contrasting it with Behaviorism. Whereas Behaviorism focuses on the external, the behavior that can be seen, Constructivism focuses on the internal, what is going on in our minds. As you probably know or guessed, while Behaviorism links to teacher-centered learning and extrinsic motivation, Constructivism links to student-centered learning and intrinsic motivation. The term Constructivism derives from its central concept that people individually construct their own learning based on the interaction of, on one hand, their prior knowledge, interests, and abilities, and, on the other hand, what they take in from the outside, including from other people. Teachers and peers can scaffold that construction. (Please remember scaffolding from the subsection on Sociocultural Theory.)

In the 1970s, at least in academia, Constructivism replaced Behaviorism as the dominant view of what shapes human behavior. Gardner (1987), about whom we will hear more in the subsection on Individual Differences, wrote a book about cognitivism titled *The mind's new science*. In this century, with greater recognition of the role of the social, as highlighted throughout the present chapter, most people use terms such as social constructionism or social cognitivism. Furthermore, with the development of neuroscience's ability to show us exactly what is happening in our minds as we learn, a new field has blossomed: social cognitive neuroscience (Lieberman, 2010). In fact, Lieberman (2013) produced an enjoyable, example-filled TED Talk titled 'The social brain and its superpowers.'

Cognitive psychologists, including Wittrock (1974), Craik & Lockhart (1972), and Brown & Palincsar (2018), studied how people take in, process, and store information. The following metaphorical three-part model, termed the Information Processing Model, presents a simple version of what takes place in our minds.

Part 1 is called the Sensory Register. There, our five senses take in information from around us, with most of this information quickly being lost. The question is, what information will students focus on? Will they focus on the learning task before them or on a bird in a tree outside their classroom? With cooperative learning, students have one more reason to focus on their learning task: they are learning not just for themselves, but also for their group.

Part 2 is called the Working Memory. There, students use their existing knowledge to understand the information from the Sensory Register on which they decided to focus. For instance, in a class learning Chinese, in which they are reading a text in Chinese, their existing knowledge of Chinese allows them to understand the text. If they have insufficient existing knowledge, perhaps their groupmates can help.

Part 3 is the most exciting part of the Information Processing Model, as this is where the information goes into students' Long-Term Memory. This storage process takes place in two overlapping ways. First, by repetition, just as we might repeat a phone number to ourselves in order to help us remember it. However, this repetition need not be a form of rote learning. Instead, students can repeat the information with their groupmates, e.g., by taking the information in the text they read in Chinese and transferring it into a table or other graphic organizer. Second, they can use elaboration, e.g., giving examples, disagreeing, or adding more information. The key point here is that our minds do not store information in isolated pieces; instead, we store information in networks of related information. A slogan we will see in the Individual Differences subsection of this chapter is 'The more ways we teach, the more students we reach.' The extension to this slogan goes, 'The more ways we teach, the more students we reach and the more ways we reach each.' This slogan reminds learners and teachers to connect new information to many different networks in learners' minds.

This 'more ways we reach each' part connects with a famous concept from Cognitivism, Bloom's taxonomy of education objectives: cognitive domain (Bloom et al., 1956). Over the years, the taxonomy has been reinterpreted in various ways. However, the main point is that thinking in different ways increases the learning and use of new information. Students can work together to learn to ask and answer questions at each of the six levels of the taxonomy. The examples here refer to a famous soy-based food, tempeh, which is thought to have originated in Indonesia.

a. Knowledge – remembering information, e.g., What bean is usually used to make tempeh?

b. Comprehension – going deeper to show understanding, e.g., How does the fermentation process add to the nutritional value of tempeh?

c. Application – using the information, e.g., How could you use tempeh to replace meat in a popular dish?

d. Analysis – comparing or looking at the parts, e.g., How are tempeh and tofu similar and different?

e. Evaluation – assessing, e.g., Which is better, tempeh from soybeans or tempeh from chickpeas?

f. Creation – making something new, e.g., What other food can you ferment that has not been fermented? What would you call this new creation? How could you include it in a meal?

Reflective Break

1. What stands out for you in Lieberman's TED Talk?
2. For the Sensory Memory part of the learning process, what strategies do you use to encourage students to focus on what you believe are the important parts of the learning tasks?
3. One benefit of Bloom's taxonomy is that it encourages a wider range of thinking, as too often, students focus only on Knowledge questions. What about you? Do you and your students use questions from various parts of the taxonomy?

Critical Pedagogy

Critical Pedagogy is perhaps less of a theory about how to help students learn and more of a philosophy of what should be included in education. Paulo Freire (2000) was a leader in Critical Pedagogy. As a language teacher in Brazil during a time of dictatorship, he worked in literacy education, but he saw learning to read and write as also a part of civic education, i.e., students learned to read words in order to learn about and improve the world (Crookes, 2013; Shor, 1992). In this way, Freire echoed Dewey's ideas about how education should not serve individual benefit, e.g., someone getting a business degree only so that they may start the next Amazon or Facebook. Instead, when students learn about business or anything else, they consider how the application of their learning could benefit society generally. This resonates with the social goals of cooperative learning and positive interdependence with others, instead of individual goals, rugged individualism, and negative interdependence with others.

Freire argued that language is not neutral. Furthermore, language can change. We see this in many debates about usage in English and other languages. For example, if we use 'A doctor should care for his patients' and 'A nurse should care for her patients,' does that stereotype doctors as male and nurses as female? Does the use of *firemen* exclude females from that profession, while the use of *firefighters* makes it easier for females to enter that profession? Porreca (1984) found instances of sexism in ESL textbooks, involving not just language but also the different roles played by the sexes.

While Porreca's study was many years ago, issues of the intersection of language and society continue to abound. Examples include the language we use with non-human animals. Chau & Jacobs (2021) argued that the use of the relative pronoun *who* should not be restricted to humans. Marcus (2021) offered a guide to 'neopronouns,' i.e., a relatively new set of pronouns that do not express gender. What are students to do when learning a new language? Even native speakers may be walking into a minefield by using new forms of the language; how much more may learners of the language?

Auerbach & Burgess (1985), teaching in the US, talked about their use of critical pedagogy to help poor people overcome power imbalances, just as Freire had done in Brazil. Even if many students and their families do not suffer from poverty and other socially-induced ills, the internet offers large amounts of credible evidence that billions of other people do. For instance, undernutrition causes an estimated 3.1 million child deaths annually, that is, more than 8,000 daily (UNICEF, 2018). The overlapping factors of absence of sanitation facilities and clean water kill hundreds of thousands of children before they reach the age of five (World Health Organization, 2019). A United Nations estimate states that more than 50% of the world's population lacks access to safely managed sanitation (Harvey, 2020). Plus, the rapidly deepening climate crisis exacerbates all these problems.

But wait a minute, please. Is this book about language teaching or social studies teaching? Will talking about rising ocean levels and starving children upset students who already face the anxiety of trying to learn a new language? What about when students live in countries that take a dim view of citizen action generally and an even dimmer view of student action? Yes, the world faces many problems, but a great deal of progress has been made (Kristof, 2021). Should we celebrate instead of complaining? These questions and more confront teachers and students who want to do something about the problems described in the previous paragraph and others. Answering those questions goes beyond the scope of this book, but certainly cooperative learning can help in at least two ways. First, it provides a forum for students to learn from and discuss with peers and teachers whether to take any action. Second, if students decide to take action, there is power in numbers.

Reflective Break

1. Are you, family members, or friends involved in addressing any of the problems mentioned in this subsection; for example, by donating to help poor children?
2. Is your school or at least one of your colleagues involved in using the school to address social issues, such as world hunger? If not, why not? If so, could more be done?
3. How can you find time in your teaching for doing critical pedagogy?

Theories from Second Language Education

See Long (2017) for a much deeper and more nuanced look at some of the theories that impact second language education.

The Input Hypothesis

According to the Input Hypothesis, second language acquisition requires comprehensible input (Krashen & Terrell, 1983). Input consists of language that goes into our brains, either via our eyes (reading) or our ears (hearing), whereas output consists of language that goes out from our brains, either via our mouths (speaking) or our fingers (writing). The other part of comprehensible input, 'comprehensible' means that we can understand what we hear or read. Teachers of second language learners, and indeed all language learners, need to exercise caution; otherwise, the input students receive may not be comprehensible. From a Sociocultural Theory perspective, too much input that lacks comprehensibility could be considered outside students' ZPDs and in their Panic Zones.

How does the Input Hypothesis link with cooperative learning? Peers provide another source of comprehensible input in addition to input from teachers and course materials. For instance, in extensive reading (Extensive Reading Foundation, 2011), students do large quantities of reading of texts that are at their independent reading level, i.e., they can understand most of what they read without outside assistance. Nonetheless, peers can add to the quantity of comprehensible input in several ways:

a. They can recommend which books to read and which books to avoid, thereby increasing students' motivation to read and encouraging students to reflect on their reading choices.

b. Peers can assist each other in understanding what they read, e.g., understanding some of the context involved in a book from another time period or culture.

c. Often reading becomes more enjoyable when people have opportunities to reflect on and discuss what they are reading and have read, including their reactions and learnings. This discussion promotes thinking. As Freire (2000, cited in Crookes, 2013, p. 62) stated, 'Only dialogue, which requires critical thinking, is also capable of generating critical thinking. Without dialogue there is no communication and without communication there can be no true education.'

Despite the many potential advantages of comprehensible input from peers, concern does arise that the flaws implicit in students' current less-than-sterling version of the target language might lead to peers incorporating each other's errors. Krashen & Terrell (1983) did not seem concerned: 'our experience is that interlanguage [intermediate forms of the L2] does a great deal more good than harm, as long as it is not the only input the students are exposed to. It is comprehensible, it is communicative, and in many cases, for many students it contains examples of i+1 [language slightly above students' current level of competence]' (p. 97). Various studies have supported this view (Bruton & Samuda, 1980; Jacobs, 1989; Pica & Doughty, 1985; Porter, 1983).

Reflective Break
1. In your experience as a second language learner did you/do you ever encounter input that was/is not comprehensible?
2. Do your students do much extensive reading?
3. What is your reaction to the concern that students will pick up each others' errors?

The Interaction Hypothesis

The Interaction Hypothesis (Hatch, 1978; Long, 1983) follows from the Input Hypothesis and highlights the role of social interaction in increasing the amount of comprehensible input that students receive. The interaction includes both how people modify their language to make it more comprehensible to learners as well as what learners do to repair comprehension breakdowns. An example of modifying input to increase comprehensibility can be seen in the graded readers used in many extensive reading programs (Extensive Reading Foundation, n.d.). Graded readers are books, both fiction and non-fiction, intended for language learners. The term 'graded' means that the books are designated according to their level of difficulty. Some graded readers are modified from original works by simplifying the vocabulary and grammar, while others are specially created at a particular level, e.g., using only the 500 most common vocabulary items in the target language.

Learners can interact with others to increase the comprehensibility of the input they receive (Cho & Larke, 2010). Examples from spoken interaction include asking for repetition, for increased volume, for the spelling or definition of a word, and for time to use translation software. Such repair strategies form a common part of language learning curricula. However, students may be hesitant to admit their lack of understanding in front of the teacher and the entire class. Perhaps, such anxiety can be eased by the use of cooperative learning, as in groups of 2–4 members, students may be able to develop feelings of trust.

Cooperative learning also fits with the Interaction Hypothesis, as it provides students with multiple opportunities to interact. Information Gap tasks (Pica, Kang, & Sauro, 2006) facilitate this by creating situations in which students need to exchange information in order to close information gaps. For example, in a group of two, each student might need to write a paragraph, accompanied by a table, in which they compare their family with that of their partner on a number of variables, e.g., number of members, occupations, favorite foods and pastimes, and exciting stories. In this case, each person needs to provide information and understand the information provided by their partner.

Reflective Break
1. Have you ever taught with graded readers?
2. In your own life outside of your teaching, do you use repair strategies? If so, give an example.
3. What are some information gap tasks that your students do?

The Output Hypothesis

The Output Hypothesis (Swain, 2000) can be seen as complementing the Input and Interaction Hypotheses. It states that, yes, learners need comprehensible input, and interaction plays an important role by increasing the comprehensibility of input. However, learners need to supplement that comprehensible input by also producing comprehensible output, i.e., using the target language to speak and write in a way that others can understand. Cooperative learning serves this need admirably. For instance, in a class of 32 students in which teacher-centered interaction predominates, students have little opportunity to produce output and to see whether their output is comprehensible. Why? Because most of the time the teacher talks, and when the teacher provides an opportunity for student talk, that opportunity often goes to only one student at a time. Thus, in a 50-minute class, each student might produce less than one minute of output.

Let us contrast this situation with that of another 32-student class that uses cooperative learning. For example, the cooperative learning technique Write-Pair-Square is used, in which students begin by individually working alone to write in response to a prompt, e.g., 'What is one of your favorite memories of one of your grandparents or other older family member?' That is the Write step. For the Pair step, students form groups of two and share their written memory with their partner. For the Square step, two pairs combine to form a group of four (a square). In the foursomes, each student in turn shares their partner's story with the other pair, who ask questions and make comments. Obviously, in the same 50 minutes, due to cooperative learning, students produce much more output. [Note: In order to increase output time even further, students can do the Write step in Write-Pair-Square as homework.]

Reflective Break

1. In your own experience as a second language learner, what percentage of the time was input and what percentage was output? Did the percentage differ according to your stage of development in the language? For example, at early stages of language development, input might greatly exceed output.
2. Do your students have much opportunity outside class to produce output in the target language? What about inside class?
3. Did you notice that the Write-Pair-Square task involved information gaps?

INDIVIDUAL DIFFERENCES

The next two sections of this chapter do not involve theories or hypotheses, but they do address big-picture matters in language acquisition. The first of these big-picture concepts makes the point that everyone is different, and these differences can make important differences in learning. The concept of individual differences calls on students, teachers, and other curriculum developers to take into account the fact that a great deal of variety exists among any group of students, even if they share a common nationality, religion, age, ethnicity, and gender (Dörnyei, 2014; Robinson, 2002).

To illustrate the point about individual differences, let us review a story from more than 70 years ago about designing seats for pilots (Rose, 2016). Researchers measured 4,063 pilots on the 10 physical dimensions, such as sleeve length, thereby arriving at the dimensions of the 'average pilot.' Next, the researchers calculated the middle 30% of the range of values for each of the 10 dimensions. The result shocked everyone: not even one pilot was within the average range on all 10 dimensions. In other words, we are all unique!

We teachers need to understand something about these differences and take them into account in our teaching, because 'One size does not fit all' and 'The more ways we teach, the more learners we reach.' Just a short list of differences among students, in addition to those mentioned earlier in this section, includes: personality, such as extroversion/introversion; aptitude, such as aptitude for language acquisition; impulsivity/reflectivity, i.e., acting quickly in contrast to wanting time to consider; and intelligence profile. Next, we will examine two of these individual variables – extroversion/introversion and intelligence profile – in relation to cooperative learning.

It might be common sense to believe that extroverts would learn new languages more quickly and more effectively than introverts, as extroverts would produce more output and engage in more interaction (Ali & Shah, 2018). However, Jacobs (2017) questioned this view. First, it should be understood that the extroversion/introversion variable lies along a continuum, rather than being either/or. Thus, no one is 100% one or the other. Second, the meaning of introversion needs to be examined. Characteristics of introverts include a preference to have time alone, to be away from the center of attention, to interact in small groups including pairs, to take part in deeper conversations, to have time to think and write before speaking, and to ask rather than answer questions. Can these preferences be accommodated in language learning? Yes. Indeed, cooperative learning provides environments in which introverts can blossom, at the same time that cooperative learning offers extroverts much more opportunity to speak than does a typical teacher-centered environment.

Christison & Kennedy (1999) explored the role of Multiple Intelligences Theory (Gardner, 1993) in the learning of languages. Briefly, this theory optimistically says that many intelligences exist, everyone possesses all these intelligences to various degrees, and everyone can increase their intelligence in all areas. Gardner posits that at least eight intelligences exist. Students probably do better, try harder, and enjoy the learning experience more when tasks involve intelligences which they possess to a relatively greater degree. The intelligence that fits most obviously with cooperative learning is interpersonal intelligence, i.e., enjoying some time spent with others, caring about and seeking to understand others, and understanding how groups function.

At the same time, Cohen & Lotan (2014) advocated the use of tasks that involve a range of intelligences, toward the goal of lessening status hierarchies among students. Their thinking flowed as follows in the context of language learning. Students high in what Gardner called verbal/linguistic intelligence likely will excel in language class, where they will do well on assessments and, in the context of cooperative learning, be the ones often helping their peers for whom verbal/linguistic is not currently one of their stronger intelligences. Thus, a status hierarchy could result, in which some students hold higher status than others. To counter this status gap, group tasks could involve a number of intelligences, e.g., drawing (visual/spatial intelligence) could be used in language classes. This would give opportunities to shine to those group members relatively high in that intelligence, thereby making status hierarchies less likely.

LEARNER AUTONOMY

In student-centered language learning (Jacobs, Renandya, & Power, 2016; Sloan, 1992), students have freedom to make choices, and they have more control over what and how they learn. For instance, in extensive reading, students often choose what books to read, and if they are not enjoying a particular book, they can stop reading it and choose another. As Palmer (1998, p. 6) put it, 'I have no question that students who learn, not professors [or teachers] who perform, is what teaching is all about. Teachers possess the power to create conditions that can help students learn a great deal – or keep them from learning much at all. Teaching is the intentional act of creating those conditions.'

Student-centered teachers hope to create conditions that will encourage students to become lifelong learners, e.g., to continue reading, whether from print sources or online, for the rest of their lives. Along with choice, control, and lifelong learning, resilience is another frequently heard term in student-centered education. It emphasizes that failure, while inevitable, can be beneficial when students see it as a learning opportunity, i.e., as a way to strengthen themselves and peers for the hardships that life inevitably brings. Learner autonomy (Benson, 1997, 2013) encapsulates the attitudes and behaviors that student-centered curricula hope to develop.

The previous paragraphs do not seem to have much to do with cooperative learning. However, in reality, strong links do exist between learner autonomy and cooperative learning. Autonomy is about choice, and students would be wise, for all the reasons discussed in various sections of the current chapter, to choose to sometimes work with others and to be resilient and resourceful when groupmates' performance does not live up to expectations.

Furthermore, doing cooperative learning does not mean always working together; it does not mean students surrendering their own ideas and doing whatever groupmates say. As will be discussed in Chapter 2, individual accountability, i.e., everyone needs to do their fair share, constitutes an essential cooperative learning principle. Students often work alone before and after exchanging ideas with partners, and they often have individual roles in their groups. Additionally, disagreements among group members play a key role in helping groups make better choices.

Another point linking learner autonomy and cooperative learning involves from whom students seek to be autonomous. Usually, students try to move somewhat, but not completely, away from dependence on teachers. After all, learner autonomy promotes lifelong learning, and teachers do not follow their students for a lifetime. Fortunately, peers in education and elsewhere in life provide alternative support (Murphey & Jacobs, 2000). Peers together have much more power than an individual student standing alone. Therefore, student voices can be heard more clearly, and are more likely to be accorded respect, when groups of students speak in unison.

Reflective Break

1. What do you do to facilitate a student-centered environment among your students?
2. Do students seem receptive or do they prefer to depend on you? A minor example might be – if you offer your students opportunities to choose what to read or write about, do they choose, or are they more likely to say, 'Teacher – you choose for us'?
3. If you are currently teaching, do you and your colleagues exercise some autonomy from your institution's administration? If so, how?

COOPERATIVE LEARNING AND COLLABORATIVE LEARNING

As noted near the beginning of this chapter, we see a variety of terms used to describe the theme of this book. We have decided to use 'cooperative learning,' but we also like the other terms. 'Collaborative learning' may perhaps be the most popular of the other terms to describe students interacting to learn more, learn better, and enjoy the learning experience.

Table 1.1. Issues along student-centered and teacher-centered continua

Issue	Student-centered	Teacher-centered
The main perspective on how learning takes place	Knowledge construction – Teachers facilitate students' learning, as students work with groupmates to construct their own understandings	Knowledge transmission – Students work in groups to master what teachers/course materials have taught them
Who chooses what will be studied	Students can make some choices in areas such as what topics their groups study	Choices of topics to study are exclusively made by teachers
Who chooses materials	Students find, select, or create some of the learning materials for their group activities	Teachers and administrators find, select, or create all the learning materials for the group activities
The main type of motivation	Intrinsic motivation	Extrinsic motivation
Assessment of students	Assessment by teachers is supplemented by peer- and self-assessment	Assessment by teachers only
Number of students per group and which students work together	Students decide how many members will be in their group and who those members will be	Teachers decide on group size and membership
How group seating is arranged	Students decide	Teachers decide
How well students can work together	Trusting students to work together well	Explicit teaching of collaborative skills and teacher monitoring of the use of these skills
How student interaction will be structured	Students decide how they will interact with groupmates and other students	Teachers decide how students will work together, e.g., will each member take a turn to speak, will they first work in groups of two and then groups of four, etc.
Whether students will care about the learning of their groupmates	Trusting students to want to help each other	Social engineering to encourage students to care about their groupmates' success, e.g., rewarding groups based on how well each member does compared to their past performance, with all group members receiving the same reward

While some experts differentiate between cooperative learning and collaborative learning (Brody, 2009; Bruffee, 1993; Panitz, 1999), we prefer cooperative learning, because we feel comfortable with it, and because we feel it has a rich history. In Table 1.1, we attempt to explain what other educators mean when they differentiate collaborative learning from cooperative learning, and we do so in the spirit of Sever (2016) who cautioned that no two educators use the same definition for any term, just as in the famous story from India, none of the five people gave the same description of the elephant they encountered.

In short, some educators see collaborative learning as more student-centered than cooperative learning. Table 1.1 (adapted from Jacobs, 2015) explores this possible distinction via a number of continua. These continua offer students and teachers a range of options from which to choose.

To interpret the table, four points need highlighting:

a. To restate, the table is about continua, not dichotomies.

b. When classes use group activities, whether it is called collaborative learning or cooperative learning, the fact that students are in groups already orients them toward student-centeredness. For example, students seated together are likely to speak a larger percentage of the time compared to when teachers stand at the front of the class.

c. Teachers and students by necessity exercise flexibility. Yes, we all have preferences, but how anyone teaches or learns varies based on such variables as the policies of the institution and the overall cultures of the school where students are studying and the communities where they are living, and in any particular class, who are the other people in that class and what are their experiences, skills, and preferences. Sometimes these variables facilitate the characteristics in Column 2 of the table, sometimes not.

d. Well over a hundred diverse techniques have been self-described as cooperative learning techniques. Some of these techniques might be closer to the student-centered ends of the various continua in the table, while other cooperative learning techniques lie closer to teacher-centered ends.

Here is one cooperative learning technique, Circle of Speakers. After understanding the steps in in the technique, consider where the technique stands on the issues in the table. Also contrast the Circle of Speakers technique with typical teacher-fronted interaction.

Step 1 – Each student has a number, e.g., in a group of three, the numbers are 1, 2, and 3. Each person takes a turn to speak on the designated topic. These turns can continue going around in a circle for multiple rounds.

Step 2 – Students can ask questions, lend assistance, and make comments on what their groupmates have said.

Step 3 – The teacher calls a number, e.g., 1, 2, or 3. The group members with that number stand up and share not their own individual points, but their partners' points and/or points raised in their group discussion.

Circle of Speakers could be implemented in a rather teacher-centered way. Conversely, it could also be done in a more student-centered manner, e.g., students can participate in choosing the topic, and they can provide peer feedback and self feedback. Thus, as with any cooperative learning technique, its place along the continua in Table 1.1 can migrate based on the students and teachers who are using it.

Other self-described cooperative learning techniques, such as Group Investigation (see Chapter 8) seem to have student-centeredness built into their design.

RESEARCH ON COOPERATIVE LEARNING

A large body of research suggests that student–student interaction is associated with better results on a wide range of variables including achievement, thinking skills, interethnic relations, liking for school and teachers, and self-esteem (for reviews, see Bossert, 1988–1989; Cohen, 1994; Johnson, Johnson, & Stanne, 2000; McGroarty, 1989; Sharan, 1980; Slavin, 1995). Notice the dates of these research reports. The fact that these studies were reported more than 20 years ago suggests that there has long been a consensus among researchers in a wide variety of areas of education that cooperative learning can promote gains in both affective and cognitive variables. However, the key word here is 'can.' How to realize cooperative learning's potential, how to harness the social element in education, provides the focus of much of this book's other chapters, for we know that impressive research results and scholarly endorsements may convince ministries of education and individual schools and teachers to dip their toes in the water of various teaching methods, but what actually happens in classrooms may not always be so golden.

Research on cooperative learning continues. For example, a 2021 search on Google Scholar using 'cooperative learning research second language' as the search terms located many studies. Below are the first four that had sufficient bibliographic details. Latip-Panggaga (2021) studied the use of cooperative learning in the teaching of vocabulary and reading to Grade 6 students in the Philippines. Gardihewa (2021) looked at the possible impact of cooperative learning on engineering students in Sri Lanka. Karmina et al. (2021) investigated how teachers in Indonesia implemented cooperative learning in their various contexts. In the last of the four research reports, Arunsirot (2021) explored the use of cooperative learning in an English course at a Thai university.

Certainly, as the saying goes, 'The proof of the pudding is in the eating.' Long-term implementation of any methodology only takes place when teachers and students enjoy the sweet taste of success. Teacher reflection involving student input and reporting of results to students and other stakeholders constitute vital taste tests, because education needs to honor teacher wisdom, and evidence-based teacher reflection supplies a path for teachers to further develop that wisdom. We will revisit this in Chapter 5 on teacher reflection for cooperative learning.

For the authors of this book, yes, we have read many studies involving cooperative learning, including those listed in the first paragraph of this section, and we also know about the various theories supporting the use of cooperative learning. Nonetheless, what impresses us most, what sustains us most strongly in our drive to create environments in which our students can collaborate with peers, are our own life experiences, in and out of education. These experiences power our will to continue learning about student–student cooperation and how to enhance it. In our own lives, we have experienced the joy of human interaction and seen the benefits that it can bring. In addition to our own experiences, we have watched as people combined to perform plays; we have listened as the members of bands and their audiences have exalted in their musical creations, and we have savored the tastes produced in family kitchens as people created meals to be cherished by those close to them.

Reflective Break

1. Do you pay much attention to research that appears in academic publications or is presented at workshops or on the internet? If so, how do you access that research?
2. Are you familiar with ideas in education that have succeeded and become a regular part of teaching? What about ideas that failed to catch on? Why do some ideas sustain while others fail to thrive?
3. What is one happy collaboration experience that you have had outside of the education space?

CONCLUSION

This chapter has provided background on cooperative learning by talking about some of its history, theories in education and language learning which support the use of cooperative learning, as well as the large body of research on the use of cooperative learning. It has also dealt with the frequently asked question of whether cooperative learning differs from collaborative learning. Our view is that they do not differ. We hope this background facilitates your reflection on cooperation in your own life in and out of your career in education, as well as on whether cooperative learning syncs with your views on education. Chapter 2 will look at some of the elements that help cooperative learning succeed for students and teachers, in particular eight principles of cooperative learning.

Chapter 2

Eight Principles of Cooperative Learning

INTRODUCTION

This chapter centers on eight principles of cooperative learning. Different educators have different lists of cooperative learning principles. Probably these differences flow from a matter of emphasis. We are in no way competing with these esteemed educators. Our principles resulted from our reflections on our own experiences, and this book is designed, based on the template of the book by Farrell, the series editor, to enable you to develop your own principles. We want to stress that the various lists of cooperative learning principles are MUCH more similar to each other than different from each other, and there is no need to stress about the differences. Instead, we recommend that teachers focus on what works for their students in their particular contexts, in the midst of a world in which, as the saying goes, 'The only thing permanent is change.'

The list below contains eight cooperative learning principles highlighted in this book.

a. Positive interdependence
b. Individual accountability
c. Equal opportunity to participate
d. Maximum peer interactions
e. Group autonomy
f. Heterogeneous grouping
g. Teaching cooperative skills
h. Cooperation as a value.

POSITIVE INTERDEPENDENCE

As you will recall from Chapter 1, positive interdependence denotes the feeling among group members that their outcomes are positively correlated. In other words, they sink or swim together. Like the Three Musketeers in the 19th-century Dumas novel, groupmates believe in the spirit of 'One for all and all for one.' This, however, does not have to be a 'Till death do us part' kind of bond. According to one cooperative learning expert we spoke with, positive interdependence can be seen as a form of 'enlightened self-interest,' i.e., by helping others, we are *not* sacrificing our own well-being for that of others. Instead, we are being smart about how to help ourselves. For example, by helping the billions of people in the world without food, clean water, or sanitation, more fortunate people are actually helping themselves, too, because this empowers more people to play a fuller role in the world. Maybe the world's next great inventions in physical sciences, social sciences, and humanities will come from people who otherwise would have died in childhood from diseases of poverty, such as diarrhea and cholera, or whose brain development would have been permanently stunted by malnutrition. Students also benefit from helping others in more everyday settings, such as explaining ideas to their classmates. In the words of Seneca (see the history of cooperative learning in Chapter 1), 'Those who teach learn twice.' Therefore, while students help their groupmates learn, e.g., by giving them examples of concepts the class is learning, they are also deepening their own understanding.

Reflective Break
1. Had you heard of enlightened self-interest before? What do you think of the concept?
2. As a teacher, do you often experience 'Those who teach learn twice'?

Eight Types of Positive Interdependence

At least eight ways exist of promoting positive interdependence among students (Johnson, Johnson, & Holubec, 1994). These eight are goal, resource, role, environment, celebration/reward, fantasy, identity, and outside enemy. Any one cooperative learning activity can include multiple types of positive interdependence. Remember that the goal lies in students believing that their outcomes are positively correlated.

Below, each of the eight types of positive interdependence is explained with an example based on a cooperative learning technique. We begin with Jigsaw

(Aronson, 1978), a well-known cooperative learning technique. Jigsaw, developed in the US, has a history that spotlights the power of Social Interdependence Theory (see Chapter 1). Even though slavery was officially ended in the US in 1863, and Black children from that point had the right to an education, often it was a separate and inferior education. In the 1950s, separation of schools by race was made illegal. Nonetheless, even when children of different races attended the same school, they were only together in the classroom; in the cafeteria, in the playground, after school, etc. children of different races tended not to mix.

Jigsaw was developed to address this problem (see Aronson, 2021 for his own account), inspired by the work of another social psychologist, Allport (1954), a student of Lewin. Allport's team attempted to address ill-feeling among different races living in public housing in New York City. They developed the Contact Hypothesis which states that intergroup contact under a specific set of conditions can reduce ill-will among people from different social groups. Their 1954 study involved people of different races, but subsequently, the same ideas have been applied to many other intergroup situations. According to the Contact Hypothesis, to facilitate development of social harmony, three specific conditions need to be met: (1) everyone has a common goal, (2) they interact under conditions of equal status, and (3) their interactions have the approval and encouragement of the government or other official bodies.

Aronson and team developed Jigsaw to fulfill these three conditions. The four steps of Jigsaw involve the following. Note that Jigsaw can be modified, bearing in mind the principles explained in this chapter, as can every single one of the many cooperative learning techniques described in this book, as well as all the hundreds of other cooperative learning techniques not found in this book. Cooperative learning has no magic formulas. Therefore, you, your students, and your colleagues should not be shy to change any cooperative learning technique or even invent your own. It would also be productive to reflect on why you did or did not modify techniques.

Reflective Break

1. Do you ever modify what is stated in a Teachers' Guide or other curriculum document?
2. In the middle of a lesson, do you ever get an idea for making the lesson better?
3. Have you ever witnessed your students doing something the 'wrong' way and said to yourself, 'Hmm, maybe this is actually better.'

The Steps in Jigsaw

Step 1 – Students form groups of approximately four members, and everyone in each group has a number 1, 2, 3, or 4. These are their Home Groups. Home Groups are heterogeneous, such as with members of different nationalities or different proficiency levels. Each group member receives a different piece of the same text. For example, a text about Greta Thunberg, the climate activist, could be broken into four pieces: (a) her childhood before she became an activist, (b) her family and their reaction to her activism, (c) her early activism, and (d) her 2019 trip to North America. Students work alone to read their individual pieces.

Step 2 – Students leave their Home Groups to form temporary Expert Groups of approximately four members with students who have the same piece. If, for example, the class consists of 40 people, 40 divided by 4 equals 10; so, maybe there would be ten Home Groups of 4. When students form Expert Groups, one possible arrangement would be three Expert Groups for each of the four jigsaw pieces, with three Expert Groups of 2 members each, and one Expert Group of 4 members. The Expert Groups have two purposes. First, they need to check that everyone in the Expert Group understands their piece. Second, they need to make a plan for teaching their piece when they go back to their Home Group. What should *not* happen is that students return to their Home Groups and just read their piece aloud to others. That is not teaching. Peer teaching can be aided by such means as mind-maps and other visuals, examples of key concepts, and brief quizzes. To help experts to prepare, people could visit Expert Groups with the same piece of the jigsaw to compare notes on how to teach that piece. For instance, one person from each #4 Expert Group could visit another #4 Expert Group. Also, teachers could circulate among groups as well as assist in other ways, including checking that the pieces are not too difficult and preparing guide questions for the Expert Groups.

Step 3 – Students return to their Home Groups and take turns to teach their members. Time can be allotted for questions after each person teaches. Also, to avoid Home Groups finishing Step 3 in widely disparate amounts of time, each person can have a designated amount of time to teach their piece, and another person in their group can serve as timekeeper. In Step 2, students can be informed of this time limit, and they can rehearse their presentations with the time limit in mind.

Step 4 – Students individually take a quiz which requires knowledge of all four pieces.

Let us look again at Jigsaw, bearing in mind three conditions in the Contact Hypothesis. First, everyone has a common goal: to help themselves and their groupmates do well on the quiz in Step 4. Second, everyone has equal status during the peer interaction, as everyone has unique, valuable information. Third, teachers and the school generally are encouraging students to cooperate.

Reflective Break

1. Have you ever experienced Jigsaw as a student or teacher? If so, did you like it?
2. Does the Contact Hypothesis make sense to you? Have you ever begun working with people and felt uncomfortable, but as you worked together toward a common goal, and everyone contributed to the effort, you started to feel more comfortable, and maybe you even became friends?

Eight Types of Positive Interdependence as Seen in Jigsaw

Now, let us look at the eight types of positive interdependence explained earlier in this chapter and see how they are encouraged in the Jigsaw cooperative learning technique (Aronson, 2021). These types of positive interdependence are goal, resource, role, environmental, celebration/reward, identity, fantasy, and outside enemy.

1. Goal positive interdependence

Goal positive interdependence means that students share a goal. In Jigsaw, the goal lies in everyone doing well on the quiz in Step 4 of Jigsaw, the quiz that requires knowledge of all four parts of the text. Students should be aware of this goal when Jigsaw begins.

2. Resource positive interdependence

Resources can be divided into two types: knowledge/information and materials/equipment. It is not resource positive interdependence because all group members have resources, such as important information. It is only resource positive interdependence if each group member has *unique* resources. Each person must have unique resources, and they must need to share them for the group to succeed. In Jigsaw, we are talking about information resources. In the Greta Thunberg example, each Home Group member has unique information about one of four areas of her life, and everyone needs to learn all four pieces of that information for the quiz which is taken individually.

In addition to information, the other kind of resource for resource positive interdependence consists of equipment. A simple example of unique equipment resources would be different color pens, if, in groups of four, students' goal is to all contribute to the making of a mind-map, and the mind-map needs to have equal amounts of four different colors: black, blue, green, and brown. No one can accomplish the goal alone, because just as each group member has a different information resource about Greta Thunberg, here, each person has a different color pen.

> **Reflective Break**
> 1. In language teaching, in many common activities students have unique resources. For example, students often interview each other about their families, their opinions, etc. Do your students ever do such activities?
> 2. What kind of equipment do your students use? Could this ever be distributed so that each student has unique equipment?

3. Role positive interdependence

With role positive interdependence, everyone has unique roles that they need to perform in order for the group to succeed. These roles could be the same role which they all must do at different times. In Step 3 of Jigsaw, everyone needs to play the role of teacher in order that all group members can do well on the quiz in Step 4. While one group member acts in the traditional role of teacher, dispensing information, the other three play the traditional role of student, attempting to learn the information dispensed by the person in the teacher role. Of course, the teacher and student roles can be done in a student-centered mode, with teachers learning along with students, and students contributing to the learning, e.g., as each member has unique information about the same overall topic (in our example above, the topic was the life of Greta Thunberg), they might be able to contribute to a fuller understanding of their partners' pieces.

Many other roles can serve the success of cooperative learning groups. Here are ten examples.

a. Facilitator – helps the group stay on task and encourages everyone to participate

b. Questioner – asks questions to push group members to achieve more complete understanding

c. Example generator – encourages the group to develop examples of their ideas

d. Roster creator and checker – develops a roster of the tasks each person should do and the date by which they should do a particular task; and then, reminds people of their tasks

e. Tech whiz – assists group members with technical problems and suggests software and other tech tools that might increase the group's efficiency

f. Mental health advisor – reminds members of the need to take breaks in order to reduce harmful stress

g. Reflection ringmaster – reminds the group of the need for periodic reflection

h. Courteous conflict creator – in the words of a Russian proverb, 'an enemy will agree but a friend will argue'; thus, groups need someone who introduces differing opinions

i. Summarizer – summarizes what the group has discussed and done, with an emphasis on the positive, and suggests what should be done next

j. Praiser – praises group members for their contributions to the group.

A few overall points about roles should be noted. The person with a specific role is not the only person who can perform that role. For instance, the praiser is not the only person who can praise others; after all, someone should praise the praiser. Also, roles should rotate so that everyone can learn to do all the various roles. In the same spirit of promoting everyone's overall development, the person who is best in the group in a particular role should seldom do that role, instead they should guide others. For example, for the role of graphic designer, who uses IT tools or traditional tools, such as color pencils, to create graphics for the group, the best graphic artist in the group should act as guide on the side to help their groupmates develop their graphic design skills.

Reflective Break

1. So many roles need to take place for classrooms to function well. In a teacher-centered class who usually does those roles, such as the ten roles mentioned above?

2. In addition to the ten roles listed above, what other roles can students do?

4. Environment positive interdependence

Nowadays, everyone is justifiably very concerned about the damage we humans do every day to the environment, in particular how we accelerate the climate crisis. However, environment positive interdependence does not deal with this issue. It deals with how students are configured when they interact with each other. For instance, sometimes from the other side of the room we can identify a well-functioning group, because students are comfortably close together; their posture shows their interest in what group members do and say. Environment positive interdependence certainly comes into play in both the Home Groups and the Expert Groups in Jigsaw.

This kind of conducive environment facilitates interaction even when group members interact online. For example, virtual learning often takes place more effectively when everyone has their cameras on and their face is centered so that their facial expressions can be seen. In this setting, people can see if everyone is attentive, or if they seem bored. Similarly, having the sound at an optimal level facilitates communication. At the same time, research suggests that virtual learning environments may be more stressful (Bailenson, 2021); thus, caution may be warranted as to how long cameras should be turned on.

5. Celebration/Reward positive interdependence
Sports teams provide great examples of the sink or swim together nature of cooperative learning. Either the entire team wins or the entire team loses. It does not matter how close the score might be. In a basketball game, if one team wins 100–99, everyone on that team wins, even someone who scored 0 points, and everyone on the other team loses, even someone who scored 39 points. Moving this into the classroom, note that the presence of a celebration or a reward does not determine whether the activity promotes celebration/reward positive interdependence; only whether everyone in the group earns the right to the same celebration or the same reward. For example, in Jigsaw, grades sometimes motivate students to study, but on the quiz in Step 4, some Home Group members might receive a grade of A, while others might receive lower grades, even F. Thus, celebration/reward positive interdependence does not feature in the standard version of Jigsaw. (The important topic of assessment in cooperative learning is discussed in Chapter 4.)

Celebration/Reward positive interdependence previously was solely called Reward positive interdependence. We are not sure why 'celebration' was added, but probably to move away from a sole emphasis on extrinsic motivation. Indeed, grades often comprise the most common type of rewards in education. Celebrations seem less high-stakes than grades, and might fit better with internal measures of success. A well-used cooperative learning technique that does promote Celebration/Reward positive interdependence is Student Teams-Achievement Divisions (STAD) (Slavin, 1995). Briefly, in STAD, students are in heterogeneous groups of four (see the discussion of heterogeneous grouping later in this chapter) who study together in preparation for a quiz. The slightly tricky part of STAD is that students earn points for their group based on a comparison of their personal score on the current quiz with their past average quiz score. In this way, students are rewarded for improving and helping their groupmates improve. Groups *celebrate* when they receive certificates for improvement, or they celebrate by doing their self-designed team cheer.

Reflective Break
1. What is your view of the pros and cons of extrinsic and intrinsic motivation? How do you use the two in your teaching, as well as to motivate yourself?
2. Have your students ever used improvement scoring?

6. Identity positive interdependence

Identity plays a major role in many people's lives. Countries build a common identity among their citizens by such means as flags, anthems, popular foods, iconic buildings or places of natural beauty, and pledges. Sports teams have names, such as Tigers or Reds, fight songs, mascots, colors, and logos. Cooperative learning groups can also take advantage of these tools to promote the feeling of 'One for all and all for one' among their members. Examples we have seen include group names, handshakes, slogans, favorite songs, and logos.

7. Fantasy positive interdependence

Fantasy positive interdependence might seem to be the weirdest, most impractical kind. Students have to use their imaginations to pretend the group are all different people or a different species (maybe chickens), or the same people but in a different time (maybe one hundred years in the past or future), in a different place (maybe in a country on the other side of the world or in different climate zone), in a different culture (maybe a different social class, as in Mark Twain's *The Prince and the Pauper* in which a prince and a boy from a poor family change places), or in different walks of life (maybe being journalists instead of students). Such perspective-taking can expand students' horizons and give more meaning to their tasks.

8. Outside enemy positive interdependence

Cooperative learning and positive interdependence are supposed to be about working *with* other people; so, it might seem strange to hear about enemies in a type of positive interdependence. However, life can often be complicated, and positive and negative interdependence can both be felt in the same situation. For example, two female K-Pop bands in Korea might compete to be the most popular girl group. In that way, they might feel negatively interdependent with each other. At the same time, if one of the groups uses new dance steps, and fans seem impressed, that pushes the other band to try new dance moves.

Thus, this situation, in which improvement by one band leads to improvement by the other, could be seen as facilitating feelings of positive interdependence. In many societies, competition commonly serves as a tool for motivating businesses, sports teams, schools, students, and even teachers. In such situations, other people play the role of outside enemy, i.e., enemies who are outside of our group. However, as explained in the K-Pop example, competitors do not have to be enemies; we need not hate our 'enemies,' and we can enjoy a mutually beneficial relationship with our enemies.

Furthermore, outside enemies need not be people. For instance, standards can serve as outside enemies. A simple example would be if a class has a weekly reading quiz, and in a group, the average score so far this term is 72. The outside enemy becomes 72, and to 'beat' the outside enemy, the members of the group need to help each other raise their score so that the average this week exceeds 72. Maybe one group member's individual average stands at 62. That person can contribute to victory even if this week their individual score rises to only 68, still below 72. This is a bit similar to the improvement scoring used in STAD, discussed above in the point on celebration/reward positive interdependence. Other non-sentient enemies could be disease (everyone reminds each other to regularly wash their hands, drink water, and eat lots of fruit and veggies), rising greenhouse gas levels, or bullying in their school and online.

Reflective Break
1. Do you ever feel both negative interdependence and positive interdependence in the same situation?
2. What might be a non-human outside enemy which your students and you could attempt to defeat?

Eight Types of Positive Interdependence All in One Non-School Example

Many of the theories that support the use of cooperative learning have applications not just in education but in many other areas of life. For instance, in Chapter 1, we saw that one person used ideas from Behaviorism to change the behavior of their spouse. In an example of how using ideas outside education strengthens teachers' ability to facilitate the same concepts with their students, an elementary school principal told us that before teachers at their school used Positive Psychology (Seligman, 2012; Seligman & Csikszentmihaly, 2000), the teachers spent a year using Positive Psychology in their lives outside of school. This familiarized teachers with Positive Psychology and convinced them of its efficacy. Similarly, positive interdependence springs from Social Interdependence Theory, and people participate in groups in many parts of their lives. The following example shows eight types of positive interdependence in a teacher's life outside school.

Zahra and Hasan, a married couple, both teach secondary school in Surabaya, on the eastern side of Indonesia's island of Java. Zahra teaches Internet Technology and Hasan teaches English. They live with Zahra's parents, Isnita and Fuad. Zahra and Hasan are planning for an open house on the Indonesia Independence Day holiday on 17 August. Their *goal* is to delight the relatives, friends, and colleagues who will visit their house that day.

Hasan does very good calligraphy, and he has a special set of pens for that; thus, his *resources* are the pens (equipment) and knowledge of calligraphy (information), and his *role* will be to create an invitation card. Zahra is, not surprisingly, very good with IT, and she has an app with beautiful images; thus, her *resources* are the app (equipment) and knowledge of how to use it (information), and her *role* will be to add images to Hasan's invitation and to email or WhatsApp the card to the people they are inviting. Zahra and Hasan share a common *identity* as a married couple, and some photos of them together, from their wedding 20 years ago, as well as more recently, will be displayed at their home for the visitors to see.

For *outside enemy* positive interdependence, Zahra and Hasan remember the Independence Day gathering last year at a colleague's home, and they want to create an event at least as pleasant. Of course, food features prominently at such events, and Zahra and Hasan are especially proud of the small but powerful chillies they grow in their home garden, a photo of which adorns the invitation. *Environmental* positive interdependence will be in evidence as they work together in their garden tending to the chilli and other plants. As a *fantasy*, the two teachers imagine that some family members who passed away before Indonesian independence in 1945 are still alive and will visit their party, so that Zahra and Hasan can explain about Indonesia's progress since then, especially in education. Last but not least, for *celebration/reward* positive interdependence, the couple will rejoice at their guests' pleasure and compliments, as well as the pride that Zahra's parents display.

As a recap, listed in Table 2.1 are the ways the two teachers use eight types of positive interdependence to inspire themselves as they prepare for an open house at their home.

Table 2.1. Non-school examples of eight types of positive interdependence

Ways to promote positive interdependence	How Zahra and Hasan operationalized them
Goal	A successful Independence Day open house
Resource	Hasan: equipment – calligraphy pens, knowledge of how to do calligraphy; Zahra: equipment – an image app, knowledge of how to use the app
Role	Hasan: write the card; Zahra: add images and send the card
Identity	A couple who have been married more than 20 years, with photos showing highlights from those years
Outside enemy	A similar party held last year at another home
Environment	Working closely together in their garden
Fantasy	Family members who passed about 75+ years ago will attend in spirit
Celebration/Reward	The satisfaction and compliments of their guests, and the pride of Zahra's parents

INDIVIDUAL ACCOUNTABILITY

Individual accountability is the term used for a second cooperative learning principle. Whereas the previously discussed principle of positive interdependence aims to provide students with peer support, individual accountability aims to exert peer pressure on students to do their fair share in the group. Please note that the term is *fair* share, not equal share. In different contexts, different group members' fair share will differ and take different forms. For instance, in mathematics class, perhaps one student's mother works as a mathematician and enjoys spending time preparing that student for the next day's mathematics lesson. As a result, that student may be able to do more to empower their group to succeed in mathematics class.

The cooperative learning principle of individual accountability answers a frequently heard complaint about group activities: one or more group members try to be 'sleeping partners' and get others to do all the work for them. This situation is very unfortunate because not only do the others do all the work, they also do all the learning. The hard-working group members seldom appreciate their sleep partners' 'gift' of learning opportunities; instead, the hard workers get turned off to group activities and, thus, deprive themselves of future opportunities to reap the rewards that cooperative learning offers. By promoting individual accountability, teachers wise in the ways of cooperative learning contribute to students' collaborative experiences.

Fortunately, the cooperative learning literature offers a treasure trove of ideas for promoting individual accountability. Before we look at some of these ideas, it must be clearly stated that, as all teachers know from happy, sad, and somewhere in between experiences, nothing in education comes with guarantees. Sometimes, a lesson or technique can be a big success, but the same lesson with a similar class, or even the same technique with the same class can end up in need of emergency surgery to save the day. Teachers need a well-stocked toolkit of emergency fixes, and as you will see throughout this book, cooperative learning has a plethora of such tools.

Reflective Break

1. Do you ever have students who try to be sleeping partners? How do you and the other students respond to them? What about in your life outside of the classroom? Do you ever have colleagues or people in your home or elsewhere in your life who try to let others do the work? How do you respond?
2. Do you think that reflection (Farrell, 2019) could help students assess their contributions to the group?

Returning to the specific case of promoting individual accountability in cooperative learning activities, the following cooperative learning tools often help.

1. Roles

When each student has a different role, as in role positive interdependence, they all need to do that role, and each person has been designated that role, so that everyone knows what everyone else's role is and can see whether they are doing that role. An example would be the cooperative learning technique Jigsaw, explained earlier in this chapter. Everyone has the role of teacher in Step 3 of Jigsaw, and they have been given time and assistance to prepare for that role in Steps 1 and 2. Their fellow Home Group members are counting on them to perform their role so that the rest of the group will be prepared for the Step 4 quiz. Thus, the peer pressure should be felt on each person's shoulders.

2. Resources

Distributing unique resources or students bringing their own unique resources, as in resource positive interdependence, means that each student is the only one in their group with those resources. As a result, they need to use their resources in order for the group to succeed. Mind-Map-Pair-Square, described below, is a cooperative learning technique in which students create unique resources, in this case mind-maps.

Mind-Map-Pair-Square: A simple example of using resources to promote individual accountability can be seen in the cooperative learning technique Mind-Map-Pair-Square. The steps go like this in groups of 4 (squares) divided into pairs.

Step 1 – Everyone works alone to create a mind-map on a topic agreed by the class.

Step 2 – Students discuss their mind-map with the other person in their pair.

Step 3 – In their foursome (square), students take turns to tell the other pair about their partner's map and the discussion the two had about it. If one student has written nothing, what can their partner tell the other pair? Returning to resource positive interdependence, this can be promoted when the topic in Mind-Map-Pair-Square involves information which is likely unique to each person, such as writing about the oldest member in their extended family and their background.

3. Taking turns

Turn-taking provides another tool for facilitating individual accountability. Circle of Speakers, explained earlier, is a cooperative learning technique that uses turn-taking. Circle of Speakers can be done in groups of 2, 3, or 4. In a group of 3, for instance, everyone has a number: 1, 2, or 3. Starting with #1, everyone takes a turn to speak, and the turns can go around the group multiple times. The last step in Circle of Speakers is for someone at random to share with others what one of their partners has said. The point is that when it is one student's turn, either to speak or to share what a groupmate has spoken, the pressure falls on them to do the necessary.

4. Calling on group members at random

Too often when students study together as a group, teachers call on a group, not an individual, to report for their group. And, who answers for the group? Usually, the same person every time represents their group. What about individual account-ability in such situations? Sadly, students can easily hide, because they know that if the teacher calls their group, the star of the group will answer for them. What is the alternative? Instead, the group representative can be selected at random, thereby encouraging all group members to be ready and to help all the other members to be ready. Random selection was seen in Circle of Speakers in the above paragraph.

5. Positive interdependence

Before closing this discussion of individual accountability, we need to talk about what may be the most important way of encouraging students to do their fair share in their groups: positive interdependence. That's right – when students care about their groupmates, when they care about what their group wants to achieve (see the 8th cooperative learning principle – cooperation as a value, to be discussed below), no special tricks, such as the four mentioned earlier, e.g., turn-taking or calling on members at random, need be used.

> **Reflective Break**
> 1. Do you usually call on students as a group or on individual students at random? Why?
> 2. One problem we have is that even when we ask students to share a part-ner's ideas, students nonetheless share their own. How do you think we can improve this situation?

EQUAL OPPORTUNITY TO PARTICIPATE

The cooperative learning principle of individual accountability urges students to do their fair share in the group, while the principle of equal opportunity to participate provides students with chances to do that fair share. Why do we call this principle equal *opportunity* to participate instead of equal *participation*? Kumiko Fushino, an ESL teacher and teacher of ESL teachers, is the person behind this principle (Fushino & Jacobs, 2017). Dr Fushino correctly noted that in any situation, each person has different readiness to participate, and some may wish to listen, research, and consider before sharing. Nonetheless, even though these people may not participate immediately, they still retain their right (their opportunity) to participate when they feel ready. Thus, the principle of equal opportunity to participate seeks to counter the complaint that too often one or two members dominate their group, thereby depriving the group of the wisdom of the other group members and depriving those members of learning opportunities.

Below are ways to facilitate equal opportunity to participate. Note that the same tactics that contribute to individual accountability can also facilitate equal opportunity to participate.

1. Small groups

Some people believe that two members do not constitute a group. Wrong. In fact, groups of two possess important strengths. First, as David and Roger Johnson stated at a workshop that one of us attended, 'It's impossible to be left out of a pair.' In other words, each student has more opportunities to participate in a group of two because their partner has no one else with whom to interact. In contrast, the larger the group, the easier it becomes for someone to be left out of the group's interactions. A second benefit of twosomes lies in the fact that smaller groups are easier for students to manage.

On the negative side, with only two members per group, students have fewer minds to contribute ideas and information. 'Two heads are better than one,' and by the same logic, 'Four heads are better than two.' No worries. In cooperative learning, many times students can begin in a pair, and then pairs combine to form foursomes, such as in Write-Pair-Square. Thus, students enjoy the benefits of the smallest size of group, two, as well as the benefits of groups of four.

2. Talking Tokens

This technique calls students' attention to the need for everyone to have equal opportunities to participate. Here are the steps in Talking Tokens (Kader, 2013).

Step 1 – All group members begin with the same number of tokens, such as two or three. Tokens can be coins, poker chips, pieces of a discarded box, etc. The group decides on a discussion topic or they continue discussing their group's task.

Step 2 – Each time someone talks, they put one token into the center of the group. Once they have surrendered all their tokens that group member cannot talk, except to ask questions to those who still have tokens.

Step 3 – When no one has any tokens remaining, all the tokens are returned and the process begins again.

Usually, in Talking Tokens, it quickly becomes apparent who talks a lot and who talks much less frequently.

3. Multiple Ability Tasks

Multiple Ability Tasks (Cohen & Lotan, 2014) resonate with Multiple Intelligences Theory (Gardner, 1983), the idea that everyone is smart in different ways and that everyone can become smarter in all these various ways. Cohen and Lotan were concerned about status differences in classrooms, with these status differences leading to some students dominating their groups, i.e., depriving others of equal opportunity to participate. For instance, in language classes, those high in what Gardner called verbal/linguistic intelligence would be the ones dominating groups in those classes. How to address this disparity? Instead of using tasks based solely on language ability, use multiple ability tasks – for instance, ask students to do a skit based on a short story they have read or create a mind-map based on the short story. As a result, more students would have opportunities to be the stars of their groups and to participate more fully.

4. Writing instead of speaking

Yashima (2002) and Fushino (2010) talked about students' 'willingness to communicate' in a second language, one point being that some people are reluctant to produce output when they worry that their output will be error-laden. Writing, especially online asynchronous writing (people writing at different times, instead of everyone writing at the same time), may increase students' willingness to communicate, as writing affords more time to consider and correct one's output, especially with electronic tools, such as spell check and grammar check (Mancilla, Polat, & Akcay, 2017). Writing promotes thinking and can be done in so many different phases of the collaborative process, and peer feedback can also take place in writing. For example, journal writing, also known as diary writing, is a well-known language learning technique (Novariana, 2021), but normally, teachers act as the sole feedback providers. Instead of, or in addition to teachers, students can supply written feedback on their peers' journal entries.

5. Students' cultural and personality differences

Green et al. (2017) highlighted the role of culture in differentiating students in terms of their hesitancy or keenness to interact with others. Teachers need to be knowledgeable about the various cultural backgrounds of their students because, yes, cooperative learning can work regardless of culture, but how to facilitate cooperative learning might vary across cultures (Baker & Clark, 2010; Huber et al., 1992). At the same time, here, as with individual accountability, positive interdependence can play a role in facilitating equal opportunity to participate. Just as in the research that Aronson and colleagues did in the development of Jigsaw (e.g., Aronson & Bridgeman, 1979), working toward common goals (as in goal positive interdependence) can enable cooperation to succeed despite cultural differences. When students see their peers' contributions and learning as necessary to the overall success of the group, they become more willing to make sure that everyone has chances to share their valuable knowledge and perspectives.

Perhaps even more common than cultural differences among students are personality differences. With regard to the cooperative learning principle of equal opportunity to participate, a relevant area of variation in personality may be the extroversion-introversion continuum (Sadriyeva, 2021). For many years, the view in language learning and society generally seemed to be that extroverts performed better at learning new languages and at most other important activities in life. However, that view seems to be changing to a more balanced picture in which both extroverts and introverts bring valuable strengths to their own learning and that of their groupmates (Cain, Mone, & Moroz, 2016; Jacobs, 2017).

Reflective Break

1. Do some students ever dominate group or class discussion? Why do you think that happens?
2. What do you think about the distinction between equal participation and equal opportunity to participate?
3. Do you tend to be more of an extrovert or an introvert? How does that affect your learning and teaching?

MAXIMUM PEER INTERACTIONS

Peer interactions create the power that leads to the magic of cooperative learning. Yes, teachers remain very important, as are learning materials, including from the internet and apps, as is time alone for each student. Nonetheless, peer power sits on the throne as #1 for achieving the affective and cognitive gains associated with cooperative learning. How to maximize these gains? That is what we seek to accomplish with the cooperative learning principle of maximum peer interactions.

Maximum Quantity of Peer Interactions

'Maximum' has two meanings: maximum *quantity* of peer interactions, and maximum *quality* of peer interactions. Let us start with maximum quantity. The typical classroom tilts desperately to one side, to the side of teacher talk, with teachers talking 80% of the time and more. In all these years, after so many workshops and courses about student-centered pedagogy, our experience suggests that most teachers remain tied to their places at the front of the classroom, faithfully doing their best to follow in their own teachers' footsteps by being sages on stages, even though they know this may not be ideal. Furthermore, even when teachers are not talking, usually only one student is talking, the one student called upon by the teacher.

To categorize the patterns of peer interaction seen in classrooms, we can say that three major interaction patterns exist:

a.   Zero peer interactions – teachers are speaking
b.   One peer interaction – one student is speaking to the teacher and their classmates
c.   Maximum peer interactions – students are speaking to each other in groups.

To illustrate these three patterns at work in a class of 50 students: When the teacher speaks to the class, zero peer interactions are taking place (not counting the students communicating without the teacher's knowledge). When the teacher calls one student and that student speaks, 49 students are listening (or at least they are supposed to be listening) and one is speaking. Thus, we can say one peer interaction is taking place – that certainly is not the maximum quantity of peer interactions. However, both no peer interactions and one peer interactions have an important place in learning. Teachers can give mini-lectures (Au, 2020) to act as guides on the side, and when one student speaks to the rest of the class, everyone can learn from that one classmate and the feedback the teacher provides to that student. The point that we are making with the maximum quantity of peer interactions is that we need a much better balance of the three interaction patterns. Peer interactions are so valuable, they should be happening much of the time, not just once every Friday afternoon to reduce the boredom.

Now, let us look at that third interaction pattern, where students are speaking to each other in groups of 2, 3, or 4, or occasionally larger sizes. In our class of

50 students, in groups of two, we have 25 peer interactions, in threesomes, there are approximately 16 peer interactions, and in foursomes approximately 12 peer interactions: so much more than 0 or only 1. What else can we do to promote peer interactions? One idea looks at what we do at the end of the group activity. Let us say our 25 groups of two students each have been telling the other about the different books they have read as part of their extensive reading program (Renandya, Ivone, & Hidayati, 2021). What should happen next? In a typical class, a few students might be called by the teacher to share with the class about their partner's book. That has value, as it encourages all the pairs to speak clearly and listen carefully to each other, and maybe other students will want to read the same book that they heard about when one student was reporting to the class. Despite the benefits, one student talking to the teacher and classmates means only one peer interaction.

What could we do to maintain the maximum *quantity* of peer interactions? Instead of a few students one at a time reporting to the entire class, we could have pairs report to pairs. In that way, we could have 12 peer interactions simultaneously. And, of course, the internet offers so many more ways for multiple peer interactions. For instance, staying with extensive reading activities, for many, many years, movies have had movie trailers – short advertisements. Now, books have book trailers (Zhang & Xiong, 2020). Students can make book trailers for books they enjoy and share them online in safe places for classmates and others to view.

Maximum Quality of Peer Interactions

Even more important than the quantity of peer interactions is the *quality* of these interactions. Viewed from the perspective of Bloom's taxonomy (Bloom et al., 1956), we can categorize peer interactions into one of two categories: (1) do the interactions stay at the knowledge level in the taxonomy? or (2) do the peer interactions involve the other cognitive levels on the taxonomy: understanding, application, analysis, creating, and evaluating? This distinction is also known as the difference between lower-order thinking and higher-order thinking. Another way to understand the same two categories would be to ask whether or not the interactions go *beyond the information given* to students by teachers, learning materials, etc. (Bruner, 1973). For example, if a student asks a partner, 'When is the assignment due?' although the question is important, that probably constitutes lower-order thinking, because the teacher has probably already announced the assignment's due date, or the class has already decided. In contrast to asking about information that has already been given, if the same student asks their partner, 'How do you think I could make this paragraph clearer?' the response calls for higher-order thinking. Higher-order thinking, going beyond the information given, takes more work but here lies what makes cooperative learning special, where students scaffold for each other, where 1 + 1 = 3.

An African proverb captures the spirit of 1 + 1 = 3: 'If you want to go fast, go alone; if you want to go far, go together,' i.e., easy tasks can be done by one person, but challenging, important tasks often require many minds. The following two quotes from Nobel Prize-winners reflect the same idea.

a.   'Nothing new that is really interesting comes without collaboration' – *James Watson, co-discoverer of DNA*

b.   'The magic was what happened next [after one of the pair had shared an idea with the other]: the uncritical acceptance, the joining together of their minds. "I have the feeling that I initiate a lot, but the product is always out of my reach, ...".' – *Michael Lewis in* The Undoing Project *(2017, p. 470), describing the chemistry among the Nobel Prize-winning pair of Amos Tversky and Daniel Kahneman, with a quote from Kahneman*

Two other aspects of maximum quality of peer interactions involve using cooperative skills and doing reflection. We discuss these in other parts of this chapter and later in this book. While both involve higher-order thinking, we treat them separately, as they deserve extra attention.

Reflective Break
1. In your teaching, approximately what percentage of the time are each of the interaction patterns present:
    Zero peer interactions
    One peer interaction
    Maximum peer interactions?
2. Were you already familiar with Bloom's taxonomy and/or lower-order and higher-order thinking? Is it easy to facilitate higher-order thinking among students?
3. Do you enjoy higher-order thinking yourself?

HETEROGENEOUS GROUPING

When doing cooperative learning, a key question involves which students will be groupmates. In the cooperative learning literature, the usual answer lies in forming heterogeneous groups such that each group reflects the diversity of the overall class. To give a simple example – but life is almost never simple – if a class consists of 50% females and 50% males, each group of four members would have two females and two males. In the real world, achieving such exact mixtures in each group presents difficulties, as people differ in so many ways. For instance, people differ as to gender, race, religion, ethnicity, social class, nationality, past achievement, age, personality, other languages, multiple intelligences profile, and interests. With so many variables, we usually need to focus on only a small number of them when forming groups. One of the variables on which most teachers focus is past achievement, as having a wide range of past achievement levels in each group makes it more likely that students will be able to learn by helping others and receiving help from others.

One way to form heterogeneous groups is to list all the students in a class in order according to past achievement. (If at the beginning of the term, you have no data on their achievement level, wait a while to form ongoing groups.) After listing students in order of past achievement, use a second variable. For example, if you teach at a girls' school, and about half the students in your class are Ethnic Group A and the other half belong to Ethnic Group B, form groups with one student near the top as to past achievement, one near the bottom, and two from near the middle, exercising care to have two in each foursome from Group A and two from Group B.

One issue may be that as 'Birds of a feather [prefer to] flock together,' students may not feel comfortable in their new groups. Four ways to address this are given below.

1. Explain to students why heterogeneous grouping can be useful, e.g., (a) in most jobs and other life contexts, we cannot choose who we need to collaborate with; (b) society is heterogeneous, meaning that in a harmonious society, we need to get on well with anyone; (c) heterogeneity benefits us by providing different perspectives and resources.

2. Allow students to play a role in choosing their groupmates, provided that the groups indeed are heterogeneous.

3. Start new groups with relatively easy tasks so that students can become comfortable with their new groupmates.

4. When groups first form, spend time for everyone to learn everyone else's name. With 50+ students in a class, that can take time; in smaller classes, it can happen faster. The following ideas facilitate this process of learning each others' names.

   a. Students decide what name they would like to be called, e.g., some students have nicknames.

   b.   One idea is for everyone to say the name they like and one object, activity, or place they like, e.g., 'My name is Oksana and I like basketball.' This may help with remembering names because people can form a visual image, for instance, of Oksana playing basketball.

   c.   Teachers also learn students' names and use them.

   d.   Students develop the cooperative skill of using people's names when speaking with them. Russell (2014) quotes the famous self-help educator, Dale Carnegie, 'A person's name is to him or her the sweetest and most important sound in any language.'

Use team-building activities to create familiarity and trust among group members. One of our favorites is 'A Surprising Fact about Me.' It uses the procedure of the cooperative learning technique Think-Circle of Speakers, although all cooperative learning techniques are generic as to topic; in other words, we can use any cooperative learning technique with any content. First, students think alone to come up with a surprising fact about themselves, e.g., I volunteer at an animal shelter, my whole family goes bike-riding together on the weekend, or my favorite dessert is sliced mango with dark chocolate sauce. Students take turns, one by one, telling groupmates their surprising fact, and after each person has shared, the rest ask questions.

One of our favorite stories about seemingly incompatible groupmates was recounted to us by a teacher who had two students who told her they could not possibly work together and insisted that the teacher move them to other groups. The wise teacher responded, 'I'm happy to move you once you show me that you can work together.' Of course, once the two students were working together successfully, they did not want to move to other groups. This story demonstrates the power of positive interdependence. As Allport (see Chapter 1 above) and others have demonstrated, striving together to achieve common goals works wonders to create bonds.

Finally, it should be stated that, as with most other aspects of cooperative learning and other areas of good teaching, principled flexibility must prevail. Therefore, homogeneous, not heterogeneous, grouping may sometimes be the best choice. For example, if the class has decided to prepare presentations about the different countries represented among their classmates, perhaps the groups preparing those presentations should be homogeneous as to nationality. At the same time, the groups could be heterogeneous as to past achievement, e.g., there could be two groups of students from Mexico, each with a fairly even distribution of students according to their current level of language ability.

Reflective Break
1. What are some of the main variations among your students?
2. Would 'A Surprising Fact about Me' work with your students?
3. Do you ever have students who strongly resist working together?
4. Have you ever thought you would not be able to work with someone, but in the end, you jelled?

GROUP AUTONOMY

A big advantage of cooperative learning flows from the fact that it greatly expands students' support network. With groups, in addition to their *one* teacher, students can find support from their *many* fellow students. Sociocultural Theory, discussed in Chapter 1, says that this support, known as scaffolding, plays a crucial role in learning. Furthermore, as discussed earlier, students benefit by helping each other; thus, scaffolding for peers is a two-way street with everyone scaffolding for and learning with each other. Nevertheless, even though peer assistance is so readily available with cooperative learning, too often students have difficulty breaking their old habit of immediately turning to teachers the second complications, doubts, and concerns arise.

Yes, teachers usually do know best: they are the ones who have spent years learning about teaching and the relevant content knowledge. However, a big reason why cooperative learning has become so important lies in the fact that society needs people who can learn without teachers being there day and night to guide them; society needs lifelong learners, and lifelong learners need to know how to find and manage peer support. Cooperative learning prepares students to do that. The principle of group autonomy says that groups should try to rely on peers, not teachers, although teachers remain ready to help, but only as a last resort.

Two slogans capture the essence of group autonomy:

1. 3 B4 Me – When a student has questions or problems, they should first seek assistance from their three groupmates before (B4) going to the teacher (here 'Me' is the teacher, as this is the teacher speaking to the students).
2. 3 + 1 B4 T – '3' means a student's three groupmates, as in the previous slogan; '1' means one other group of students; 'T' is the teacher. When a student has questions or problems, they should first seek assistance from

their groupmates or another group before asking the teacher. In this way, students expand their support network beyond their small group. We will talk more about this in our discussion of the cooperative learning principle of cooperation as a value.

> **Reflective Break**
> 1. Do you have students who seem to turn to you right away at the first difficulty? How do you deal with that?
> 2. Who provides your own support network as a teacher? To whom do you turn in the face of difficulties?

TEACHING COOPERATIVE SKILLS

The cooperative learning principle of group autonomy facilitates students looking first to peers for help. However, many people feel uncomfortable asking for and giving help. In particular, helping others is not easy. After all, we teachers go to university for many years to learn to do it, and even after we have become teachers, we continue to study the art and science of teaching, going for courses and workshops, reading articles and websites, doing reflection and other types of research. Thus, we should expect students will need some help in teaching others. This is not to mention the difficulties of heterogeneous groups in which students need to collaborate with people from different backgrounds. On top of that is the skill needed in managing groups. Libraries are full of books written on that very valuable skill.

As a result of the difficulty in mastering the arts of cooperation, the cooperative learning principle of teaching cooperative skills should not be ignored. Sometimes, miracles do happen, and a class just seems to work together marvelously. Unfortunately, such happy circumstances seldom occur. Instead, students may benefit if they spend time learning cooperative skills. Fortunately, these skills are also language skills; thus, we feed two birds with one bowl when we teach cooperative skills in language class.

Many cooperative skills exist. We list 10 of these skills in Table 2.2.

Table 2.2. Ten cooperative skills

Cooperative skill	Explanation
Checking that others understand	Remember that in cooperative learning, no one's task is done until everyone in the group has learned the necessary information and skills.
Thanking others	This seems like something most people were taught in pre-school, but too often too many people miss too many opportunities to thank others.
Praising others	Similarly, praising others can make both parties feel better, and it makes it more likely that the praised person and those who hear the praise will repeat the praised action.
Disagreeing politely	Disagreement can spark thinking, but when disagreement is not done politely, it is more likely to spark ill-will, not thinking.
Asking for reasons	In the section above on the cooperative learning principle of maximum peer interactions, we discussed higher-order thinking. Asking for reasons provides a great tool for facilitating such thinking.
Providing reasons	Many cooperative skills come in pairs, e.g., Thanking others goes with Responding to thanks. Asking for reasons does not do much to improve group discussion unless groupmates respond by Providing reasons.
Summing up	At various points in a group's activities, it can be useful to summarize what the group has discussed and done so far and what might be done next.
Reminding about responsibilities	The cooperative learning principle of individual accountability encourages everyone to do their fair share for the group. This skill is about giving gentle nudges toward that goal.
Health checking	The pandemic has reminded everyone of how important health is. Showing concern for groupmates' health and encouraging them to practice behaviors that promote mental and physical health, e.g., drinking enough water and expressing gratitude, are important to successful groups.
Reflecting	It is easy for groups and individuals to forget to practice reflection. Thus, students need the skill of reminding people and organizing times to reflect (Farrell, 2019).

Cooperative skills overlap with language skills, which makes it especially important and especially convenient for students learning language to include cooperative skills in their curriculum. This can be done via the cooperative learning technique Tell/Paraphrase (disseminated by the former MAACIE [Mid-Atlantic Association for Cooperation in Education] in 1998) which works as follows with students in pairs.

Step 1 – One student makes a statement, such as 'The new bicycle path near my home is great. I like it because it is wide, and there are many trees nearby.'

Step 2 – Their partner tries to paraphrase what they said, e.g., 'There is a new place to ride bicycles close to where you live. Two good things about the place are that it has a lot of space and you can see a lot of trees while you ride your bike.'

Step 3 – The original speaker checks the paraphrase, for instance, maybe their partner misunderstood. Sometimes, misunderstandings are the listener's fault, but other times, they are the speaker's fault, because the speaker was not clear. Still other times, misunderstandings are no one's fault. If the paraphrase was not acceptable, the pair can try other communication strategies (Tarone, 1980) such as using drawings to clarify meaning.

Step 4 – Now, the two partners switch roles, and the person who spoke first now is the one who listens and paraphrases.

Tell/Paraphrase is actually a series of techniques for developing students' cooperative skills. Others include Tell/Ask for Repetition, Tell/Disagree Politely, Tell/Ask for Spelling. In the latter, students use the repair strategy (Tarone, 1980) of asking the people with whom they are speaking to spell words that students have trouble understanding. Repair strategies fit with the Interaction Hypothesis (Chapter 1) in which students interact with people in order to increase the amount of comprehensible input that they and their interlocutors (the people with whom they are communicating) receive.

> **Reflective Break**
> 1. Does your school put any emphasis on how students interact with other people: teachers, peers, and others?
> 2. If you had to choose one cooperative skill – listed in the table or not – and try to increase your students' use of that skill, which skill would you choose, and what would you do to encourage your students to use it more often?

COOPERATION AS A VALUE

We started this list of eight cooperative learning principles by discussing the principle of positive interdependence. We will end this list with a cooperative learning principle, cooperation as a value, that seeks to expand the feeling of positive interdependence beyond classroom groups of 2–4 members. To be clear, achieving well-functioning groups in just one classroom is by no means a minor achievement. That said, to achieve the vision of Dewey, Freire, the Johnsons, and others cited in Chapter 1, we need the feeling that our outcomes are positively correlated with those of others to blossom forth to embrace many, many others beyond small classroom groups. Do you remember the story at the beginning of Chapter 1 about all the people on all the continents who cooperate to bring us the candy bars we buy in stores? That is not to mention all the people who transport the ingredients and the bars, and who look after the health of all those people, and who educate those people's children and the people themselves as lifelong learners, and the police, military, firefighters, and civil defense workers who protect their countries.

The cooperative learning principle of cooperation as a value asks if we can learn a little about these people from all over the world and wish them well. Maybe we can start with a single classroom. Can we have common goals for all the groups in that single classroom? For example, maybe the class can have the goal that each group will create their own book, and then they can publish all those books in hard copy and online, and then have a class celebration to launch the books. That sounds like fun, and we will have so many more books for everyone to enjoy.

Then, how can we expand the feeling of positive interdependence beyond our single class to a single grade or a single school? Maybe we could have a healthy behaviors campaign, maybe to drink more water and fewer drinks with added sugar (Irwin et al., 2019). The campaign can begin with a survey to collect baseline data on the drinking habits of students, teachers, and others in the school community. Next, every class can do their own push to educate people about drinking healthier beverages, and students can each reflect on their habits and how these habits impact their own health and their learning. Finally, we can collect data again, and celebrate. Even if the numbers did not improve, we can be optimistic that they will – as more people will have learned about the issue, and that learning can, we hope, aid them throughout their lives.

Feeling positively interdependent with people we see every day may be easier than caring about people we have never met and probably will never meet, even people in other countries. However, it can be done. The United Nations tries to do this with its 17 SDGs (Sustainable Development Goals) (Al Amin & Greenwood, 2018). The goals (see https://sdgs.un.org/#goal_section) include very basic needs, such as everyone having food, clean water, sanitation, and education. What might your students do to help the world meet the SDGs and other worthy goals? That sounds like a good question for students to discuss, and cooperative learning principles can facilitate this discussion. To review the principles let us look at Table 2.3 which lists each principle, its meaning, and the role the principle could play in this discussion of working toward the SDGs or similar goals.

Table 2.3. Review of eight cooperative learning principles in light of Sustainable Development Goals

Principle	Meaning	Role in discussing the SDGs
Positive Interdependence	Everyone cares about the success of others.	The group can promote resource positive interdependence by each member investigating one of the SDGs.
Individual Accountability	Everyone does their fair share.	Each member needs to do a presentation suggesting what their group might do to advance the goal they investigated.
Equal Opportunity to Participate	Everyone can take part in the group's activities.	Everyone has 10 minutes for their presentation to the group plus 5 minutes Q&A by their groupmates.
Maximum Peer Interactions	Students frequently interact with peers and those discussions sometimes involve higher-order thinking.	When each group is deciding which SDG to work on, one group member can visit another group to share ideas. Groups need to explain their reasons for the SDG they chose and how to advance it.
Heterogeneous Grouping	Classroom groups mirror the diversity present in the classroom as a whole.	Having people from different backgrounds in a group provides more perspectives to help the group's decision-making.
Group Autonomy	Groups look first to their members for support, using teachers as the last option.	Each group needs to make their own decision; they cannot let the teacher decide for them.
Teaching Cooperative Skills	Students improve their ability to cooperate with others.	While discussing, students practice the cooperative skill of asking for reasons.
Cooperation as a Value	'All for one and one for all' expands beyond a single classroom group.	Students imagine how much better the world will be if all the SDGs are achieved.

CONCLUSION

Whereas Chapter 1 provided a big-picture view of cooperative learning, including history and background as to philosophy, theory, and research, Chapter 2 has dug into why cooperative learning can be worth using. The chapter explored eight principles that underlie effective peer interaction. What are your reflections? Do these principles resonate with your thinking on how learning best takes place to promote student growth in terms of cognitive, emotional, and social growth? Drilling down to an even more detailed level, Chapter 3 will examine the nuts and bolts – the practical issues – for students and teachers to consider when using cooperative learning.

Chapter 3

Nuts and Bolts of Cooperative Learning

INTRODUCTION

Some critics of cooperative learning maintain that only lazy teachers choose cooperative learning, because when students learn together in cohesive groups, the teacher can just sit back and relax; the students do all the work. Hahahaha. That only happens in our dreams! And, how do people think these imaginary students become such academic angels? How do they continue to spread their wings?

Actually, in some ways, cooperative learning and other forms of student-centered learning can be more complicated than teacher-centered instruction. When teacher talk dominates, as long as teachers have prepared their presentations (no simple task), the lesson seems under control; the show will go on. In contrast, with cooperative learning and other student-centered forms of learning, if the students just sit there as spectators in the teacher's show, the lesson has flopped; the show cannot go on. In student-centered learning, we teachers want to be 'Guides on the Side,' but if students do nothing, what is there for us to guide? Thus, we not only need to prepare our part of the show, we must also figure out how to facilitate environments that encourage students to actively engage with each other, with the content to be learned, discovered, and constructed, as well as with us, their teachers.

This third chapter highlights nuts-and-bolts matters related to cooperative learning. It raises questions for students and teachers to figure out together. Chapters 1 and 2 focused on more conceptual matters, while this chapter ponders practical issues that we deal with in our own teaching and that fellow teachers often ask cooperative learning practitioners about. No doubt, as you are reading and reflecting on this chapter during the Reflective Breaks and at other times, and while discussing with students and colleagues, more issues will arise.

SEATING

A fundamental question to answer when facilitating cooperative learning revolves around how students will sit or perhaps stand together. Classrooms and classroom furniture come in many varieties, not to mention that younger students sometimes sit on the floor, and at other times, students study virtually. Of course, low-income schools struggle with special problems, such as overcrowded classrooms, lack of furniture, etc. while classrooms in more fortunate schools provide students with the space, furniture, big screens, wifi, etc. to facilitate a wide range of classroom configurations. The above notwithstanding, the key point of this section on seating is that, while some setups make cooperation easier, cooperative learning can be done regardless of the available resources in terms of seating and related matters.

Harmer (2015) highlighted four seating arrangements: standard rows (Figure 3.1), circle (Figure 3.2), horseshoe (Figure 3.3), and small groups (Figure 3.4). The first three class settings seem to promote teacher-centeredness. However, as emphasized in the previous paragraph, cooperative learning and other student-centered learning strategies can function regardless.

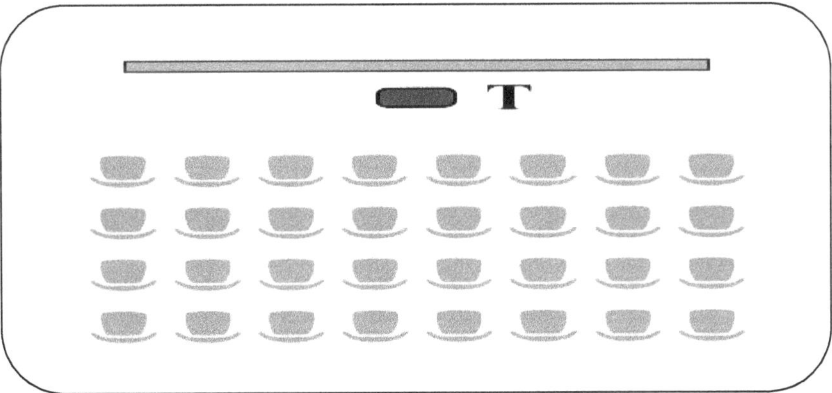

Figure 3.1. Standard rows seating

In our experience, standard rows as shown in Figure 3.1, is the most common seating arrangement, with varying numbers of rows and often with space between columns for teachers and others to walk around to observe and advise students. This seating arrangement can work well with students seated in pairs, e.g., Figure 3.1 has eight columns which can be grouped in pairs into four columns. Working in pairs fits well with the quantity aspect of the cooperative learning principle of maximum peer interactions, e.g., in a class of 50 students engaged in pairs, 25 peer interactions take place. These pair interactions could lead to the cooperative learning technique Write-Pair-Share, which works as follows:

Step 1 – Each student works alone to write.

Step 2 – Pairs compare ideas and give each other feedback. Students can change what they have written after this discussion.

Step 3 – One member of some of the pairs is randomly chosen to share with the class. This person shares their partner's ideas or the group discussion, rather than their own pre-discussion ideas.

Similarly, feedback on what the randomly chosen person says goes to the entire pair, not just to the person who speaks.

Groups of Four in a Standard-Rows Arrangement

While groups of two have advantages, larger groups, such as foursomes, also have their own advantages, because students can get more ideas from additional partners. Also, with larger groups, teachers have fewer groups to observe. In standard rows, to form foursomes, half the pairs can turn around to face the pair behind them. Thus, standard rows can work when cooperative learning takes place in groups of four, for example in the cooperative learning technique Write-Pair-Switch, a variation to Write-Pair-Square (Chapter 1). Here are the steps in Write-Pair-Switch:

Step 1 – Students work alone to write. Each member of the foursome has a number: #1, #2, #3, or #4. #1 and #2 sit in front of #3 and #4, with #3 behind #1 and #4 behind #2.

Step 2 – Students form pairs to discuss what they wrote.

Step 3 – Students switch partners. For example, if students #1 and #2 have formed a pair, and students #3 and #4 the other pair, now #1 turns around and forms a twosome with #3, and #2 turns around to form a pair with #4. The new partners share with each other the discussion they previously had with their original partners. One more step can be added to Write-Pair-Switch in which the pairs switch back, #1 and #2 turn around to face the front of the class again, and students tell their original partners about the discussion they had after switching partners.

The story behind how we learned about Write-Pair-Switch may be of interest. One of us had been teaching cooperative learning to a class of teachers. This was a once-a-week class over ten weeks, and after each class, over the week before the next class, we encouraged the teachers to try out the cooperative learning techniques and other ideas they had experienced during the just-concluded class. One week, we had experimented with Write-Pair-Square, and in the next class one of the teachers reported that one foursome of students had done the technique 'wrongly' – instead of staying with their partners, they had switched partners within the foursome, and each told their new partner about their first partner's ideas and the discussion that took place around them. Rather than chastising the students for not following directions, this teacher wisely looked for the good in what the students had done, and, in consultation with the students, found a great deal of good. We concurred, and 'Write-Pair-Switch' was born. In a smaller way, as Fleming accidentally discovered penicillin (Letek, 2020) and saved untold numbers of lives, this teacher accidentally discovered Write-Pair-Switch and enlivened untold numbers of classes. Of course, chances are that other classes in other schools and in other countries, or in workplace or community organizations, etc. had invented something very similar to Write-Pair-Switch many years or even centuries earlier.

When in the standard rows seating arrangement, half the class has turned around, after a while, the teacher may want to speak or lead a whole-class discussion. In such circumstances, the pairs who have turned around turn back to face the front, so as to more easily take part. Also, periodically, perhaps every other day, the pairs could change seats so that it is not always the same pair that needs to turn around.

Other Seating Arrangements

In addition to standard rows, other seating arrangements also lend themselves toward teacher-centered learning, although, as mentioned previously, they too can be adapted for cooperative learning and other student-centered arrangements.

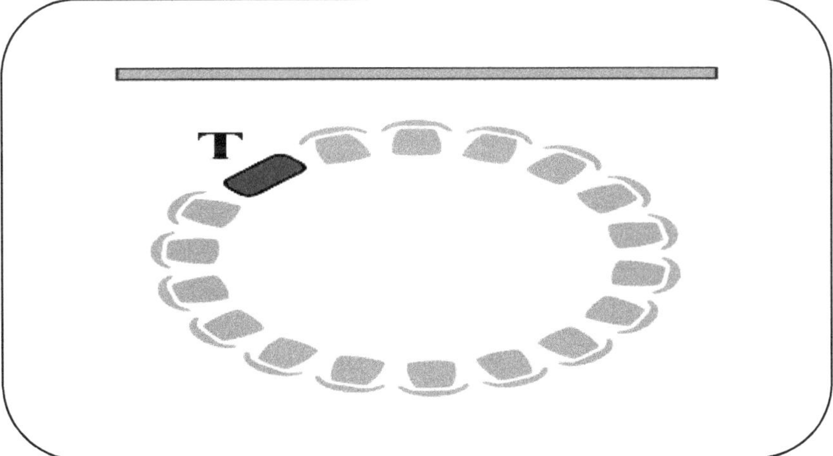

Figure 3.2. Circle class seating

The circle seating arrangement (Figure 3.2), similar to standard rows, naturally caters for whole-class or very large group discussions. However, as we saw with standard rows (Figure 3.1), small groups remain possible. Also, we must remember that using cooperative learning does not mean that students always interact in small groups; students can learn alone and cooperative learning also takes place when they study as a whole class or in other large group formats.

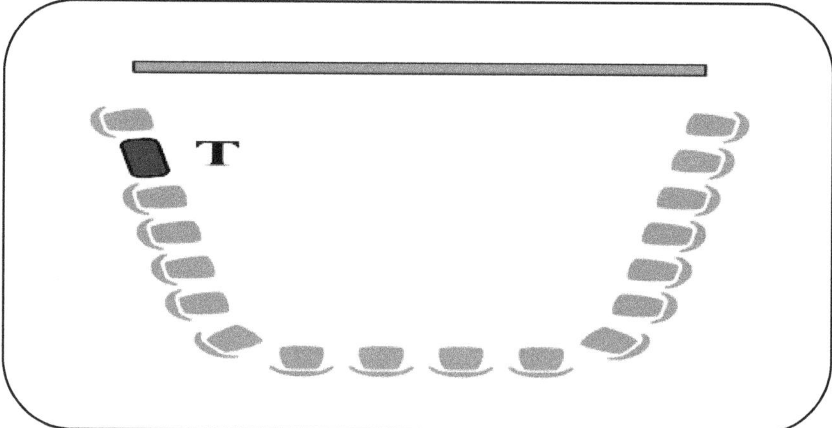

Figure 3.3. Horseshoe class seating

As with circles, the horseshoe arrangement (Figure 3.3), also known as semi-circle, provides for whole-class and large-group discussions in a more open atmosphere than the standard rows. Teachers hold less of a 'sage on a stage' position, and students can form small groups before and after teacher-led discussions. For example, the cooperative learning technique Group Investigation (see Chapter 7) could use circles and horseshoes in the whole-class discussion steps at the beginning and end of the technique.

Figure 3.4 presents one form of seating that promotes student-centeredness. Note that in this seating arrangement, at the same time students are seated in groups, they all have a clear view of the teacher and the whiteboard, projector screen, and whatever else is at the front of the class. However, the two people at the ends of each group are fairly far from each other, making it a little difficult to see each other's work and to hear each other without speaking at a volume that might disturb other groups.

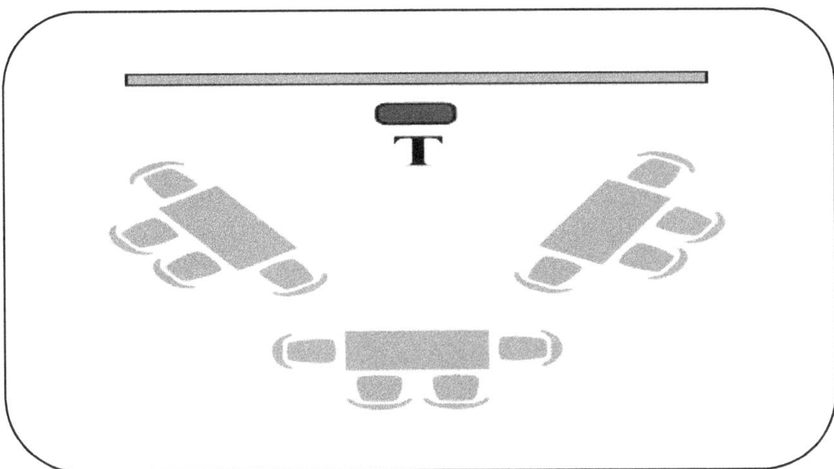

Figure 3.4. Small group seating

Figure 3.5 illustrates small-group seating in a more student-centered setting where teachers are not the center of attention. Here, teachers have surrendered the grand stage and their role as classroom royalty (Tamah & Priyambodo, 2015), and are now together with their people – the students. McCaughey (2018) labelled this arrangement a 'moveable class' design. The class is filled with mushrooms of small groups of students who spend most of their time in their groups while the teacher moves from one group to another to offer assistance when needed.

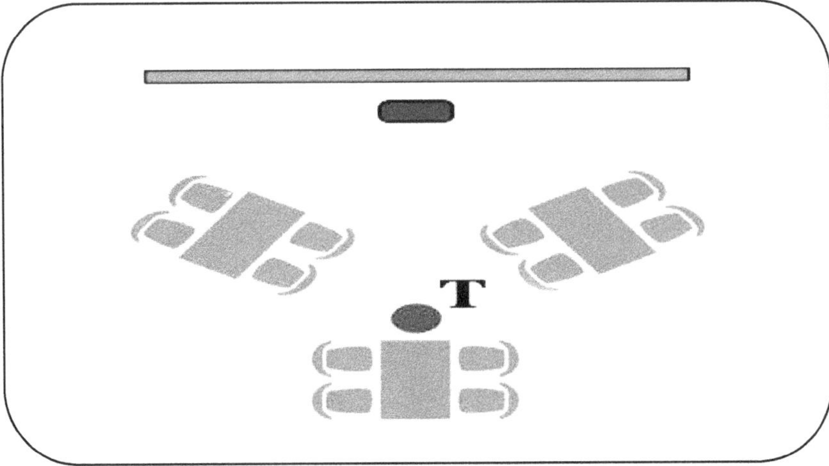

Figure 3.5. Student-centered class seating

Being Accustomed to Being on the Move

In teacher-centered instruction, students are often in the same seat the entire class or even the entire day. This stationary situation can also occur in cooperative learning; however, when students learn in cooperative groups as part of a cooperative classroom, they may need to accustom themselves to being on the move, within their own group as well as between groups. Examples of cooperative learning techniques that involve intergroup movement are 7S, Friendly Spy, and Everyone Can Explain Mobile, to be explained later in this chapter. Also, from Chapter 2, recall 3 + 1 B4 T, which flows from the cooperative learning principle of group autonomy. In 3 + 1 B4 T, when students have questions – either of the 'I don't understand' variety or of the 'I'd like to know more' kind – they are encouraged to consult first with members of their own group (3) and then with another group (1) before seeking teacher (T) assistance. Looking for and extending assistance beyond one's own group also fits with the cooperative learning principle of cooperation as a value, which seeks to expand students' feeling of positive interdependence beyond their small classroom group. Also, movement within the classroom adds variety to learning and encourages students to be lifelong, self-directed learners – able to seek resources – which also helps them prepare themselves for many careers (Lemmetty & Collin, 2020). Students need to rely on, believe in, and develop their capabilities for learning cooperatively with peers. Of course, enabled by online communication, students can also turn to others beyond their class to collaborate, as in the spirit of Communities of Learners (Ghosh, 2021; Rogoff, Matusov, & White, 1996).

In order for students to rely more on each other and less on teachers, teachers themselves need the willingness to leave not just their grand stage at the front of the classroom. Teachers, even when not at the front of the class, can still dominate, quickly intervening whenever students have questions, encounter difficulties, or seek feedback on their work. Too often, students have been trained to look to their teachers. After all, we teachers are the experts; we are the ones with the degree or degrees. Plus, students only need to raise their hands and, faster than a food delivery driver, teachers speed to their assistance. In Singapore, many students call their teachers 'cher,' short for 'teacher, and need not even raise their hands; all that is required is to open their mouths and chirp 'cher, cher' and help quickly arrives. No need for students to rise from their seats and seek out peer assistance.

For example, when we teachers visit groups to observe their interactions, the interaction pattern too easily shifts (Pennings et al., 2018), and soon, instead of talking to each other, students are talking to us. We have become the center of attention, almost as though we were back at the front of the class, except with fewer students. How to reduce the chances of this happening? One idea is to stand between two groups so that we can toggle our attention between them, and we do not seem too attached to any one group. Another idea involves recommending that students visit particular other groups, e.g., if we witness that one group has done something well, we can send other groups to them for help.

Reflective Break

1. Do you sometimes observe students when they are working in groups? How do you avoid becoming the center of attention?
2. How do you feel about giving up your place as the focus of the classroom? Do you feel as though you are not doing your job? Do you feel bored, as your main job has been taken away from you?

AVOIDING CONFUSION OVER COOPERATIVE LEARNING TECHNIQUES

So far in this book, in Chapter 1 which introduced cooperative learning and Chapter 2 which explained cooperative learning principles, we have used a variety of components of cooperative learning techniques: Think, Write, Draw, Mind-Map, Pair, Share, Square, and Switch. Other chapters contain other components, including Stand, Stir, Sip, and Explain. Without a doubt, students and teachers can create more components. Furthermore, the order of components can also be manipulated, but always based on reflection about what might help students learn better and enjoy more. For example, alongside Write-Pair-Square, we could create Write-Pair-Square-Journal, in order for students to reflect in journal entries about what they experienced, learned, and wanted to learn more about as they did Write-Pair-Square.

With all the many cooperative learning techniques, not to mention all the components that can be mixed, matched, and invented, students can easily be confused about what to do. Here are some means of reducing confusion:

a. Use the same cooperative learning technique multiple times rather than changing techniques with every activity. Some teachers might feel that frequently switching techniques adds variety, thereby reducing the chances of students becoming bored with cooperative learning. However, using interesting content, providing students with choice as to that content, experimenting with different types of thinking, e.g., giving examples, disagreeing politely, providing negative examples, playing with hypothetical thinking, and seeking to inject humor, may be more effective ways to vary cooperative learning.

b.   Provide steps in a cooperative learning technique in writing for students to refer or ask one student per class or per group to repeat the steps.

c.   Allow for variation in how a cooperative learning technique is done. Remember the invention of Write-Pair-Switch.

d.   Ask one group to demonstrate for the rest of the class or to make a video demonstration.

TARGET LANGUAGE USE

Among the more controversial issues in language teaching are those that revolve around the role of students' various language(s) in the classroom. Complications also arise over the question of which variety(ies) of the target language should be used in both learning and assessment (Rakab, 2021; Smidt et al., 2021). Rather than debating these issues in the pages of this book, in the spirit of cooperative learning being a way to increase student decision-making and to model democratic discussion and execution of decisions, we prefer to encourage classes to consider the various options, formulate policies, try out those policies, and periodically evaluate and reconsider their own choices. Indeed, language issues provide fertile ground for reflection on such topics as students' history of language use, how language and identity overlap, and goals for future language use. Furthermore, this reflection must be based not on off-the-top-of-my-head thinking but on reflection about and a deepening understanding of each student's past, present, and future contexts, because certainly, one size does not fit all.

Members of cooperative learning groups often have roles, and language monitor can be one of those roles, gently nudging groupmates to adhere to the policy decided by the group/class. Periodically, each group can engage in group, peer, and self feedback on their language policy and its use, remembering that feedback can be positive, not just negative. Plus, feedback can be subjective, as well as objective (Dyrendahl, 2012). For instance, in addition to including what people did in terms of which language they used (objective), feedback can include how people felt as they were using or not using languages (subjective). Students can also interact about their language use in various settings outside of class, whether they are satisfied with the current situation, and how they might wish to change it.

Along similar lines, cooperative learning groups can facilitate students' use of goal-setting, i.e., when students set out what they hope to achieve, perhaps by the end of a term, and how they plan to achieve it (Al-Bataineh et al., 2019). Goal-setting, also known as learning contracts, fits with a key tenet of student-centered learning: self-directed learning (Zhou & Li, 2020). Normally, goal-setting and making of contracts takes place between students and their teachers. With cooperative learning, peers can help each other formulate and achieve goals.

Reflective Break

1. What is your view about students' use of the target language in and out of class? Do your students usually say that they agree with you, and do their deeds match their words?
2. Does your class ever have discussions about how the class should function, such as which language(s) should be used in class?
3. Do your students ever do goal-setting or other forms of self-directed learning?

BUILDING A GROUP IDENTITY

As mentioned in Chapter 1, one means of promoting a feeling of positive interdependence among group members involves building a common identity within the group. Similar strategies can be used to build solidarity across a class. This can inject fun into learning. For example, groups can develop their own handshake. Boyd, Jarmark, & Edmiston (2018) stressed that the handshakes should be co-authored by the students, not imposed on them by teachers. This fits the student-centered spirit of cooperative learning, and it is fun to witness students' creativity in action.

Group Names

Group names can also build cohesion. Here are two cooperative learning techniques – Forward Snowball and Reverse Snowball (Kearney, 1993) – that can be used (even in tropical climates ☺) in combination to choose a group name. The name Forward Snowball comes from the fact that the group makes a list that grows as the game progresses, just as the size of a snowball increases as it progresses down a hill.

The general steps are as follows:

Step 1 – Each member of a foursome individually makes a list, such as a list of foods. When time is up, students each count the number of things they listed and write that number at the top of the paper.

Step 2 – Pairs within the foursome read and explain their lists to each other and then each makes a combined list. They can also add additional words sparked by words from their partner's list. For example, if their partner's list included 'noodles,' that might lead students to think of specific types of noodles, such as elbow noodles, spaghetti, udon, or rice noodles. When the time limit is reached, students count the number of words they now have on their list and write that number with a circle around it at the top of their paper. The circled number should be larger than the first number written at the top of the page.

Step 3 – Pair One and Pair Two get together and make a combined list. Again, more items can be added based on sparks generated by other lists. When the time limit is reached, students count the number of words they now have on their list and write that number at the top of their paper, this time with a square around the number. The class compare the three numbers from when they worked alone, collaborated with a single partner, and worked as a group of four. Normally, this number increases with each collaboration, thereby supporting the idea that cooperation can be beneficial.

To further implement the idea of going for a growing list when playing Forward Snowball, students can solicit words from other groups or spend more time discussing, thinking alone, or consulting research tools to continue growing their list. Comparison of the numbers achieved by various groups is not encouraged, as the goal is not to spur competition between groups. A fun way to play Forward Snowball in language class is to start with a long word, such as 'vegetarian' and see how many words students can make from the letters in the word (in the case of 'vegetarian,' the number is far north of 100 words). Students with smaller vocabularies can take assistance from a dictionary, but they need to learn the meanings of the words they discover. Another good language topic for Forward Snowball can be verbs.

The companion of Forward Snowball is Reverse Snowball. As you have probably guessed, instead of the list becoming larger with each round, it becomes smaller. Here is the general Reverse Snowball procedure.

Step 1 – Each person in a group of four lists a total of 10 items, such as 10 songs they like.

Step 2 – Pairs explain their lists to each other and then make a list of three items common to both lists, e.g., three songs they both like. If they do not have three common items, they can brainstorm until they discover them.

Step 3 – The two pairs in the foursome repeat the same process, trying to come up with at least one common item among the group.

Applying Forward and Reverse Snowball to choosing a group name, the group can begin by playing Forward Snowball to list their likes, such as items (mangoes) and activities (skateboarding). This listing offers a way for group members to get to know more about each other. Once their long list is completed, the group uses the list to play Reverse Snowball, and the final 'like' in Step 3 of Reverse Snowball can be the basis for the group's name, e.g., if they all like mangoes, their name can be the Magical Mangoes.

Beyond the Name

Once the groups have their names, each can build from the group's name to a group motto (A mango a day keeps the blues away) or a poem, such as an acrostic poem (Nugroho & Wiyatmi, 2019).

> **MANGO**
> **M**akes our minds happy
> **A**fter we finish a project
> **N**othing says 'Congratulations' better
> **G**et us more, please
> **O**h, they taste so good

Other ideas for promoting group identity include group logos, memes, videos, songs, recipes, cheers, and websites.

Reflective Break
1. Do you think your students would enjoy any of the ideas offered here for boosting the identity of cooperative learning groups?
2. What might be another way not mentioned here of promoting the feeling of positive interdependence among group members?

GAMES TO BOOST TEAM SPIRIT

Cohen (1994) suggested that when groups first form, discomfort may exist among group members who may not be familiar with each other or may come from different backgrounds. Even weeks or months after groups have formed, difficulties can arise, as relationships of all kinds have bumpy moments. Thus, some educators recommend team-building activities at regular intervals. Klein et al. (2009) reported that team-building can be effective especially for affective and process outcomes. In contrast, we have known other educators who do not believe in spending time on team-building activities. Of course, as with many matters, a continuum exists. Team-building activities can take less than a minute, for instance, with groupmates praising each other for something they did as the group was tackling a task; or team-building can last as long as an hour or more, e.g., groups work together to build something out of noodles and then debrief each other about their interaction on that task. Similarly, team-building can be done frequently or only very occasionally.

Alternatives to time specifically dedicated to team-building can be careful attention to promoting various forms of positive interdependence and other cooperative learning principles during cooperative learning activities, as well as using content that inspires student engagement. One source of engaging activities can be found in the use of games. The term 'gamification' has justifiably become popular this century (Zainuddin et al., 2020). In the next subsection are ideas for making games more cooperative, but first we consider some reasons why games help in language learning (Jacobs, 2019).

a.   Games boost student effort (Wright, Betteridge, & Buckby, 2005). As one teacher in Japan put it, 'I use games much of the time, as I teach a lot of students whose motivation to learn English is very low. Games come to my rescue.'

b.   Games offer many opportunities for language use which leads to more input (Krashen, 1982), output (Swain, 1993), and interaction (Long, 1981).

c.   A multitude of games exists, involving all language skills, not to mention the games that students and teachers can create (Kim, 1995).

d.   Games provide a form of student-centered activity, as in games, students are active and play a variety of leading roles. Along the same lines, many games are or can be played in groups.

e.   Students can continue to play games after class, which encourages them to use the target language outside class time (Ellis, 2005).

Reflective Break

1. Do you think your students would enjoy having group names, handshakes, mottoes, etc.?
2. Do your students ever play games in class?
3. When you attend courses/workshops, are there ever team-building activities? If so, do you find them to be time well-spent?

Cooperative Games?

When most people think of games, they think of winners and losers. Indeed, most games have many losers and only one winner, or in the case of team games, many losing teams and only one winning team. Competition does have its plus points; however, some of the disadvantages of competition are that it may demotivate those who lose, discourage cooperation, focus students on winning rather than on learning, promote cheating, and stigmatize weaker participants (Kohn, 1992). Life is complicated, as is the competition/cooperation divide. Competition and cooperation can coexist, e.g., students can cooperate with group members to attempt to win a game at the same time they compete to defeat other groups. Just as in assessment (Chapter 4), many options exist as to competing and/or cooperating, e.g., as in ipsative assessment, each student can compete only against their own past achievement. Additionally, groups and classes can compete against a standard, not against people.

Remember that competition often serves as a tool to attempt to motivate people, including teachers (Aliyyah et al., 2020), to work harder and better. How does competing fit with the cooperative learning principle of cooperation as a value? Many people believe that competition makes us stronger and that competition lies in our nature. Bregman (2020a) attempted to counter much of the pro-competition evidence, e.g., the famous novel, *Lord of the Flies*, which tells the story of how a group of boys stranded on a deserted island soon began attacking each other. In contrast, Bregman (2020b) recounted the more hopeful true-life story of a stranded group of boys who cooperated with each other.

Reflective Break

1. What is your view about competition and cooperation, both in education and outside education?
2. Is it possible for students to enjoy the benefits of both competition and cooperation?
3. What have you observed when your students compete against each other versus when they cooperate?

Making Games Cooperative

Should students and teachers sometimes wish to make games cooperative, many strategies exist (Jacobs, 2019; Orlick, 2006). Here are just six of those ways:

1. Play but do not keep score
Young children just play for the fun of it. Older kids, teens, and adults can learn from them. For example, Pictionary, also known as Win, Lose, or Draw, is a

popular commercial game that can be used for vocabulary-building. Groups compete to earn points when one group member draws to represent a word and their groupmates try to identify the word being drawn. One advantage of just playing without keeping score is that whenever someone draws, everyone can guess the word, rather than only the groupmates of the person currently drawing. At the same time, the cooperative learning principle of equal opportunity to participate must be remembered.

2. Act like The Three Musketeers

The Three Musketeers (by Alexander Dumas, 1844) is a novel about three people whose motto is 'All for one, one for all,' the feeling that lies at the heart of the cooperative learning principle of positive interdependence. Scaffolding for each other (Wertsch, 1986) provides a powerful way to implement this motto. When scaffolding, students support each other's success by providing demonstrations, explanations, hints, etc. In contrast, in competition, students do not scaffold for others, because they hope their competitors will fail. This equates to negative interdependence.

Scaffolding can be done in many games in language class, including Twenty Questions. In the typical competitive version of Twenty Questions, students take turns to be the Answerer, who thinks of an individual, place, concept, or object, and the Guesser(s), who attempt to guess who/what the Answerer has in mind. The game is called Twenty Questions because the Guessers can ask the Answerer a maximum of 20 Yes/No questions. If they guess prior to or by the time they have asked 20 questions, they win; if not, the Answerer wins.

If students decide to play a cooperative version of Twenty Questions, the Answerer scaffolds for the Guessers, for example, by answering the Yes/No questions with additional clues, such as, if the object is a book, and the question is 'Is it made of trees?' the Answerer might reply, 'Yes, the object is usually made of trees, but electronic versions also exist.' In the cooperative version of this game, we hope players feel the same as the Three Musketeers, so that if the Guessers arrive at the right answer before asking 20 questions, both the Answerer and the Guessers win.

3. Develop common goals

Goal positive interdependence can be easily forgotten. It means that students share a common goal, a goal that they all reach or none of them reach. Teachers may see the goal(s) that students should try to achieve, but maybe we need to do better at helping students see the goal(s). An example of a goal would be for a group or class to improve on their average score on the last quiz or last writing task, to accumulate a certain number of total points, or to put on performances that achieve a rating above a certain level. A group's goals must include the strengthening of each individual member of the group. For instance, a group has not fully succeeded if they reach a particular goal but one of the group members has not learned via the experience.

The game Just a Minute (Lee, 1995) provides a common goal to a group, plus a strong way to promote the cooperative learning principle of individual accountability. In Just a Minute, students each have a topic. The goal involves speaking for a minute on that topic with no hesitations (e.g., uh), repetitions, or changing of topics. Just a Minute resembles Table Topics, an activity from Toastmasters, an international club where people practice public-speaking skills. Students begin with a practice round. The goal is that all students will improve on their practice round score in each subsequent round. To achieve that goal, group members give each other tips and let them practice and redo.

4. Rotate roles

Role positive interdependence is a frequently used way to encourage cooperation. Each group member takes on a role that aids the group's functioning and learning, and each member is necessary in achieving the group's goal as they play a cooperative game. Roles encourage all group members to feel that they have value in the group; everyone plays a part in the team effort. Furthermore, everyone can improve the way they implement their role. Additionally, roles should rotate so that everyone develops more fully.

An example of students taking on roles in their groups when playing a game could be in the commercial language game Scrabble, in which each student has tiles, each tile has a letter printed on it, and students earn points by forming words with the letters of their tiles.

Roles that might make Scrabble a better learning experience include player (who forms a word with their tiles), advisor (who gives advice to the player before they put down their tiles), checker (who uses a dictionary to check that the player's word is correct), scorekeeper, and speaker (who uses the word to say something, in order to check that everyone knows at least one of the meanings for the word). Those roles rotate each time. You may have noticed that we just listed five roles, but usually our groups grow to no larger than four members. Thus, one student can perform two roles.

5. Go for a group best

Here, applied to games, is an idea we have mentioned before: the group collaborates to exceed a standard. The inspiration for this idea comes from celebration/external challenge positive interdependence. Instead of the external challenge coming from other people as in a competitive version of a game, students cooperate to surpass a previously determined goal. An example would be to play the game Forward Snowball, explained earlier in this chapter, and set a goal for how many words the group will have at the end of the game. Other groups can help if necessary.

6. Convert favorite competitive games to become cooperative
This section has provided ideas to bring groupmates and classmates closer together by playing games that simultaneously build their language skills. The various ways described for emphasizing cooperation when playing games are generic ideas that can be applied to a large number of games, including ones that people usually play in competitive mode. Plus, students may come up with their own ideas for converting favorite games from competitive to cooperative and perhaps strengthening the language element. For example, while chess is a silent, competitive game as usually played, language could be added by playing in a group of four divided into pairs, with the partners consulting together before making moves. Alternatively, when played by only two people, the game could pause every five/ten minutes for players to share their strategies, to praise each other, or ask each other questions.

> **Reflective Break**
> 1. Do you play indoor games with family and friends? If so, could your students play the same games (in cooperative mode)?
> 2. Would you be able to use any of the strategies for creating cooperative games?

OBSERVING, DISCUSSING, AND MODELING EFFECTIVE COOPERATIVE LEARNING

A frequently mentioned caution when students learn in small groups is that the expected cooperation does not automatically appear. We cannot expect effective cooperation to emerge by itself just because students are in small groups. What often happens instead is that students prefer to do assignments individually, even though they have peers sitting just next to them. Or students may collaborate but this collaboration falls far short of what is envisioned by the cooperative learning principle of maximum peer interactions. For example, some students may ask peers to share their answers and then copy them, with no discussion when answers differ and no consideration of how to elaborate on answers.

One way to help students learn what cooperative learning looks and sounds like can be to use the glass bowl technique, also known as the fish bowl technique

(Al Ghozali, Barnawi, & Pratama, 2019). Glass bowls allow others to witness what takes place inside. The essence of the technique involves two groups. The first group, usually smaller and often much smaller, are the people in the metaphorical glass bowl. They sit within the second, outside, group. The first group is the more active group, while the second group is active too, but as observers and recorders. The special part of this technique occurs when the two groups discuss what happened in the inside group, and they all reflect on what can be learned from that experience.

Another modelling idea is for the teacher to act as a group member and perhaps train one, two, or three students to act as the teacher's partners. The rest of the class can attempt to identify behaviors that empower the group to collaborate better. In order to add interest, the teacher or some of the teacher's group might intentionally engage in counterproductive behaviors to see if the rest of the class identify them. Somewhat similarly, groups can present skits to illustrate pro- and anti-learning group behaviors; and to fit with the cooperative learning principle of maximum peer interactions (quantity), instead of one group performing their skit for the entire class, groups can take turns performing for other groups, with post-skit discussion in which the audience seeks to identify the pro- and anti-behaviors inserted into the skit.

Reflective Break

1. Do you have any other ideas for helping students to think about how groups should interact?
2. What about taping group interaction, either audio only or both video and audio? Would that be workable in your context?

CONCLUSION

Human behavior is an endlessly fascinating area, with endless variations and interactions. This chapter has attempted to provide some practical ideas for encouraging cooperative behavior among students. These ideas include attention to seating, discussion of what languages to use in what situations, building group identity, and playing language games. As humans are innately social, perhaps we can optimistically imply that students really do want to cooperate with peers; they just need some friendly guidance to reach that self-fulfilling goal. As you read and reflected on the ideas in this chapter, did these ideas fit with your vision of a class that you would enjoy teaching? The book's next chapter takes up the topic of assessment when cooperative learning is used.

Reflective Break
1. Could you mention any ideas or issues related to improving group functioning that were not mentioned in this chapter?
2. After the first three chapters of the book, how are you feeling about cooperative learning? More or less favorably than when you started the book? Are you more or less clear than when you started the book?

Chapter 4

Assessment in Cooperative Learning

INTRODUCTION

If you are like us, the authors of this book, you love to teach, but when it comes to assessment, such as marking homework or tests, your enthusiasm shines significantly less brightly. However, when we stop to think about it, assessment is something we all do so often in so many other parts of our lives. For instance, when we wake up, we assess how well we slept the night before and whether we might want to try to grab another five minutes of shut eye. When we do get out of bed, as we prepare breakfast for ourselves and our families, we assess the quantity, nutrition, and taste of the food we are preparing. After we bathe, we have more assessment tasks, as we use our knowledge of the likely weather, where we are likely to be later that day, with who, and doing what in order to select what to wear and what to bring along with us when we leave home. Finally, when the day nears an end, maybe about 15 hours later, we are looking for something relaxing to read, play, or watch, with the internet providing so many options for us to assess before making a choice, and then, five minutes later, upon further assessment, maybe changing our choice. Thus, assessment in non-academic aspects of our lives is an inescapable and sometimes even enjoyable activity. We do not expect that this chapter will convince you to enjoy the academic assessment you do, but we do hope that discussing and reflecting on assessment will make you feel a bit more positive toward this vital element of education. It worked for us.

This chapter considers a number of questions about assessment generally, as well as questions about assessment when cooperative learning takes place. Three points that we find to be of particular value concern frequent assessment aided by the fact that in cooperative learning, students are available to aid teachers in assessing peers and themselves; ipsative assessment, in which students compare their current performance with their previous work; and combination grades, in which groupmates' results and evaluations impact one another's grades.

QUESTIONS ABOUT ASSESSMENT

In the earlier days of education, many of the key decisions regarding assessment lay out of the hands of classroom teachers, as high-stakes term-end or year-end exams mattered more than any other kind of assessment. Now, teachers and even students exercise a bit more control over how both teachers and students are assessed. Table 4.1 looks at some of the questions that need to be considered when doing assessment, especially when students are doing cooperative learning. These questions are discussed in greater detail in the text that follows.

Table 4.1. Assessment questions to consider when cooperative learning is used

Assessment questions	Options
1. How often are students assessed?	• Summative = Long (such as three-hours long) assessment instruments at the end of a term or year • Formative = Short assessments (as short as a couple of minutes) done many times a day, or assessment combined with learning tasks
2. Who does assessment?	• Teachers • Peers • Individual students assess themselves
3. With whom or what are students compared?	• Norm-referenced – Students are compared with peers, in the same class or even in an entire country or across countries • Criterion-referenced – Students are compared with a standard • Ipsative – Each student is compared only with themself
4. Are groupmates' grades linked?	• Each student receives an individual grade unconnected to groupmates' grades • Students' grades are a combination of their own grades and their groupmates' grades • The entire group receives the same grade • Students collaborate and learn without grades; assessment occurs, but not in the form of grades

<table>
<tr><td>5. Are ungraded tasks used?</td><td>• Students can earn points for their group, and these points count for recognition (such as attainment of a level or a certificate) for the group, but are not part of grades
• Groups work for enjoyment, intrinsic motivation, or to learn for future purposes</td></tr>
<tr><td>6. Are cooperative skills assessed?</td><td>• Cooperative skills are part of students' grades
• Using cooperative skills enhances groups' learning, but this contributes only indirectly to grades</td></tr>
<tr><td>7. Who creates assessment items and assessment rubrics?</td><td>• Only teachers and other education professionals
• Students sometimes also participate</td></tr>
<tr><td>8. What alternative rewards exist other than grades?</td><td>• Groups who succeed can receive certificates and recognition
• Digital badges offer another possibility
• We can also try to wean students off rewards</td></tr>
</table>

Reflective Break
1. Would you add any questions to the eight questions about assessment for cooperative learning?
2. Before you read the rest of the chapter, you might want to consider tentative answers to some of the questions.

How Often Are Students Assessed?

Alternative assessment is a term for a wide range of assessment practices that differ from traditional teacher-centered assessment (Murniati, 2008). First off, it must be clearly stated that assessment does not always mean grading, especially in the case of alternative assessment. Formative assessment constitutes one part of alternative assessment. Formative assessment (Tamah, 2020), assessment <u>for</u> learning (McSweeney, 2012, 2014), contrasts with summative assessment, assessment <u>of</u> learning. These two terms can be understood by looking at the first syllable of each word. The 'sum' in summative refers to the fact that summative assessment takes place at the end of a lesson, a unit, a term, a year, etc. to sum up what students have learned. Teaching has stopped; now comes the assessment to tell us what students learned during the teaching. In some countries, as much as a month can be spent twice a year, at the end of each of the year's two terms, on nothing but assessment, with each of the many exams lasting several hours. To be fair, teaching continues during these two months, but now students are teaching themselves or being taught by family members or paid tutors perhaps at private tuition centers, aka cram schools. Teachers are often too busy preparing, monitoring, and marking exams to do much teaching.

The first syllable in formative is 'form,' which means that the purpose of formative assessment lies in forming how and what students will learn going forward. Formative assessments are usually short and take place during and as part of learning activities, not after them. For example, when students do a writing activity in cooperative groups, that can be a formative assessment activity, as the students can be doing self-assessment of their own writing skills, and peer assessment of their partners' writing skills. Plus, as teachers observe groups, we also do formative assessment. Furthermore, more than writing skills can be assessed. Assessment can also be done of students' knowledge of the content of their writing task, e.g., global warming, as well as assessment of students' cooperative skills and their thinking skills, not to mention teachers' skills at teaching all the above learning elements.

When differentiating summative and formative assessment, as with differentiating almost any two concepts, we have to remind ourselves that most differences can be best understood as continua or spectrums, rather than as either/or dichotomies. For example, when considering the difference between extroversion and introversion, no one human being is either 100% extrovert or 100% introvert (Cain, 2012); we all lie somewhere along a continuum. Similarly, we should appreciate the overlaps between summative and formative assessment. For instance, the focus of attention should not be on the form of the assessment, e.g., a multiple-choice quiz, a skit, or website construction, or on the content of the assessment, e.g., grammar vs listening and speaking (Dixson & Worrell, 2016). Rather, what differentiates these two types of assessment lies more in how we use the results of the assessments.

The focus of formative assessment rests on students and teachers more consciously using what they learn from formative assessment to enhance learning and teaching. We say 'more consciously' because we are always doing formative assessment. For instance, when we are at the front of the class explaining something to students, we are probably scanning their faces for some signs of understanding. In fact, one challenging aspect of online teaching arises when, for whatever reason, we cannot see some of the students' faces.

In some ways, formative assessment resembles reflection on life and teaching, because formative assessment takes place as students are learning, just as reflection on life takes place as we are living (not at our funeral!) and reflection on teaching takes place as we are teaching, not after we retire. In this way, formative assessment, just like reflective practice on life or teaching presents as an optimistic approach to learning, living, and teaching. We can improve; we can self-care, self-heal, and self-improve. Plus, we can do all this caring, healing, and improving even better when we do this with others.

One more point links formative assessment and reflection; although, to a lesser extent, it also links summative assessment and reflection. Formative assessment can be short, so we can do many formative assessments. But even if we and our students can do 1000 formative assessments a day, it will not amount to a hill of beans unless we: (a) reflect on the results of those assessments; and (b) take action based on those reflections. To give a non-academic example, teachers can look down and notice their bellies getting bigger and step on the scale and notice their weight going in the wrong direction, but all that will do is make them depressed. What they really need to do (and this applies to at least one of the authors of this book) is to take some actions to reverse the situation; otherwise the assessments and reflection are for what?

Reflective Break

1. Do your students do many summative assessments? Are these supplemented with formative assessment?
2. The concepts of summative and formative assessment actually lie along a continuum, rather than either/or. What other concepts are also continua? Could teacher-centered and student-centered learning also best be understood as a continuum?

The following story presents a context that might illuminate formative assessment. A teacher nears the end of a lesson in which they have been standing at the front of a class, using video and slides to present information to the fairly attentive class. The teacher pauses and takes a quick peek at the clock. Yikes! Unfortunately, only five minutes remain for the lesson, but at least eight minutes of information remain in the presentation. That remaining information will be tested in the exam at the end of the term (a summative assessment). What should the teacher do? From a teacher-centered, summative assessment perspective, the teacher should speak faster and should definitely not stop for a quick cooperative learning activity. After all, the teacher's job is to cover all the materials in the syllabus. But, isn't the teacher's real duty not to cover the syllabus but to <u>un</u>cover it? As teachers, can we really feel satisfied just by virtue of having 'downloaded' the information into students' brains or, put another way, having poured the knowledge into the empty vessels that, according to the theory behind teacher-centered instruction, are students' minds (Rodriguez, 2012)?

A teacher in the exact same situation but coming from a student-centered, formative assessment perspective might make a very different decision. They might think to themself, 'Whoops – I got carried away, and I've been presenting my students with information almost the entire period, without giving them a chance to process the information, without a chance to connect that information to what is already in their minds and to elaborate on it [see the section on Constructivism in Chapter 2]. Maybe I should use the last five minutes for a quick cooperative learning activity. During that time, the students and I can do some formative assessment to see how much has been learned and to get an idea of what to do in the next class.'

Maybe this class could use the 3-2-1 technique. Like all cooperative learning techniques, this can be done multiple ways, one of which is described here.

1. In a foursome, after reading, listening to, or watching something, each student works alone to write **3** pieces of information or ideas that they want to remember, **2** questions based on what they did not understand or want to know more about, and **1** way they can use what they learned. [As the class only has five minutes, maybe a reduced version would be better, e.g., **1** piece of information they want to remember, **1** question, and **1** way they can use what they learned.]
2. Students exchange their 3-2-1 with one partner. They read and discuss, in class or electronically.
3. For homework, they each make one or more comments on their partner's 3-2-1. The comments could be a short list of similarities and differences in their 3-2-1s, an attempt to answer some of their partner's questions or ideas about where to look for answers, and the information learned from the partner's 3-2-1.

Reflective Break
1. Have you ever been in the situation of having five minutes left in class but eight minutes of material left? What might you do?
2. What do you think of 3-2-1? Have you ever done something like that?

Another difference in perspective often seen between summative and formative assessment can be expressed in the terms *performance orientation* and *learning orientation*. Performance orientation tells students, 'Okay, we've taught you; now it's your turn to show us what you've learned.' To paraphrase what one teacher wrote in a book, *900 shows a year*, describing teachers' work: We teachers have been up at the front of the class 'performing' for you; now, it's you students' turn to perform (Palonsky, 1986). In contrast, a learning perspective emphasizes the positive by focusing on what students have learned and how to build on that learning. With summative assessment, students' work is seldom returned. 'You're done. That's it. You've had your chance. Better luck next time, if you get a next time.' However, formative assessment invites students to examine and reflect on what they have done, and there will definitely be a next time. After all, a learning perspective and formative assessment go hand-in-hand with lifelong learning. You can see that formative better fits the strengths of cooperative learning, although some of the research on cooperative learning has used summative assessment instruments to measure student learning.

Portfolio assessment (Wiggins, 1998) offers one example of a learning perspective and formative assessment. When constructing a portfolio, students preserve (hard or soft) copies of some of their work – including quizzes, essays, reports, videos, poems, book advertisements, etc. – and then write a reflection on what their work shows about their learning, their strengths and weaknesses, their plans for learning and using what they learn, what promoted and hindered their learning, and insights into their emotional, not just their cognitive, journey. Peers can take part in choosing portfolio items, in comparing them, and in giving feedback on each other's reflections. A scaled-down version of a portfolio can involve just two pieces from different times in the same term or even two drafts of the same piece of work, and again, peers can aid each other.

Why does the summative/formative continuum matter when it comes to cooperative learning? It matters because peers' roles in summative assessment differ greatly from their roles in formative assessment. Peers can help each other prepare for summative assessments. In fact, from a scaffolding perspective, peers' roles can be seen as part of the scaffolding process. The scaffolding (Gagné & Parks, 2013) starts with teachers teaching, and it continues with peers coaching each other, before finally students stand on their own when, ready or not, they do the summative assessments. When the authors of this book were students, we sometimes formed study groups with peers to prepare for summative assessments.

The situation differs greatly with formative assessments. Here, fellow students can be right there, working on the same assessments, whereas when students do summative assessments any helping is viewed as cheating and punished accordingly. Also, unlike with summative assessment, with formative assessment, peers can take part in evaluating each other's work. Thus, cooperative learning can be valuable regardless of the type of assessment, but with formative assessment, peers play more multifaceted roles.

Reflective Break

1. Have you experienced anything like portfolio assessment, either as a student or a teacher?
2. Do you ever notice your students scaffolding for each other? If so, what kind of help do they provide their peers? Do you ever make suggestions to them about how to scaffold?

Who Does Assessment?

In teacher-centered instruction, the answer to the question 'Who does assessment?' is too obvious for anyone to even ask it. In fact, from the perspective that guides teacher-centered instruction, it might even be considered malpractice if teachers do not do all the assessment. After all, teachers know the most; so, they should be the sole judges of students' work. Plus, wouldn't students assessing their peers and themselves (as in self-assessment) be like 'the helpless assessing the clueless'? Please keep an open mind about this question until you have finished reading this subsection.

Let us begin by saying that one of the many advantages that cooperative learning offers in comparison with a steady diet of whole-class instruction accrues from the fact that when learning in cooperative groups, students can receive more and faster feedback (Kulkarni, Bernstein, & Klemmer, 2015). As a teacher, how many times late at night have you wisely decided that relaxation and sleep were more important than that big stack of students' work you had brought home to assess in hopes of substantially diminishing its size? Peer assessment and self-assessment offer a better way of downsizing teachers' workload. Plus, complementary non-teacher feedback can not only increase teachers' lifespans, it can also increase student learning. Of course, it should be stressed that peer assessment and self-assessment, as already noted, complement – they do not replace – teacher feedback.

The following represent some of the advantages of peer assessment and self-assessment.

a. For teachers to successfully hand over some of the assessment responsibility to students, teachers need to make it clear what is going to be assessed, i.e., students cannot assess everything teachers assess. We also need to make assessment criteria public, clarify the assessment criteria with examples, and facilitate student skill in using them. For example, one of the authors of this book sometimes earned extra money by being a marker for the entrance exams a university gave. Before the markers could begin their task, the people in charge did 'rater training' (Wang et al., 2017) in hopes that the job would be done in a fairly uniform manner. Rater training involved everyone reviewing criteria, followed by everyone individually marking the same few scripts, then a whole-group discussion of the grades they had given and why, and finally a return to the criteria to perhaps rewrite them. Our students need similar training.

b. Peer assessment can be faster than teacher assessment, as classes have many students but usually only one teacher (Stenger, 2014).

c.   There being so many more students compared to teachers also means that students see and hear more of their peers' behavior, much more than one teacher observes. Therefore, student assessment adds substantial data to teacher feedback. One possible peer assessment system involves students giving each of their group members a percentage mark. For example, in a group of three, student C has two groupmates, A and B. If B and C feel that A contributed their fair share to the group, they give A a mark of 100%; if A and C feel B contributed only half of their fair share, they give B a mark of 50%. Then, if the teacher gives the group's work an overall grade of 80, student A receives the full 80 points (100% of the group's score of 80), but student B receives only 40 points (50% of 80).

d.   By assessing their peers' work, students become more aware of the qualities of competent work. For instance, they might recognize and later emulate their peers' positive examples and avoid their peers' negative examples.

e.   Students can then apply this awareness to self-assessment of their own efforts.

f.   Students can give feedback on areas that lie within their competence, allowing teachers to focus on those areas that lie, for now, beyond students' competence.

g.   As well as giving feedback on the language and content aspects of peers' work, students can also evaluate the evaluators. For example, did they use cooperative skills (Chapter 2) when assessing each other's work? 'Feedback Sandwich' is the name of one idea that promotes socially skilled assessment (Procházka, Ovcari, & Durinik, 2020). Just as a normal sandwich places two slices of bread, one atop and the other below the 'meat' of the sandwich, in a feedback sandwich, any criticism is accompanied on either side by praise. Of course, people perhaps can learn more from praise than from criticism, although praise itself has many variations (Zarrinabadi, Lou, & Darvishnezhad, 2021).

Reflective Break

1.   Do you trust students to do peer assessment? What is your evidence for this view?

2.   Self-assessment and reflection are linked. Do your students often do reflection activities?

With Whom or What Are Students Compared?

Three main assessment options exist for comparing students' work. Which options we choose impacts our use of cooperative learning.

The two most common assessments are *norm-referenced* comparisons and *criterion-referenced* comparisons. In norm-referenced assessments, we compare students' results with those of other students. These other students could all be in the same class, or they could be anywhere else in the same school, city, province, country, or anywhere in the world. Norm-referenced is also called 'grading on a curve' (Austin Community College, 2015). Here, 'curve' refers to the bell-shaped curve which distributes students such that the majority of scores are in the middle, with fewer and fewer the closer one goes to the two far ends of the curve. When true norm-referenced assessment takes place using the grades of A, B, C, D, and F, approximately 2% of students would receive As, 14% Bs, 68% Cs, 14% Ds, and 2% Fs. (It should be noted that while some form of norm-referenced assessment dominates at many education institutions, in the experience of the authors of this book, often a modified, less severe version of grading on a curve is applied.)

The essential point to note is that with norm-referenced assessment, the grade students receive depends on the outcomes of the students with whom they are compared. For example, a score of 90 out of 100 on an exam could be an F in a class in which 98% of the other students scored above 90, yet it would be an A in a class where 98% of the other students scored below 90. Similarly, a score of 25 on the same exam could be either an A or an F or anything in between, again depending on the scores of the other exam takers. As Johnson et al. (2004) pointed out, such a situation does not promote student–student cooperation, because students (and their families and friends) might think that students are negatively dependent (see Chapter 1) on each other, i.e., one group member's gain causes a loss to their groupmates. Thus, norm-referenced assessment might discourage peer cooperation. However, Jacobs & Greliche (2017) demonstrated statistically (see the online article for details) and logically that positive interdependence should still apply even when norm-referenced assessment takes place in small groups and even more clearly when it is used on nationwide or international standardized exams taken by perhaps hundreds of thousands of other students.

As to why, logically, students should feel positively interdependent with groupmates even when norm-referenced assessment prevails, Webb and her colleagues have conducted many studies (e.g., Webb et al., 2009) suggesting that cooperative learning derives much of its magic from the phenomenon expressed in the principle of maximum peer interactions (Chapter 2), i.e., that students need to have many peer interactions (maximum quantity) and that these must be quality interactions (maximum quality), in particular interactions where students explain to each other, rather than only tell each other answers. In such quality interactions, both the students receiving explanations and those giving explanations benefit cognitively. Most people would easily agree about the benefits to *recipients* of explanations, but many would wonder about benefits to *givers* of explanations. Are the givers wasting their time going over what they already know, when instead they could be taking on more advanced, challenging work, work at the right level for them? We teachers see the wisdom of Webb and colleagues' endorsement of properly conducted cooperative learning. We know that 'Those who teach learn twice,' that by lighting the path for others, we also help ourselves move forward.

Reflective Break
1. Do your students do norm-referenced assessments? If so, with what other students are your students normed?
2. What is your view on whether students should still feel positively interdependent with groupmates even when norm-referenced assessment is used?

Criterion-referenced assessment constitutes the second major way that student performance is compared. The term 'criterion-referenced' derives from the fact that comparison of students takes place not with other people but with an established standard of quality, i.e., the criterion, and the quality of work that each student demonstrates. For instance, people who want to be plumbers need to demonstrate that they can perform important plumbing tasks to an acceptable standard. Meeting the required criteria does not mean that these would-be plumbers can fix any problem in the fastest and least costly manner; it only means that their work rises to a standard deemed to be sufficiently good. Unlike with norm-referenced assessment, people who undergo criterion-referenced assessment are compared only with the criterion, not with each other. If 100 people take the same criterion-referenced exam, all can pass or all can fail, or any combination in between, e.g., 82 can pass, and 18 can fail.

Therefore, with criterion-referenced assessment, students should be able to easily see that by helping peers, they do not damage their own chances. Furthermore, as explained in Chinese and other cultures, by helping others, we build a reputation as dependable people, and we build a reservoir of favors we have given others. Later, we might be able to successfully seek favors in return from the recipients of our favors (Jacobs, 2013). Additionally, students have been found to register emotional gains from helping peers (Binfet, 2015).

Ipsative assessment represents a third, less known, option for assessing a student's performance on a test. With ipsative assessment, instead of comparing the performance with the performances of others (norm-referenced) or with a standard (criterion-referenced), the comparison is with previous performances of the same student. In some sports, we see this when athletes, such as runners, talk about their personal best (Burns, Martin, & Collie, 2019), i.e., their fastest times over particular distances, the goal being for the runners to continually improve on their personal bests. As with criterion-referenced assessment, ipsative assessment seems less likely than norm-referenced assessment to generate competitive feelings among groupmates, thereby increasing the likelihood of the blossoming of feelings of positive interdependence.

Ipsative assessment can also be called improvement scoring, because it calls attention to the possibility of students registering improvement in their proficiency, should it occur. Of course, we need to remember that any score or other form of assessment necessarily only provides a partial picture of students' capabilities. For instance, many people credit Albert Einstein as the originator of the oft-quoted phrase, 'Not everything that can be counted counts, and not everything that counts can be counted' (Bloomfield, 2017). In other words, it may be difficult to give a score to many of the important aspects in life, e.g., trustworthiness, and many of the aspects of life that can be easily scored may not actually be very important, e.g., ability to divide large numbers in one's head. [Note that disagreement exists as to who originated the quote (Quote Investigator, 2010).] Later, this chapter discusses the use of ipsative assessment in a prominent family of cooperative learning techniques, including Student Teams-Achievement Divisions (Slavin, 2011).

> **Reflective Break**
> 1. Either as a student or teacher, do you have experience with criterion-referenced assessment?
> 2. Outside of Education, have you personally used ipsative assessment with yourself? For example, many people use ipsative assessment for body weight, although in this case, often the goal is to record a lower, not a higher, score.
> 3. What do you think of the Einstein quote? For example, some people would say that students' scores on grammar tests do not count for much; instead, what counts is how well they can communicate.

Are Groupmates' Grades Linked?

One of the most controversial issues in cooperative learning arises over whether to link groupmates' grades in any way. We present three options here, along with a fourth option that may not be feasible in many cases.

Option 1 – Same Grade for All (aka Group Grades)

If a group of four students do a project together or all four take the same quiz, some teachers may give the entire group the same grade. Reasons for this choice include:

a. Many times, outside of Education an entire group succeeds or fails together. Examples include sports teams, orchestras, and businesses. They really do sink or swim together. A team can have the worst player in the league, but if the rest of the players compensate for their weak link and/or help that person improve their performance, they can still win. Conversely, if a theatre troupe has the world's premier singer/actor, but some of the others mess up their lines or laugh when the script says to cry, the performance probably will flop. Thus, Option 1 – Same Grade for All – may be the most real-life option.

b. Same Grade for All highlights celebration/reward positive interdependence, thereby motivating groupmates to assist each other.

c. Any other option provides more work for us teachers and confronts us with a difficult task: how to separate out each member's value to their group, for every group. For instance, when we observe one group, we cannot know what members of the other groups are doing.

d. Johnson et al. (2004) claimed that when groups function well, students will come to see Same Grade for All as the fairest option, and this option will do the most to build strong bonds among group members.

e. One path toward Same Grade for All that we have read about but never tried is for group members to help each other to prepare for a task, e.g., a quiz, an essay, or a presentation. Then, the teacher chooses only one group member's work to grade or the choice is made at random, and all group members receive that grade (Tamah & Prijambodo, 2014). Allowing students to choose whose work to grade might decrease individual accountability (see Chapter 2)

Option 2 – Separate Grades for All (aka Individual Grades)

This option is the opposite of Same Grade for All. Reasons for choosing the Separate Grades for All option include:

a. Group grades might strengthen positive interdependence, but they could weaken individual accountability (see Chapter 2) by opening the door to freeloading, aka, sleeping partners. Those among students, teachers, community members, and other stakeholders who already question the virtue of relying on student–student cooperation may seize on group grades to oppose cooperative learning altogether. Separate Grades for All may be the only option they will approve.

b.   Separate Grades for All may most accurately reflect each student's current ability. In contrast, with Group Grades, aka Same Grade for All, two students in different groups who put in equal effort and have equal skill could receive different grades based on the efforts and skills of their groupmates.

c.   Students who feel 'cheated' by having 'bad' groupmates may lose motivation to participate in future cooperative learning activities as a result of Group Grades.

Individual assessment can be easily done with exams and other types of assessment which students normally do individually, but what about assessment of projects and other activities that typically rely on group work? Here are some suggestions.

a.   Each student is responsible for one section of the project. Their grade is based on that section only.

b.   Students take quizzes on the content of their group's project and possibly the projects presented by other groups.

c.   The group aspect of the project, e.g., the project report, is not graded; however, individual aspects, e.g., oral presentations, receive individual grades.

How can we motivate students without using group grades? Some ideas are:

a.   Give students more choice as to what and how they study (Allred & Cena, 2020).

b.   Introduce non-grade rewards as in STAD (explained in Question 8 below), such as certificates, prizes, and celebration time. Rewards to avoid are those that might seem anti-learning, such as more recess or shorter assignments. Instead, rewards can put learning in a positive light, such as more time for silent reading or for the teacher to read aloud, or students designing their own assignments and supplementary activities.

c.   Encourage goal-setting by students, so that they set their own standards and develop their own ways of assessing whether they met those standards.

Option 3 – Combined Grade

In our experience, many teachers who use cooperative learning prefer some combination of group and individual grades. The rationale for a combined grade is that it recognizes the value of the group but also recognizes differences in the achievements and efforts of group members. Combined grades can take many possible forms; the basic idea is that each group member receives a grade that comprises a group component and an individual component. For example, on a project, 70% of each student's grade can derive from the grade on the group's project report and 30% from that student's individual project presentation. Therefore, if the group's project receives a grade of 80 and Student A's individual presentation gets an individual grade of 70 and Student B's individual presentation gets a 60, A's combined grade for the project is 77 (70% of 80 = 56 plus 30% of 70 = 21) and B's combined grade for the project comes to 74 (70% of 80 = 56 plus 30% of 60 = 18). Of course, the percentages for group and individual grade components can vary widely, with the individual component possibly outweighing the group component.

Other possible ways to construct combination grades include:

- Bonus points for everyone – Option #1: If all group members score at or above a fixed score, the entire group receives a designated number of bonus points. For instance, if the target score is 80, Table 4.2 shows the initial and final scores of four hypothetical group members.

Table 4.2. The use of bonus points when everyone needed to score 80 or above for the group to receive bonus points

Name	Score this time	Bonus points	New score
Su Min	80	5	85
Asman	100	5	105
Shara	86	5	91
Fudge	86	5	91

We may recall from Chapter 2 that with celebration/reward positive interdependence, if anyone receives a reward or a chance to celebrate, everyone in their group receives the same reward or can participate in the same celebration. However, note that even though, for instance in Table 4.2, Su Min and Asman receive the exact same reward (5 bonus points), Asman's grade that goes into the teacher's grade book is higher.

- Bonus points for everyone – Option #2: If all group members improve on their past score or past average for quizzes, assignments, etc. (except for those who previously had perfect or other very high scores, and thus had little or no room for improvement), the entire group receives a designated number of bonus points. Table 4.3 presents an example with our same four hypothetical groupmates.

Table 4.3. The use of bonus points when everyone needed to improve on their past score, unless their past score was high

Name	Score this time	Past average	Bonus points	Total score
Su Min	80	75	5	85
Asman	99	99	5	104
Shara	86	83	5	91
Fudge	76	75	5	81

Note: Option #2 employs ipsative scoring, explained earlier in this chapter. Also, if even one group member misses the set goal, no one in the group receives bonus points.

- Bonus points for everyone – Option #3: If the group average on an assessment instrument exceeds the group's past average, everyone receives bonus points. Table 4.4 shows an example where the group's past average was 70. The group's average this time is 73; so, they all receive bonus points, although this time only 2 bonus points are given.

Table 4.4. The use of bonus points when the group's average score exceeds their previous average

Name	Score this time	Bonus points	Total score
Su Min	80	2	82
Asman	60	2	62
Shara	66	2	68
Fudge	86	2	88

Note here, that just as cooperative learning techniques are amenable to many possible variations, always bearing in mind cooperative learning principles, methods to combine grades can also be very flexible, again bearing in mind cooperative learning principles. One of those principles, cooperation as a value, seeks to spread the feeling of positive interdependence beyond the same group of 2, 3, or 4 members. A way to possibly promote cooperation as a value might be via bonus points for the entire class if the class accomplishes a predetermined goal. For example, bonus points Option #2 could be used, except this time not just within a small group but across the entire class.

Reflective Break

1. Of the three options of Same Grade for All, Separate Grade for All, and Combined Grade, which would you usually favor? Why?
2. In your student days, were all three used at different times?
3. What do you think students and administrators would say if your class used Same Grade for All?

Bonus points can involve a great deal of calculations for teachers. As a result, some teachers may prefer to skip all the fuss. Alternatively, two suggestions for reducing the fuss might prove useful. One, students could be asked to do some of the calculations. This would also make students more aware of their own progress. Two, teachers and students can ease the calculations burden via use of one of a wide variety of software, such as Excel. Such software does require some initial learning but can be fun once we get the hang of it or find someone, such as a family member or student, to do the preliminary setting up.

It should be noted that in addition to their teachers, peers, and themselves, students can now receive a great deal of technologically aided feedback on the various language skills (John & Woll, 2020). Furthermore, with Artificial Intelligence, technology can assist students and their teachers in learning about students' strengths and weaknesses (Xiao & Hu, 2019).

Rather than worrying that all this technology will render it unnecessary for students to do peer assessment and self-assessment or, god forbid, make teachers unnecessary, we can see technology as allowing us humans (students and teachers) to focus on more complex areas. These complexities are exactly where two (or more) heads, i.e., cooperative learning, are particularly needed. Spell check provides a good example. Freed from cluttering our beautiful minds with the minutiae of spelling, we could focus instead on making the best word choices in order to express our developing meaning clearly, persuasively, and colorfully.

Finally, as stated earlier, assessment and grading are not the same. Not all forms of assessment have to be translated into a grade. Teachers will need to decide if they want to include peer assessment and self-assessment in their grading. The same question arises as to whether to include the quality of students' collaboration, i.e., their use of cooperative skills, as part of grades. Alternatively, some teachers give two grades, one for academics and the other for collaboration. Some of these topics will be discussed later in this chapter.

Reflective Break
1. Are you fairly good at using software, such as Excel, for compiling and analyzing data? If so, how did you learn, and is there a colleague to whom you might teach these skills? If not, do you see yourself learning in the not-so-distant future?
2. Do you help your students improve their use of technology for feedback on their language production?

Are Ungraded Tasks Used?

Many students might have started preschool or kindergarten full of intrinsic motivation, i.e., motivated from within by the twin joys of learning and accomplishment, but too often, grades, an extrinsic (from the outside) motivator, soon became their driving force. For too many students, before beginning a task, their first questions will be whether the task is graded and, if so, what percentage of their total course mark the task is worth. We hope that, by adding a team element, cooperative learning can restore some of the joy of learning and achievement, but using tasks with no grades could also help.

What are ways to motivate students without grades? One idea is to use content that attracts students' interest, e.g., some students have great interest in dinosaurs or mystery or controversies. Also, students may find certain activities to be engaging, such as drawing, using apps, or doing drama. Here again, student-centered learning, in this case connecting to student interests, promotes motivation.

Another idea for motivating students without grades is also congruent with student-centered learning (Jacobs & Renandya, 2016). This idea that combines criterion-referenced assessment and ipsative assessment (both discussed above), is goal-setting – a form of self-assessment well-established in Physical Education (Swann et al., 2021). Students set their own goals and monitor their efforts to attain them. Schippers et al. (2020) reported a study which found that students who wrote out their goals made superior academic progress compared to those who did not do written goal-setting. This fits with student-centeredness, because students have more control when they set the goals that they need to reach. Peers can discuss each other's goals and monitor each other's progress. Based on this monitoring, peer discussion, and personal reflection, students might wish to adjust their goals.

Group tests (Gilbride, 2020) offer another form of non-graded activity, although often they are in preparation for graded activity. Group tests can be organized in many different ways, including as two separate tests, one individual and the other collaborative (Zipp, 2007). As with other cooperative learning activities, group tests should be organized with cooperative learning principles (see Chapter 2) in mind. For example, heterogeneous grouping promotes peer coaching. Furthermore, everyone needs openings to try answering and explaining answers (equal opportunity to participate), and everyone must use some of those openings (individual accountability).

Students can exercise the cooperative learning principle of group autonomy on a group test by struggling and brainstorming to work out answers amongst their group, rather than straightaway seeking the teacher's assistance. Very importantly, students should not just give answers to each other; they must also explain and otherwise elaborate on their answers (maximum peer interactions – quality). Among the cooperative skills that might be useful when students do group tests (Gilbride, 2020) are encouraging others to participate, in case some group members exhibit reluctance to try answering test questions or explaining their answers, or thinking aloud.

Thinking aloud (Bereiter & Bird, 1985) mobilizes the maximum peer interactions principle, as students (often after modelling by teachers) think aloud by speaking out what is happening in their minds as they go about a task. It goes without saying that thinking aloud fits well with reflection. Also, by opening a window into students' minds, thinking aloud permits peers to learn from the strengths of their groupmates' efforts and to more easily identify and address their groupmates' and their own weaknesses. Additionally, students can also include emotions as an element about which they think aloud. In sum, thinking aloud should be considered a valuable cooperative skill.

Reflective Break
1. If a task is not graded, will your students take it seriously?
2. How good are most of your students at exercising group autonomy?
3. Do you ever think aloud while demonstrating a task to students?

Are Cooperative Skills Assessed?

As noted in Chapter 2, one cooperative learning principle states that time should be taken for students to the develop the will and the skill to cooperate well. The many, many cooperative skills include asking for explanations, giving reasons, disagreeing politely, suggesting ways to enhance group functioning, using the designated language when appropriate, and boosting group morale. However, as with anything else we feel should be in the curriculum, the teaching of cooperative skills requires time, as does the assessing of students' cooperative skills. Perhaps, for many students, the other cooperative learning principles, especially promoting positive interdependence and cooperation as a value, will suffice to encourage them to regularly use a range of cooperative skills. The logic behind this belief is that if students feel positively interdependent with groupmates and others, they will strive to use cooperative skills because the use of such skills facilitates the efficacy of what they do and makes it more likely that the group will accomplish their goals.

If you and your students decide to assess use of cooperative skills, teacher assessment, peer assessment, and self-assessment offer three ways to do this. This can be done in Steps 4, 5, and 6 of the 6-Step procedure for teaching cooperative skills that is described in Chapter 6. Jacobs, Power, & Loh (2002) offer three sample rubrics for assessment of cooperative skills (Tables 4.5, 4.6, and 4.7).

Table 4.5. Sample rubric for teacher assessment of cooperative groups

	Teamwork	Individual contribution	Cooperative skill weakness or strength
1	Unable to work together effectively	Few contributions to group progress	No thanking of others
2	Occasionally worked well together, but were not consistent	Some contributed	Needed to remind others of their tasks
3	Consistently worked well together with only a few lapses	All contributed most of the time	Monitored time remaining

Table 4.6. Sample rubric for self-assessment of cooperative groups

	Teamwork	Individual contribution	Cooperative skill weakness or strength
1	My team didn't work well together	I seldom cooperated with my team	Did not stay on topic
2	My team sometimes worked well together	I sometimes cooperated with my team	Encouraged everyone to participate
3	My team almost always worked well together	I often cooperated with my team	Came prepared

Table 4.7. Sample scoring guide for assessing of groupmates' use of a designated cooperative skill: 'Listening Attentively'

	Approaches Expectations	Meets Expectations	Exceeds Expectations
Kip Cates			
Barbara Martinez			
Rick Ginsberg			

Reflective Break

1. Would your students have trouble simultaneously focusing on learning tasks and cooperative skills?
2. As a language teacher, can you help students link their use of cooperative skills with improving their proficiency in the target language?
3. In any of your teaching contexts, is it worthwhile to include cooperative skills in assessment?

Who Creates Assessment Items and Assessment Rubrics?

In teacher-centered learning, teachers and other educators take full responsibility for creating assessment instruments, deciding how grading will be done, such as creating assessment rubrics (Wang, 2017), and doing assessment. In student-centered learning – and cooperative learning provides a vital tool in the student-centered learning toolbox – students play an active supplementary role in assessment, including formulating assessment items, such as questions.

One cooperative learning technique in which students write questions for each other is called Exchange-a-Question. Here is one set of possible steps in Exchange-a-Question.

Step 1 – The teacher begins by discussing with students what types of questions they might like to create for each other. Many websites (e.g., https://education. illinoisstate.edu/downloads/casei/5-02-Revised%20Blooms.pdf) offer question starters for the various levels of thinking featured in Bloom's taxonomy (Marzano, 2001). Note: the differences between Bloom et al.'s original taxonomy from the 1950s and what is called the 'revised' taxonomy seem rather minor. The class also discusses the topics from which questions might be drawn.

Step 2 – Students work in twosomes. They each write one or two questions of the types and on the content discussed in Step 1.

Step 3 – Before sharing their questions, students write answers for their own questions. This unusual step serves two purposes. First, just as we teachers may see weaknesses or unclear areas when we attempt to answer the draft questions we have written for students, students may see room for improvement after trialing the questions they create for their partner. Second, some students enjoy playfully teasing their partner with very difficult questions or questions which require very lengthy answers.

Step 4 – Students exchange questions only (not answers), attempt to respond to their partner's questions, and then compare answers.

Variation: Students may work in groups of four. A pair of students can work together to create questions (with answers) for the other twosome in their group.

Reflective Break
1. Do you think your students might benefit from doing Exchange-a-Question?
2. If so, what kind of questions could you teach them to write?

What Alternative Rewards Exist Other Than Grades?

A widely-used cooperative learning technique uses rewards other than grades to motivate students and to promote celebration/reward positive interdependence.

The technique is termed STAD (Student Teams-Achievement Divisions) (Slavin, 2011), and it is one of the most researched cooperative learning techniques. The first three steps in STAD are easy to follow, but the final step in this four-step technique can be a little confusing the first time you try it.

Step 1 – Students pay attention while the teacher provides instruction.

Step 2 – In heterogeneous groups of four, students do further study on the topic the teacher just taught. Later, students will each take an individual quiz on that topic, with the chance of winning points for their group.

Step 3 – Students take the quiz independently of their groupmates.

Step 4 – Follow carefully here, please. The quiz is scored by the teacher (or students). Students' scores are compared to their past average, as in ipsative scoring (Hughes, 2017). Based on the system described in Table 4.8, students earn points for their group. As with other cooperative learning techniques, STAD and its scoring system can be changed, bearing in mind cooperative learning principles.

Table 4.8. Example of a STAD team point system

Points to team	Score on most recent quiz	Examples
30	Perfect paper (no matter what the past average is)	Rex earned 30 points for his team because he got a perfect score of 100, even though he did not improve, as his past average was 100.
30	More than 10 points above past average	Ambaree's group received 30 points because her quiz score of 89 was 11 points above 78, her past average.
20	Past average to 10 points above past average	Nimrod earned his group 20 points by scoring a 92 with a past average of 88.
10	1 to 10 points below past average	Yoshi gained 10 points for her group via a score of 82 which was 3 points below 85, her past average.
0	More than 10 points below past average	Clem, sadly, got zero points for his group as a result of a score of 82 which fell 16 points below 98, his past average. Everyone encouraged Clem to put that quiz behind him and focus on the next one.

After calculating how many points, if any, each student earned for their group, the next step involves averaging those points (not the students' scores). Based on that average, the group receives recognition, such as a certificate, or their group name posted on a bulletin board (recall positive identity interdependence in Chapter 2), or the opportunity to do their group's silent cheer or handshake. The recognition points system presented in Table 4.9 can be used with STAD.

Table 4.9. STAD's team recognition system
based on average improvement points

25 or more point average	Super Team
20-point average	Great Team
15-point average	Good Team

Three Points to Bear in Mind with STAD

STAD is a widely used cooperative learning technique, but in our experience, some matters can cause confusion. We hope that taking note of the three points below can help avoid difficulties.

a. Students' grades in the grade book come solely from their individual quiz score. Grades are not the same as the number of points earned for the group. For instance, in the data in Table 4.8, Yoshi and Clem both have a grade of 82, even though Yoshi's 82 earned 20 points for her group, while Clem's 82 earned zero points for his group. In other words, grades differ from non-grade team rewards, such as the recognition a group earns.

b. STAD calls its scoring system 'Equal Opportunity for Success,' not to be confused with the cooperative learning principle of equal opportunity to participate. Equal Opportunity for Success balances the status of each group member and makes heterogeneous grouping more acceptable to groupmates, because having a low-achieving group member does not necessarily make it more difficult for groups to achieve recognition.

That is the benefit of using improvement scoring, an ipsative assessment system: each group member, regardless of past achievement, has an equal opportunity to contribute to their group. For example, in the case of a student with a past average of only 20 out of a possible 100, by improving on the next quiz only to 32 (more than 10 points above past average), they can contribute 30 points (the maximum) to their team, as many points as contributed by a high-achieving groupmate who always scores 100.

c. The recognition system used in STAD, or some variation on it, can be used in other contexts. Furthermore, recognition and group celebrations, such as silent cheers and group handshakes (Chapter 3), can be done in many different ways. For example, digital badges, aka e-badges, can serve as a form of recognition. These badges can indicate that people have demonstrated an ability, possess a quality, gained knowledge in an area, or completed an accomplishment (Roy & Clark, 2019). Something similar, but perhaps at a lower level, are the medals issued in Pokémon Go (Reynolds, 2021).

Reflective Break

1. Do some students resist being in a group with a low-achieving student? Do they ever refuse? If so, how do you address that?
2. Would some of your students respond positively to the types of recognition or celebrations used in STAD? If so, do you have ideas for alternatives?

CONCLUSION

Cooperative learning and, more generally, student-centered learning, opens many new assessment options, including formative assessment, criterion-referenced assessment, ipsative assessment, portfolio assessment, group grades, combined grades, group tests, and group tasks with no grades. These options fit well with the paradigm underlying reflection (see Chapter 5 and Jacobs & Farrell, 2001), because this paradigm seeks to widely (some would even say 'wildly') distribute learning and decision-making. To learn and to decide require the ability to assess. Thus, by students taking on some of the assessment work from teachers, and teachers and students taking on some of the assessment work from administrators and makers of standardized tests, we can achieve a more decentralized, more participatory society.

Chapter 5

Cooperative Learning and Reflective Practice

INTRODUCTION

'Great teachers teach from the heart' (Palmer, 1998, p. 5). They join the teaching profession with their hearts longing to spark the love of learning in their students. They begin their journey with other novice teachers, many of whom share the same longing. Along the way, some of these fellow teachers lose their longing as they toil the demanding path of the profession. These defeated teachers either leave the profession to embark on different paths or drag themselves into their classes each day, inflicting the pain of rote learning on their students and themselves. In contrast, great teachers manage to survive the myriad challenges and drudgery of the profession and savor every moment of joy. Between the two extremes, there are many different types of teachers who go through the ups and downs of the profession. Some are on their way to greatness, while some others are struggling to make their days meaningful through their teaching. What, then, makes teachers great? Part of the answer lies in teachers empowering their students; after all, it is students who construct their own learning, with cooperative learning weighing heavily in that construction process. Another key element of teacher self-development lies in teachers engaging in reflection, alone and in concert with others.

Reflective Break
1. Think of a teacher who has made an impact on your life. How did this teacher change you (your perspective, your behavior, or your habits)?
2. What qualities did this teacher demonstrate that impacted your life?
3. Are you a teacher? If so, what made you decide to become a teacher?

This chapter discusses cooperative learning and reflective practice as a terrain to explore and form connectedness between teachers' inner selves and their students and subjects. To be connected with students, teachers need to find ways to nurture student–teacher encounters so that students can make the content their own and enter the various communities of practice dedicated to the various content areas. Connectedness involving the students, language teaching, and teachers' inner selves is discussed as the underlying landscape of reflective practice. This chapter, then, discusses how reflective practices enable teachers to delve into the tangles of the students, the language they teach, and their own inner selves.

Through reflective practices, teachers weave these three sources of complexity into a pattern of interconnectedness. This pattern becomes a journey map to guide 'the heart's longing to be connected with the largeness of life – a longing that animates love and work, especially the work called teaching' (Palmer, 1998, p. 5).

> As good teachers weave the fabric that joins them with students and subjects, the heart is the loom on which the threads are tied: the tension is held, the shuttle flies, and the fabric is stretched tight. Small wonder, then, that teaching tugs at the heart, opens the heart, even breaks the heart – and the more one loves teaching, the more heartbreaking it can be. We became teachers for reasons of the heart, animated by a passion for some subject and for helping people to learn. (Palmer, 1998, p. 11)

THE UNDERLYING LANDSCAPE OF REFLECTIVE PRACTICE

For weaving through the complexities of the students 'minds and lives, language teaching, and their own inner self, language teachers can equip themselves with tools. One effective tool to help teachers weave connectedness with their students and the language they teach is cooperative learning. When cooperative learning interacts with teacher reflection, the whole is greater than the sum of the parts. Figure 5.1 illustrates some of this weaving process.

A great teacher finds connectedness between the inner self and the external world. In Parker Palmer's words, 'We teach who we are' (1998, p. 1). Palmer further notes the three sources of the complexities of teaching: the student, the subjects we teach, and the inner self of the teacher. In this fast-changing world, no matter how widely teachers read and delve into the subject they teach, the content of the syllabus will always be lagging behind the progress of the discipline and the unappeasable needs of the society for the knowledge. The students are even more complex than the subjects. 'To see them clearly and see them whole, and respond to them wisely in the moment, requires a fusion of Freud and Solomon that few of us achieve' (Palmer, 1998, p. 2). Understanding the subject and the students requires that the inner self expand its reach to embrace these complexities while deepening self- knowledge. The next three sections of this chapter examine Palmer's three sources of complexities: the student, the subject taught, and the teacher.

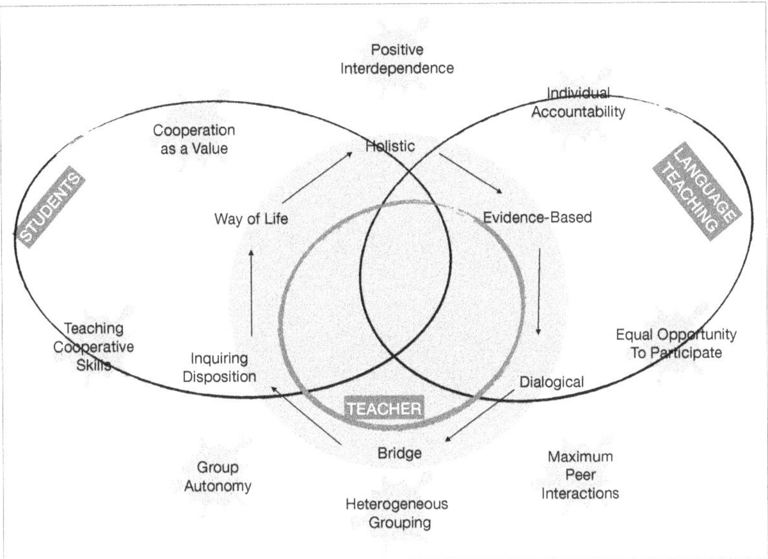

Figure 5.1. The landscape of cooperative learning through reflective practice

Reflective Break

1. As a teacher, do you encourage your students to learn in groups?
2. Do you then ask your students to reflect on their learning experiences in cooperative groups?
3. Do you gain any insights out of the reflective practices?

The Student

This section discusses the first source of complexity in the landscape built on Palmer's model, the student. One of the ultimate goals of teaching is to free students not only from the state of not-knowing but also from dependence on the teacher. Teachers design learning environments, prepare materials, facilitate activities, and guide students through learning processes. Yet, students take charge of their own learning and participate in the learning processes. No matter how well teachers design and deliver a learning process, it will not resonate with the students until they awaken their own authority to learn. Eventually, students should find, in Palmer's terms, 'the teacher within' themselves (1998, p. 29). Deep attachments cause dependence, while deep connections create freedom.

When teaching does not achieve its intended objectives, teachers begin to wonder whether their teaching empowers students to learn. Learning takes place when learners are personally engaged and allowed to discover. The shift away from teaching to a focus on learning has encouraged authority to be moved from the teachers to the students (Barr & Tagg, 1995). The literature on student-centered learning has flourished over the years in response to this paradigm shift.

Reflective Break

1. Do you remember the best class you ever had as a student? The class in which you were most confident? In which you learned the best?
2. What happened in that class? Did you discover new knowledge? Did you feel motivated to learn?
3. What led you to an intrinsic desire to learn?

Farrell & Jacobs (2020) note eight essentials for successful English language learning:

a.   Encourage learner autonomy
b.   Emphasize the social nature of learning
c.   Develop curricular integration
d.   Focus on meaning
e.   Celebrate diversity
f.   Expand thinking skills
g.   Utilize alternative assessment methods
h.   Promote English language teachers as co-learners.

All the eight essential elements relate and are connected to one another. Five of these essentials, namely learner autonomy, the social nature of learning, diversity, thinking skills, and alternative assessment, relate directly to the student and will be discussed in this section (thinking skills and alternative assessment will be discussed together). Other essentials will be discussed in the next sections: Language Teaching and The Teacher.

Frank Herbert Hayward (cited in Abualhaija, 2019) was among the early proponents of the concept of student-centered learning in 1905. The term 'student-centered learning' is also associated with the work of Piaget and of Knowles (Burnard, 1999). Carl Rogers, the founder of client-centered counseling, expanded this approach into a general theory of education (Burnard, 1999; Murphy, 1999). In his book *Freedom to learn for the 80s*, Rogers (1983, p. 25) describes the shift in power from the expert teacher to the student learner, driven by a need for a change in the traditional environment where in this 'so-called educational atmosphere, students become passive, apathetic and bored'. In education practices, Freidrich Fröbel further popularized the concept of child-centered education, urging that teachers should not 'interfere with this process of maturation, but act as a guide' (Simon 1999, p. 25). Simon (1999) further underlined that maturation was linked with the process of development or 'readiness', i.e., children will learn when they are ready.

Reflective Break
1. As a teacher, did you ever feel disconnected from your students?
2. Did your teaching ever fail to help your students learn despite all your preparation?
3. What happened then?

Learner Autonomy

In the area of second/foreign language learning, teachers may find students to be dependent on them and the prescribed coursebooks at the early stage of learning. This state of dependency may give teachers a false sense of connectedness with their students. At the beginning, teachers may feel it is their job to fill students' brains by transmitting their own knowledge to their students. However, if eventually learners fail to develop their autonomy, learning stalls. The transmission does not transform the learners. Despite all the preparation and the best teaching strategies that teachers have performed, some learners do not seem to make progress while their peers make headway. Passive learners come to the lesson unprepared and depend excessively on their teachers' direction, to the point of burdening the teachers. On the other hand, effective learners are intrinsically motivated and aware of their learning styles. Research reveals that motivation, learning styles, and learning strategies significantly affect success in second/foreign language learning (Benson, 2007, 2013). Furthermore, effective learners take charge to utilize appropriate learning strategies to enhance their learning process. The teacher's job to facilitate learning meets halfway with such learners who gather the best from the lessons. What the teacher sows the learners reap.

It is important, then, for teachers to guide learners to take responsibility for their own learning. In student-centered learning, teachers start by keeping in mind learners' backgrounds, beliefs, values, interests, and needs when planning and teaching the lesson.

Subsequently, teachers can help learners find and consolidate their extrinsic and intrinsic motivation, raise their awareness of their own learning styles, offer a repertoire of learning strategies, and give them the freedom to choose the most appropriate learning strategies so they can advance through the lessons. When teachers manage to encourage learners to take this path of autonomy, their learning journey will extend beyond the classroom. Learners will graduate from dependency on their teacher and find the 'teacher within' themselves. For some teachers, this notion may sound odd as the reverse – 'students' need for the teacher teaching them' – is so ingrained that classroom practices are grounded in the conviction that the teacher's control is paramount to the schooling operation.

Reflective Break
1. Did you ever attempt learner-centered teaching? How did it go?
2. How do you encourage your students to take responsibility for their own learning?
3. What are some of the challenges in motivating students to take charge of their learning?
4. How do you overcome those challenges?

Social Nature of Learning

To support teachers' attempts to stimulate learner autonomy, the second essential element focuses on the social nature of learning. In student-centered teaching, the social nature of learning connects with learner autonomy because by working in groups, students become less dependent on teachers and more interdependent with their peers (Farrell & Jacobs, 2020). For some students in a second/foreign language class, being fully autonomous may be frightening when they are expected to take their own path of acquiring a language they are not familiar with at the beginning of their learning journey. Being in a classroom where students are expected to express themselves in a second/foreign language may seem like such uncharted territory that their dependency on their teachers lingers on. Hence, the presence of fellow learners in their path of learning is essential. The social nature of learning was built on sociocultural theory (Vygotsky, 1978) and focuses on the cognitive and affective benefits of collaboration (Farrell & Jacobs, 2020).

Values of collaboration have been ingrained in many cultures. The Amish people still maintain a tradition of barn-raising – a collective action in which people of a community gather to build a barn collaboratively for one of the community members. Barn-raising was particularly common in 18th- and 19th-century rural North America. The tradition has diminished with modernity, but continues in some Amish communities, particularly in Ohio, Indiana, Pennsylvania, and some rural parts of Canada (today, approximately 125,000 Amish live in North America). The day of barn-raising is what the Amish call a 'frolic' event where all members of the community gather and contribute to the project based on their ability, gender, and age. Young men carry materials and build the structure, older men supervise the work, women supply food and drink, children and youth fetch tools and parts while looking on and preparing themselves to sustain this tradition in the future. All members of the community contribute voluntarily knowing that someday they may also need the community's help.

Another example of community is the value embodied in the motto 'I am because we are,' i.e., the southern African philosophy of Ubuntu made famous by the anti-apartheid activist Archbishop Desmond Tutu in his speech 'We are human only through relationships.' Archbishop Tutu described the value behind Ubuntu via the following story:

> An anthropologist proposed a game to the kids in an African village. He put a basket full of fruits under a tree and told the kids that whoever got there first won the sweet fruits. When he told them to run they all took each other's hands and ran together, then sat together enjoying their treats. When he asked them why they had run like that as one could have had all the fruits for themselves, one little girl said: 'UBUNTU! How can one of us be happy if all the other ones are sad?' Archbishop Tutu explained the story, 'we believe that a person is a person through other persons.'

On a similar note, Nelson Mandela described Ubuntu in 2006 (as cited in Oppenheim, 2012):

> A traveler through a country would stop at a village and he didn't have to ask for food or for water. Once he stops, the people give him food, entertain him. That is one aspect of Ubuntu, but it will have various aspects. Ubuntu does not mean that people should not enrich themselves. The question therefore is: Are you going to do so in order to enable the community around you to be able to improve?

What Mandela described still prevails in many rural communities in Indonesia where people take pride in the spirit of *gotong royong* which simply means mutual cooperation. In the diversity of Indonesian cultures, *gotong royong* manifests itself in different ways. In Bali, agrarian communities bind themselves with a traditional ecologically sustainable irrigation system known as *subak* (Lansing, 1987). Developed in the 9th century, it is still a widespread water management system for the paddy fields today. For the Balinese, irrigation is not simply providing water for the plant's roots, but water is used to construct a fair and sustainable ecosystem for all community members. The system consists of five terraced rice fields and water temples covering nearly 20,000 hectares (49,000 acres) binding Balinese agrarian society within the village's community center and Balinese temples. In Cancar, Manggarai, Flores Island, *gotong royong* is tied into a rice field distribution system called *lodok*. The design of rice fields is determined through a ritual as a community leader starts at a center point and draws lines outward based on the number of family or community members forming a circle. Seen from an aerial view, the rice fields resemble spider webs.

This system is designed so that everyone receives a share of the land, and this encourages everyone's involvement in the communal maintenance of the rice fields. On a nearby island, Lembata, the indigenous fishing community practices sustainable fishing rituals. When cultural leaders in charge of the sea and wind observe fishes moving into their bay, all villagers move into the sea with their sarongs on, and catch fishes in their sarongs. It is a festive event, as the whole community pours into the bay. The young hold hands with the senior members, and children play around. The local wisdom in this tradition is that the community members work together and feed themselves. They also maintain the sustainability of the ocean, as they refrain from using more powerful tools and take only what they need for the day. Furthermore, they make sure everybody in the community gets what they need, including the cultural leaders who are on duty keeping the fishes in the bay and so cannot catch their own fishes. The villagers share part of their catch with the cultural leaders. https://www.youtube.com/watch?v=A0iCZo4sF5k&t=5s

Reflective Break

1. Do you know of any other cultural/folk traditions that reveal values of cooperation, to add to those described in the preceding paragraphs?
2. What do those traditions tell us about the social nature of human beings?

Celebrating Diversity

Each individual is unique. A language class consists of learners from diverse cultural and linguistic backgrounds and social classes, and with prior experiences, values, beliefs, interests, needs, learning styles, preferences, goals, abilities, and intelligences. The fifth essential, celebrating diversity, also pertains to student-centered learning in that teachers should recognize and respect differences among students. In a second/foreign language class, students face the challenge of communicating in a new language. This challenge is exacerbated when students' ways of expressing themselves and responding to social cues at home do not conform to the norms and standards of communication expected in classrooms and may, therefore, be misunderstood and ridiculed (Lie et al., under review). Language teachers need to recognize this situation and make every attempt to understand and respect their students' frames of reference by learning more about their students' home-family relationships, their community culture, and their cultural heritage without invading their privacy (Farrell & Jacobs, 2020). During her first year of teaching in Indonesia, an American EFL teacher Barbara Hopkins was often upset when some students, in her perspective, did not show regret for their misbehavior. Whenever they showed up late in class or did not do as expected, they smiled. For Barbara, a smile was a sign of delight. But for Indonesians, and perhaps many other Asians, there are many kinds of smiles to express different feelings – happiness, shame, regret, remorse, guilt, and sadness. Later on, Barbara gradually learned to distinguish the various cultural nuances of her students' non-verbal expressions while also attempting to teach them her American way of expressing apology and regret verbally.

Recognizing and understanding students' cultural diversity helps teachers connect with their students. Irrespective of their backgrounds, students need to feel acceptance and affirmation of being who they are so they can express themselves and interact with others comfortably.

Reflective Break

1. Can you give real examples of diversity in your classroom?
2. Did you ever witness an incident in which a particular student was made to feel unwelcome and threatened in a classroom or elsewhere in a school? Analyze the situation and identify the causes and consequences.
3. How did the teacher and others deal with the situation? Do you have any suggestions for how they could have reacted more wisely to the incident?

Thinking Skills and Alternative Assessment

Expanding thinking skills is described as the sixth essential 'to bring the classroom closer to the real world and prepare students to cope with the complex world' where everyone needs to do all types and levels of thinking (Farrell & Jacobs, 2020, p. 95). A study of fifteen language teachers in three cities in Indonesia (Gozali, Lie, & Tamah, 2021) found that, in general, English teachers limited their questions to the comprehension check type, such as 'Is it clear?' or 'Is there any question?' When probed during interviews regarding their reasons for the choice of questions, some of the teachers contended that they found it hard to ask higher-order thinking questions because their students would not understand them. Certainly, the experience of the authors in this book is that even highly proficient students, including native speakers, grapple with higher-order thinking. At the same time, some teachers may avoid higher-order questions because of their own difficulty with the language involved in formulating and responding to such question. This issue will be discussed in the following part of this chapter, on The Language. All in all, some teachers' unwillingness to involve students in discussions involving higher-order thinking reveals an underestimation of students' capacity to, with patience, develop and expand their thinking skills, and thus deprives students of the chance to achieve their full potential.

The seventh essential, alternative assessment, fits into the paradigm of student-centered learning. Alternative assessments create opportunities for students to shine in different ways. Wiggins & McTighe (2005) proposed Backward Design – a three-stage curriculum approach or lesson planning in which teachers start the course design by setting learning outcomes before determining the acceptable evidence of learning, and before planning learning experiences. The second stage requires different types of assessment to determine how teachers tell what students know and assess them after identifying the desired learning outcomes. Furthermore, students should also be more involved in their own learning processes and given the chance to be assessed in various forms of assessment including self-assessment. Chapter 4 has described assessment in more detail.

> **Reflective Break**
> 1. How do you integrate thinking skills in your language classroom?
> 2. Does the lack of language proficiency obstruct the teaching of thinking skills? How do you deal with this situation?
> 3. How do you usually assess your students? Are you satisfied with your ways of assessing your students?
> 4. In what ways does alternative assessment support student-centered learning?

The Language

The second source of complexity is the subject. In this book, the subject is the second or foreign language. Language is a system of communication used by human beings to understand one another. Human language is the most unique among currently known systems of animal communication in that it is highly variable between cultures and across time, and affords a wider range of expression than other systems (Evans & Levinson, 2009), although it should be noted that advances in research continue to reveal often surprising abilities among nonhuman animals (e.g., Fishbein et al., 2020).

Language Teaching

Kramsch (1998) stated that language expresses, embodies, and symbolizes cultural reality. Language teachers help learners construct a bridge to other languages and guide them to cross that bridge and reach out to different worlds. The role of language teachers is complex. Whilst teachers may have a deep understanding of what constitutes a language, how languages are learnt, and therefore the strategies to be used to support this, they may not be expert in many languages, or even the target language learned by the students. We shall further discuss the personae of language teachers in the next section on The Teacher.

Choosing a particular field of study to teach is a personal journey. Teachers 'were drawn to a body of knowledge because it shed light on our identity as well as on the world. We did not merely find a subject to teach – the subject also found us' (Palmer, 1998, p. 25). To explain this statement, Palmer recounts Alice Kaplan's journey to become a teacher of French language and literature from a book *French lessons*. French culture gave Kaplan a way of claiming an identity and integrity she could not find in her own culture. As cited in Palmer (1998, p. 26), Kaplan reflects, 'Speaking a foreign language is … a chance for growth, for freedom, for liberation from the ugliness of our received ideas and mentalities.' Becoming a language teacher is thus guiding learners to encounter strangers in another language, understand them as fellow human beings, and gradually understand themselves better through this encounter. The regained self-knowledge of a language teacher and learner helps them reconnect with who they are through what they teach/learn.

Reflective Break
1. Reflect on your reasons for choosing the language you are teaching now.
2. What are the benefits that you have gained in teaching that language?
3. What are the obstacles that you have ever encountered in teaching the language?
4. How do you deal with those obstacles?

Language teachers do not only connect people of different cultures through the language they teach but they also connect students with other subjects. The concept of language across the curriculum offers one route for implementing a curricular integration (Chamot & O'Malley, 1994). The idea is that language competence is necessary for learning in all subject areas. The language becomes the vehicle for learning about content in various fields that connect to students' needs and/or interests. 'As language teachers we are the most fortunate of teachers – all subjects are ours. Whatever [the students] want to communicate about, whatever they want to read about, is our subject matter' (Rivers, 1976, p. 96).

Therefore, language teachers have the flexibility to work with students to venture into the curriculum. Developing curricular integration is another essential skill language teachers ought to have (Farrell & Jacobs, 2020).

Humans are meaning-making creatures. Psychiatrist and holocaust survivor Viktor Frankl posited in his 1946 book *Man's search for meaning* that the primary motivation of a person is to discover meaning in life. To teach a language effectively, teachers need to take this knowledge into account when designing and delivering a language lesson. In the day-to-day practices of language teachers, the focus on meaning needs to balance the tendency to focus on the form of the language which manifests in rote learning and memorization of the language components.

Reflective Break

1. To what extent does a second/foreign language help students learn content in other fields?
2. As a language teacher, how do you balance teaching the discrete components of the target language and focusing on the meaning?

Teachers as Co-Learners

Finally, when teachers position themselves as partners in learning with their students, they show their students a model of life-long learners. Because the world is constantly changing, everyone has to continue learning. Teachers need to practice what they preach and walk their talk. Teachers can learn with their students, from their students, and about their students. In the context of foreign language learning especially, it is important that teachers learn along with their students. In class, students may notice that their teachers' language still needs to be improved, and this is true for all teachers, whether they teach chemistry, geography, mathematics, etc. and regardless of their experience and the number of degrees they hold. Any deficiencies in teachers' knowledge of language should not affect students' respect for their teachers if the teachers continue to increase their language proficiency and show a joy for learning. As a matter of fact, the imperfections in the teachers' language can help students recognize the progression of learning and inspire them to strive forward along with their teachers. The target language becomes a shared path where teachers and learners form connectedness as partners in learning.

Reflective Break

1. What have you done to become a better user of the target language?
2. What have you done to become a better teacher?
3. What do you plan to do to enhance your professional development?

The Teacher

The third source of complexity is teachers themselves. To learn a new language in formal education settings, especially a foreign language, when one has passed the early childhood period, one usually benefits from the guidance of language teachers. The persona of a language teacher has drawn a growing body of knowledge. A Google search of 'language teachers' yields over 1.5 billion results.

Teachers are designers and facilitators of learning. Teachers help create the conditions for students to manage their own learning processes and learn collaboratively with their peers in order to become more autonomous learners. Teachers also design and facilitate projects that offer multifaceted learning opportunities. They guide students to acquire the target language through learning opportunities and assess students' learning performances.

Language teachers are responsible for creating non-threatening learning environments so that each student feels empowered to express who they are and comfortable to interact with others who are different from them in many ways. At times, teachers themselves may feel threatened when they encounter students who may be challenging the status quo and pushing them out of their comfort zone. At a conference for English teachers, a teacher from South Sulawesi, Indonesia shared her experience in facing her students' resistance to learning English. Confronting her openly, they argued that English is the language of the imperialists and does not accommodate the discourses in their religion. Another English teacher in a religiously-affiliated boarding school in East Java expressed her need for more support from the school administration and was concerned that the religious leader in the premises perceived that the English subject offered in their curriculum was merely an effort to be in compliance with the mandate of the Ministry of Education. Students were not encouraged to learn English wholeheartedly for fear that learning this foreign language would get in the way of spending more hours studying their holy book. This situation does not reflect the general attitude in such schools but is told as an example of a precarious predicament that language teachers may have to face.

A very different example was shared by a teacher in an international school using an international curriculum in Indonesia. Her students came from privileged backgrounds and spoke English very comfortably. They were also frequent world travelers. Their families had provided them with rich learning resources and exposed them to so many of life's perks that few things impressed them. Coming from a working-class background, this teacher had felt intimidated by what she had heard about the students in that school even before she started teaching there.

She wondered 'How can I teach my students about other countries they often visit while I have never traveled out of the country myself?'

Reflective Break
1. Have you ever experienced threatening situations as a second/foreign language teacher? How did you respond? Share it with a trusted colleague or write about it in your journal.
2. What do you think of the cultures of the target language you are teaching?
3. How do you introduce those cultures to your students?
4. What are your students' perceptions of those cultures?

How can teachers overcome threatening situations such as those described above? Palmer (1998) distinguishes bad teachers from good ones. There is no single set of criteria for good teachers because they vary in their teaching styles, interests, and preferences. On the other hand, bad teachers share one characteristic in common, that is, they are disconnected from their students and the subject they are teaching. Palmer further reveals that

> Good teachers possess a capacity for connectedness. They are able to weave a complex web of connections among themselves, their subjects, and their students so that students can learn to weave a world for themselves. The methods used by these weavers vary widely: lectures, Socratic dialogues, laboratory experiments, collaborative problem solving, creative chaos. The connections made by good teachers are held not in their methods but in their hearts – meaning heart in its ancient sense, as the place where intellect and emotion and spirit and will converge in the human self. (p. 11)

In reference to Palmer's reflection, the ways teachers face difficult situations determine their paths to be good or bad teachers. For language teachers to be able to create non-threatening learning environments and to empower their students to be who they are, the teachers themselves must start by recognizing and resolving their own vulnerabilities.

Reflective Break
1. Think of the bad and good teachers in your days as a student. What traits distinguished them?
2. How can teachers form connectedness with their students and the language they are teaching?

Recognizing their own vulnerabilities, teachers need to be honest with themselves and with their students. One of the authors of this book started her formal teaching career in a very diverse class many years ago. Two of her students grew up in English speaking countries and moved back to Indonesia for their college education. As a novice teacher of English, she was not confident about her own English language proficiency – her pronunciation, accent, vocabulary mastery, and her knowledge of the world. There were times that she made mistakes in class. The lingering embarrassment led to a sense of inefficacy during those early years of teaching. Fortunately, when she was honest about being a novice teacher who was still learning, the students were empathetic and respectful; their positive attitudes helped her cope with her sense of vulnerability and gradually overcome it.

When teachers promote language learning and position themselves as co-learners, they benefit along with their students in the progression of learning the target language. Teachers free themselves from the burden of demonstrating perfection in using the language and at the same time assign themselves to be models of life-long learning. Seeing such models and having honest partners in learning, students may be more motivated to strive forward and progress in mastering the target language.

Reflective Break
1. What are the advantages of teachers positioning themselves as partners in learning?
2. What are the challenges of teachers positioning themselves as partners in learning?
3. In what ways can teachers position themselves as partners in learning?

TRANSFORMATION OF TEACHING THROUGH REFLECTIVE PRACTICE

This chapter has thus far discussed the connectedness involving student, language teaching, and teacher as the underlying landscape of reflective practice as depicted in Figure 5.1. Teachers knit these three sources of complexity into a pattern of interconnectedness. Through reflective practices, this pattern becomes a journey map to guide 'the heart's longing to be connected with the largeness of life – a longing that animates love and work, especially the work called teaching' (Palmer, 1998, p. 5). To weave this pattern of interconnectedness, teachers need to equip themselves with tools. One effective tool to help teachers weave connectedness with their students and the language they teach is cooperative learning. This section discusses how reflective practices can enable teachers to use cooperative learning to sort through the tangles of the students, the language they teach, and their inner selves – and weave them into a pattern of interconnectedness.

There have been numerous cooperative learning books (Aronson, 1978; Johnson & Johnson, 1989; Slavin, 1995; Sharan, 1999), including cooperative learning for language classrooms and cooperative learning resource books in non-English languages (among others, Lie, 2002; Tamah, 2017; Tamah & Wirjawan, 2018, 2019). Most of these books postulate the compelling reasons to use cooperative learning in a nutshell and then discuss the practicalities of the techniques at great length. A great number of cooperative learning workshops have also been organized around the world. The good news is that the cooperative learning jargon has become well known in academia and the lessons from those cooperative learning books and workshops have electrified many teachers around the world. The irony, however, is that there are more teachers who do not use cooperative learning in their teaching or use it at the surface level despite its potential benefits.

Smagorinsky (1996) reported a study in which a student teacher claimed to use cooperative learning, a pedagogical tool she had been taught in her pre-service course work. She assigned her students to work in groups and share their work. The assignment consisted of a three-page summary of a story with blanks provided for students to fill in missing information. Students were placed in groups of three and told that each student should do one page independently and, when finished, the group should read the three pages consecutively for a whole understanding of the story. The teacher had a surface understanding of some features of the tool of cooperative learning, at least as articulated in professional literature, yet did not understand or promote the overall concept of cooperative learning's emphasis on interdependence.

The underlying cause of this phenomenon may be the ways cooperative learning is introduced and presented to teachers in books and workshops. Cooperative learning techniques are circulated among teacher proponents and tried out with students. In some classrooms, students seem animated during cooperative learning activities while in some others, the activities are conducted mechanistically. Those teachers who manage to engage their students meaningfully in cooperative learning activities understand the overall concepts and believe in the importance of the principles while employing the techniques. Grossman, Smagorinsky, & Valencia (1999) asked to what extent different tools for teaching are appropriated for use by teachers in different settings. To answer that question, they differentiated among five degrees of appropriation, each representing a depth of understanding of a particular tool's functions. Beginning with a discussion of why teachers might not appropriate a particular tool at all, they ranked the five degrees into

(a) lack of appropriation, (b) appropriating a label, (c) appropriating surface features, (d) appropriating conceptual underpinnings, and (e) achieving mastery. Appropriation can occur at different levels for any pedagogical tool. A pedagogical tool such as cooperative learning may be understood and appropriated as a label only or can be grasped in terms of conceptual underpinnings. An avid teacher supporter may achieve mastery in cooperative learning and mentor others to implement it. On the other hand, a lack of appropriation does not necessarily involve a lack of understanding; a teacher might understand the conceptual underpinnings of cooperative learning but reject the premises that support them. One might also understand a tool but find that the environment makes it difficult to use it effectively. A similar process occurs with students, who, in the final analysis, are the ones who cooperate or not.

Reflective Break

1. Reflect on your most successful experience in adopting or appropriating a pedagogical tool (it can be employing a particular teaching technique or achieving mastery of a lesson).
2. What processes did you experience to achieve mastery?
3. What processes did you experience in using cooperative learning in your classroom?

Learning involves the construction of identities as well as the interactions between identities and the learning environment. Cooperative learning is guided by sound principles as discussed in Chapter 2 and offers a useful set of techniques. 'Good teaching, however, cannot be reduced to technique' (Palmer, 1998, p. 11). For teachers to appropriate cooperative learning and achieve mastery in facilitating it in the classroom, they need to integrate it in their interconnectedness within themselves and with their students and the language they teach. 'Good teaching comes from the identity and integrity of the teacher' (Palmer, 1998, p. 10).

The tips, tricks, and techniques of teaching are necessary especially for novice teachers. The written instructions for techniques in many books and the taught techniques in many teacher workshops turn into impactful tools in the classroom and beyond only when their adoption and appropriation is placed within the landscape of reflective practice involving the students, language teaching, and teachers' inner selves – as summarized in Figure 5.1.

Discussions on how to teach need to be connected to who we are, where we come from, why we decided to be teachers, and why we stay in the profession. A German philosopher of the late 19th century, Friedrich Nietzsche said, 'He who has a why to live for can bear almost any how.'

COOPERATIVE LEARNING THROUGH REFLECTIVE PRACTICES

Grounded in well-supported principles and enriched with a plethora of engaging techniques, cooperative learning can serve as a useful and impactful tool for teachers who would be engaged in reflective practices. Reflective practice means that 'language teachers systematically examine their philosophy, principles, theory, and practices about teaching and learning throughout their careers.' Farrell (2019, p. 58) proposes reflective practices for English language teachers and presents six principles of reflective practice:

a.　Reflective Practice Is Holistic
b.　Reflective Practice Is Evidence-Based
c.　Reflective Practice Involves Dialogue
d.　Reflective Practice Bridges Principles and Practices
e.　Reflective Practice Requires an Inquiring Disposition
f.　Reflective Practice Is a Way of Life

Table 5.1 presents a summary of prompts to help teachers consider implementing cooperative learning across the six principles of reflective practice.

Table 5.1. Reflecting on implementing cooperative learning

Principles of Reflective Practice	Implementing Cooperative Learning
Holistic	• Why do I decide to use cooperative learning?
	• In what ways do my personal experiences lead me to choose cooperative learning?
	• How does cooperative learning help me grow into a better person and a more effective teacher?
	• How does cooperative learning help me connect with the students?
	• How does cooperative learning help me teach the target language to the students?
Evidence-Based	• What does research say about cooperative learning?
	• What is my understanding of the principles of cooperative learning?
	• What is the result of applying each of the eight principles of cooperative learning in my own class?
	• Are the results sustainable or are they dependent on contexts?
	• Do I have convincing evidence as a reason to continue using cooperative learning or abandon it?

(The words "THE STUDENTS" and "THE LANGUAGE" appear vertically in the left and right margins of the table.)

THE STUDENTS	Dialogue	• How do I use cooperative learning so far? • Do I engage my students in dialogue about what and how they are learning? How does the dialogue transform them? • Do I dialogue with a trusted colleague who shares beliefs in cooperative learning? • What can I share with this colleague about my experiences and insights in using cooperative learning? • What can I share with other teachers about my experiences and insights in using cooperative learning? • What can I learn from other people's experiences and insights in using cooperative learning so I can grow professionally?	THE LANGUAGE
	Bridging Principles and Practices	• Are my philosophy of learning, assumptions, theories, and values known to me and others, including my students? • In what ways do my philosophy of learning, assumptions, theories, and values lead me to choose cooperative learning? • How can I better translate my principles into my teaching practices? • How do I feel when my practices conflict with my principles?	
	Inquiring Disposition	• Do I question my own philosophy, assumptions, theories, and values about teaching? What do I discover? • Why is (or isn't) cooperative learning one of the right approaches for me? • Do I ever have a flow experience when using cooperative learning in my class? What happens? (Csikszentmihalyi, 1990)	
	Way of Life	• Do I engage myself in continual reflective practice? • How has reflective practice transformed me as a person and as a professional teacher? • Reflecting on using cooperative learning, how has this method helped me grow as a person and as a teacher?	
THE TEACHER			

In light of the above six principles, the following subsections illustrate how reflective practices enable teachers to appropriate cooperative learning as a tool to enhance their connectedness with their students and the target language as well as within themselves. After this, a table of reflective questions on the eight principles of cooperative learning across the six principles of reflective practice is presented to guide teachers on their journey as advocates of cooperative learning (Table 5.2).

Holistic Reflective Practice

Farrell (2019) warns against introducing reflective practice as yet another activity to be done by teachers, as this imposition may just lead to more teacher burnout. Instead, holistic reflective practice should involve not only the intellectual, cognitive, and meta-cognitive aspects of practice, but also its spiritual, moral, and emotional non-cognitive aspects; it should recognize the inner life of teachers and be integrated in the context of teachers' everyday practices both inside and outside the classroom. Holistic reflective practice leads teachers to an awareness of teaching practices as well as self-awareness and understanding that equip teachers for personal and professional growth throughout their journey as educators. Such awareness makes language teachers more integrated as they can understand who they are, where they come from, what they do, and why they do it. Palmer describes the journey toward wholeness through the metaphor of a Mobius strip, which is a continuous, unbroken shape with a single plane. There is no inner and outer; the two co-create each other, just as our inner and outer worlds co-create our reality.

Human beings need both community and solitude to do the inner work necessary to thrive. Interactions with others as done in cooperative learning groups can be further developed into 'circles of trust' to support the team members in their quest for integrity and meaning: The only guidance we can get on the inner journey comes through relationships in which others can help us discern our strengths and vulnerabilities (Palmer, 2004). Teachers can form communities of learners to understand all the principles of cooperative learning and implement them when designing and delivering the lessons. This means that students should not just be divided into groups and assigned the tasks without designing the principles of positive interdependence, individual accountability, equal opportunity to participate, maximum peer interactions, heterogeneous grouping, group autonomy, teaching cooperative skills, and cooperation as a value. All these principles need to be integratively cultivated in a cooperative learning classroom. When the group dynamics can be managed effectively, cooperative groups will be transformed into communities of learners which in turn serve as circles of trust for all team members.

In addition to community, human beings need solitude to center themselves and look into their souls. An energizing and animated class with engaging cooperative group activities is a fertile environment for learning. However, individuals also need solitude to nurture the seeds of learning in the journey of growth. Therefore, in designing a cooperative learning lesson, teachers also need to allocate some time-out when each student can engage in reflective practices individually. Palmer (2004) outlines the key practices of circles of trust, including speaking center-to-center, deep listening, asking open and honest questions, and honoring silence. These will be elaborated below.

Reflective Break
1. What is your understanding of circles of trust?
2. Where do you find your circle of trust as a teacher?
3. Do you try to facilitate circles of trust for your students in your classroom? If so, how do you do that?

Evidenced-Based Reflective Practice

Reflective practice is not about isolating yourself from the rest of the world, hiding in a cave, and meditating like a hermit. Reflective practice is an evidence-based approach in which teachers collect data about their work and then reflect on this to make informed decisions about their practice (Farrell, 2019). For example, if teachers say they have implemented the Jigsaw technique (see Chapter 2) successfully, this statement has to be supported with convincing evidence. Teachers can find evidence through several means including conducting action research and studying others' best practices. Classroom action research involves a reflective process in which teachers gather field data from their own classrooms or their fellow teachers' to improve their teaching practices. 'Engaging in evidence-based reflective practice enables teachers to articulate to themselves (and others) what they do, how they do it, why they do it, and what the impact of their teaching is on student learning,' and how they will change based on the available data (Farrell, 2019, p. 62).

In addition to collecting data about their own work, an evidence-based reflective practice can also be done by reading other teacher-researchers' studies on topics of interest, taking the lessons learned into account, and gaining insights. There is a plethora of studies on cooperative learning and anything related to cooperative learning, which teachers can refer to and compare the lessons learned with their own experiences. Implementing cooperative learning guided by the eight principles of cooperative learning needs to be supported with evidence found by the teachers or others.

The results of engaging in evidence-based reflective practice may lead teachers to continue current practices or make changes. Teachers make little and big decisions every day in regard to their teaching practices. Their decisions should not be based on impulse, hearsay, or random thoughts; informed decisions will emerge as a result of analysis of concrete evidence. One opportunity for evidence-based reflective practice arises when teachers occupy themselves in moments of solitude. Reading other people's studies and researching their own work can help those who are not used to meditating and being at peace with their true self in silence.

Dialogic Reflective Practice

After engaging themselves in moments of solitude, teachers may also carry on dialogic reflective practice. The exercises on weaving communities of learners and transforming them into circles of trust need to be carried out not only among students but also among teachers themselves. Teaching may be one of the loneliest professions. Teachers may share space and engage in discussions in the teachers' room. They may also gather in professional development forums. The truth of the matter is that the majority of teachers spend most of their working time on their own in the classroom. Any predicaments happening in the classroom too often have to be dealt with single-handedly. Few schools have a systematic and effective design of supervision, team-teaching, and mentoring. Therefore, teachers, too, need to engage with their peers through cooperative learning activities either within the school or outside. The experiences of working with peers collaboratively will equip teachers with a sense of efficacy and set them on a journey of growth. These experiences will give them the intellectual, social, and affective capital they need to design and deliver cooperative learning lessons in their own classrooms.

Farrell (2019) suggests following up evidence-based reflective practice with dialogues as a means for deeper reflection to allow for clarification, questioning, and enhanced understanding that may not be possible for a teacher engaged in self-reflection. Reflection through dialogue begins with internal conversations with the self about the teaching practices, continues with a trusted colleague, and finally enlarges into groups of teachers either from the same school or outside. Dialogic reflective practice in groups leads to the idea of building a community of practice because engagement in group discussions allows teachers to voice their ideas about various issues related to their practice and to contribute to other teachers' growth, which in turn helps them feel a sense of community while they are also receiving insights from other teachers in their group discussions.

Exercising dialogues is essential for teachers who implement cooperative learning in the classroom. Cooperative learning relies on peer interactions and equal opportunities to participate which require cooperative values and skills. Engaging in a dialogue also requires cooperative values and skills. Sometimes conflict may arise in cooperative learning activities, especially in heterogeneous groups in which members have different backgrounds, value systems, needs, interests, and achievement levels. One effective way to resolve a conflict is engaging the opposing parties in dialogue to build mutual understanding and find shared goals.

Reflective Break

1. How does dialogue with yourself help you become a better teacher?
2. Do you have a trusted colleague in school? What do you share with him/her?
3. What insights do you gain from dialogue with a group of teachers?

Reflective Practice Bridges Principles and Practice

Reflective practice connects teachers' principles comprising their philosophy, beliefs, theories, and experiences with their students and the language through their teaching practices. John Dewey (as cited in Farrell, 2019) suggests that teachers should examine what is occurring (theories-in-use) in their practice and compare it to their beliefs (espoused theories) about learning and teaching. Developing an awareness of principles and practices is a necessary starting point in reflections since we cannot grow professionally 'unless we are aware of who we are, what we do, and why we do what we do.' Sometimes teachers are not aware of the discrepancy between 'what they do and what they think they do.' A study of 192 teachers and their 3480 students (Harjanto, Lie, & Wijaya, 2018) revealed such a discrepancy about active learning. The three teachers' behaviors as perceived by the teachers themselves were different from their most dominant behaviors as observed by their students and external observers.

Not many teachers are aware of the hidden part of themselves, especially when they are not consciously monitoring their thinking processes, theories, beliefs, values, and philosophy and reflecting on how these are reflected or not in their classroom practices. Teachers should engage in systematic reflective practice to uncover their principles and connect them with their practices. When teachers are able to reflect on their principles, they can then examine how these principles are translated (or not) into actual classroom practice. When principles and practices are aligned, teachers find connectedness within themselves. This connectedness with self is fundamental to establishing connectedness with the students and with the language that is taught.

Reflective Break

1. Why are teachers' principles and their practices not always aligned?
2. How do you connect your principles to your practices?
3. In what ways do your philosophy of learning, values, assumptions, theories, and values lead you to choose cooperative learning?

Inquiring Disposition in Reflective Practice

Developing an inquiring disposition – the fifth principle in reflective practice – requires open-mindedness, responsibility, and wholeheartedness (Dewey as cited in Farrell, 2019). Open-mindedness means an attitude to listen to various viewpoints different from our own and to open up to possibilities of some truth in those viewpoints and errors in our own. Learning, according to Piaget (1970), comprises two processes in cognitive development: assimilation and accommodation. Cognitive growth is the result of constant interweaving of assimilation and accommodation. Assimilation occurs when we modify or change new information to fit into our schemas (what we already know). It keeps the new information or experience and adds to what already exists in our minds. Accommodation is when we restructure or modify what we already know so that new information can fit in better. This results from problems posed by the environment and when our perceptions do not fit in with what we know or think.

There is a second attitude or attribute associated with reflection that Dewey suggested is a prerequisite to any action: responsibility. Responsibility means careful consideration of the consequences to which an action leads. Teachers should always consider the impact of any decision and action conducted with their students, including choosing and implementing a teaching method. Responsibility is an essential part of teachers' integrity.

Finally, wholeheartedness means that teachers enthusiastically carry out their teaching practices and passionately examine what they do throughout their path as educators. As human beings, teachers may have their vulnerabilities – doubts, anxieties, and fears – as they venture into possibilities and complex connectedness with their students and learning content. When they remain true to their inner selves, they will gradually contain and resolve their vulnerabilities. Eventually, their enthusiasm will move them to carry on their teaching practices and to create a meaningful life for their students and for themselves. A meaningful life, according to Mihaly Csikszentmihalyi (1990), is one where we spend our time in a state of optimal experience called 'flow.' To live a great life, all our goals must be unified in a way that produces the maximum amount of flow. Learning how to transform any task into a flow experience will be the key to unlocking long-lasting happiness. Flow happens when our skill matches the difficulty of the task. If the task is too difficult, we will feel anxious and won't be able to experience flow. On the other hand, when skills are much higher than the challenge, we will feel bored.

Reflective Break
1. Do you remember a flow experience as a teacher? What happened? Write about it in a journal or share it with a trusted colleague.
2. Do you ever feel anxious or bored as a teacher? Why? How do you overcome it?

Reflective Practice as a Way of Life

Just as teaching is beyond technique, reflective practice, as Farrell (2019) stated, is more than a method; it is a way of life. Every human being needs to be engaged in the regular practice of ongoing reflection to have a meaningful life and to grow into a better person. Teachers, too, have this need because the world is constantly changing and so is the knowledge base of teaching. New research findings, theories, and approaches as well as new challenges concerning the students and their contexts thrust teachers into uncharted waters all the time. The Covid-19 pandemic, for instance, has caused traditional face-to-face schooling to switch into remote learning and brought unprecedented changes in education practices. For many teachers, these changes have shaken their identity and integrity, while some others who had formed their own personal theory of teaching and found an interconnectedness within themselves and with their students and the subject remained intact through the turbulence of the pandemic. All teachers have had to make major adjustments in their teaching practices but some managed the situation better than others.

Kumaravadivelu (2003, p. 17) suggests that second language teachers should enter into 'a continual process of self-reflection and self-renewal' so that they can 'construct their own personal theory of teaching.' Indeed, teachers who engage in lifelong reflective practice as a way of life can develop a deeper understanding of themselves, their teaching practices, and their students; assess their professional growth; develop informed decision-making; and contribute to the growth of other teachers. Teachers should continually reflect on how their philosophy, values, beliefs, theories, and experiences shape their teaching practices, and on the other hand how their interactions with the students and their teaching of the language transform themselves personally and professionally.

Reflective Break
1. Do you engage yourself in continual reflective practice?
2. How has reflective practice transformed you as a person and as a professional teacher?

Table 5.2. Implementing cooperative learning through reflective practice

	REFLECTIVE PRACTICE PRINCIPLES OF COOPERATIVE LEARNING	Holistic	Evidence-Based	Dialogue	Bridging Principles and Practices	Inquiring Disposition	Way of Life	
T H E S T U D E N T S	Positive Interdependence	• What do I think about positive interdependence? • How can I make team members feel safe and comfortable with one another? • How can I make them trust one another and contribute to the group goals?	• What does research say about positive interdependence in CL? • How do the students trust and support one another? • What's the result of interdependence? • What can be better next time?	• Who is my trusted fellow teacher? • What do I want to share with him/her about my experience in managing interdependence in my class? • What do I want to share with other teachers about that experience?	• What do I believe about human interconnectedness? • In what ways does my philosophy of human interdependence lead me to choose cooperative learning?	• Do I question my belief about human interdependence? What do I discover? • Why is (or isn't) cooperative learning the right approach for me?	• Do I reflect on human interdependence? What do I discover? • In what ways does my reflection of human interdependence make me grow into a better person?	T H E T A R G E T L A N G U A G E

THE STUDENTS								THE TARGET LANGUAGE
	Individual Accountability	• Do I think individual accountability is possible in CL? • How can I prevent free-riders and workhorses in the group? • How can I make students responsible for their own learning? • How can I balance group activities and individual time-outs?	• What does research say about individual accountability? • How can I assess individual accountability? • What's the result of individual accountability? • What can be better next time?	• Do I engage my students in dialogues and reflections of their share and responsibility of the group work? • What do I want to share with my trusted colleague about ensuring individual accountability in my class? • What do I want to share with other teachers about that experience?	• What do I believe about responsibility? • What is my experience in accountability? • In what ways do my beliefs and experiences lead me to choose cooperative learning?	• Do I question my belief about responsibility? What do I discover? • In what ways do my beliefs and experiences lead me to doubt the principle of individual accountability? • How do I resolve issues in individual accountability in my professional life?	• Do I reflect on human responsibility? What do I discover? • How do I make my professional behaviors accountable to my colleagues and students? • In what ways does my reflection of human responsibility make me grow into a better person?	

THE STUDENTS							THE TARGET LANGUAGE
Equal Opportunity to Participate	• What do I think about equal opportunity to participate? • What should I do when students do not participate equally? • How can I encourage everyone to participate? • How can I create a safe learning environment for every member to participate and contribute to the group?	• What does research say about participation and engagement in CL? • Are there better ways to make everyone participate? • What can be better next time?	• What do I want to share with him/her about my experience in creating a safe learning climate in my class? • What do I want to share with other teachers about that experience?	• What were my experiences with my past participation as a student? • How can I translate my principles about safe learning environment into my teaching practices?	• Do I question my belief about 'equal opportunity for all'? What do I discover? • In what ways do my beliefs and experiences lead me to doubt the principle of equal opportunity?	• Do I reflect on equal opportunity for all? What do I discover? • In what ways does my reflection of 'equal opportunity for all' challenge me as a person and a teacher?	
Maximum Peer Interactions	• What do I think about maximum peer interactions? • How can I maintain the group dynamics? • What CL techniques work best to maximize peer interactions? • Do peer interactions help achieve learning performances? Why or why not?	• What does research say about peer interactions? • What's the result of better peer interactions? • What can be better next time?	• What do I want to share with him/her about my experience in engaging students to interact constructively? • What do I want to share with other teachers about that experience?	• What were my experiences with interactions with peers in my past? • How can I translate my principles about optimal interactions into my teaching practices?	• Do I ever have a Flow experience when working cooperatively with others in my class? What happens? • How can I maximize interactions among my students so they can have their Flow experience?	• Do I reflect on human interactions? What do I discover? • In what ways does my reflection of human interactions help me implement cooperative learning?	

THE STUDENTS							THE TARGET LANGUAGE
	Heterogeneous Grouping	• What do I think about heterogenous grouping? • What are the obstacles of heterogeneous grouping? • How can I overcome these obstacles? • What are the benefits? • How can I help students to connect with one another?	• What does research say about grouping? • Why do I group students hetero-geneously? • What's the result of different ways of grouping? • What can be better next time?	• What do I want to share with him/her about my experience in grouping students? • What do I want to share with other teachers about that experience?	• What were my experiences with group work as a student? • In what ways do my principles about grouping align with my teaching practices?	• Did I ever have unpleasant group work experiences? • What are the advantages and disadvantages of heterogeneous grouping? • How can I make heterogeneous grouping beneficial for my students?	• Do I reflect on human diversity in this world? What do I discover? • In what ways does my reflection of human diversity help me implement the principle of heterogeneous grouping?	
	Group Autonomy	• What do I think about group autonomy? • Can a group be too autonomous to the point of undermining teachers' authority? • How can I facilitate groups to be autonomous? • What are the benefits for students and myself as a teacher?	• What does research say about group autonomy? • What factors lead to group autonomy? • What's the result of making groups autonomous? • What can be better next time?	• What do I want to share with him/her about my experience in facilitating group autonomy? • What do I want to share with other teachers about that experience?	• What were my experiences with group work as a student? • In what ways do my principles about group autonomy align with my teaching practices?	• What is my understanding of group autonomy? • Do I question my own philosophy, assumptions, theories, and values about group autonomy? What do I discover? • How can I help my students achieve group autonomy?	• Do I reflect on group autonomy? What do I discover? • Why are some groups more autonomous than others? • In what ways does my reflection help me implement the principle of group autonomy?

THE STUDENTS							THE TARGET LANGUAGE
	Teaching Cooperative Skills	• What do I think about cooperative skills? Are they teachable? • How can I teach cooperative skills more effectively? • What are the benefits for students now and in the future?	• What does research say about group autonomy? • What's the result of teaching cooperative skills? • What can be better next time?	• What do I want to share with him/her about my experience in teaching cooperative skills? • What do I want to share with other teachers about that experience?	• What were my experiences learning cooperative skills? • How can I teach cooperative skills more effectively?	• Do I question my own principles about teaching cooperative skills? What do I discover? • Is teaching cooperative skills necessary for every student? Why or why not?	• Do I reflect on my own experiences acquiring cooperative skills? What do I discover? • In what ways does my reflection help me teach cooperative skills more effectively?	
	Cooperation as a Value	• What do I think of cooperation as a value? • How can I cultivate cooperation as a value? • What are the benefits for students now and in the future? • How can they make the world a better place with this value?	• What does research say about cooperation as a value? • How have students changed through cooperation? • What can be better next time?	• What do I want to share with my group about my experience in cultivating cooperation values in my students? • What do I want to share with other teachers about that experience?	• What are my values regarding cooperation? • How can I instill the value of cooperation in my students? • How can I handle potential conflicts of values among my students?	• Is the value of cooperation universal across cultures? • Is promoting the value of cooperation necessary for every student? Why or why not?	• Do I reflect on the value of cooperation across cultures? Do I see differences or similarities? • In what ways does my reflection help me instill the value of cooperation in my students? • Why should I do that?	

THE TEACHER

To sum up this chapter, Table 5.2 presents reflective questions on the eight principles of cooperative learning across the six principles of reflective practice. This is not an exhaustive list of reflective questions, but it aims to guide teachers on their journey of cooperative learning. Teachers are encouraged to add their own questions.

CONCLUSION

This chapter has described the underlying landscape of reflective practice which involves students, the target language, and teachers themselves. These three aspects in the landscape may act as sources of complexity that language teachers need to deal with. Within this landscape, transformation of teaching and learning takes place through the interconnectedness of those three sources of complexity. The transformation occurs when teachers engage themselves in reflective practices. Teachers may choose and implement cooperative learning effectively when they integrate their choice with who they are as teachers. Reflective questions have been listed to help teachers explore their reasons, preferences, reservations, and decisions.

When cooperative learning interacts with teacher reflection, the whole is greater than the sum of the parts. Cooperative learning is grounded on humanistic principles of learning and offers various methods and teaching techniques that would help language teachers manage their class more effectively. The techniques and practicalities are pedagogical tools that teachers can use and keep in their repertoire. In light of the landscape visualized in Figure 5.1 at the beginning of this chapter, choosing which techniques to use should be based on recognition of self, on the students, and on the lessons. In the teaching and learning process, the techniques and cooperative learning activities should help teachers experience the connectedness of the three. Then, through continual reflective practices, teachers can deepen the connectedness and look forward to better teaching practices.

Chapter 6

Teachers Cooperatively Reflecting on Their Students' Use of Cooperative Learning

INTRODUCTION

This chapter focuses on how language teachers can reflect together to learn more about how to facilitate their students' use of cooperative learning and other student-centered learning methods. The chapter begins with thoughts on the nature of knowledge. Next, we propose benefits of teacher–teacher cooperation before delving into Farrell's definition of reflective practice. The bulk of the chapter attempts to answer the question of how cooperative learning principles, explained in Chapter 2, can apply to groups of language teachers working together to strengthen the role of their schools in making for more cooperative classrooms and a more cooperative world.

THE NATURE OF KNOWLEDGE

All of us teachers have so much to learn. Even for our most experienced colleagues, who may have taught the same subject, at the same level, such as 10th grade (15–16 years old), at the same school their entire career, so much remains unknown. A great deal of knowledge remains not only partial but also biased by teachers' own perspectives. The story from India of the blind people and the elephant illustrates this point (All About Philosophy, 2020). To recap, five visually-impaired people each touch a different part of the elephant – trunk, tail, ears, etc. – and each comes away with a very different take on what the animal is. Each person in the story – just like each of us – has only limited data. Thus, we all need to exercise caution before we can claim a big-picture view, and should seek to expand our knowledge of any situation and the range of perspectives we bring to bear in our analysis of the situation. Just like an elephant, a school is such a different place for each of the stakeholders that each of us certainly forms a very different view of what happens there and of the entire education experience.

'The Frogs in the Well,' a Chinese tale, offers another parable that highlights the partialness of understanding (Jackson, 2013). One version of that parable tells the story of two frogs who live at the bottom of a well and cannot see the world beyond the small opening at the top. The two frogs seem to be doing okay with their limited knowledge until their supply of insects begins to decrease, meaning they have to adapt or die. Forced to overcome their fears of the unknown, they hop out of the well and discover an amazing new world of opportunities but also of perils. Is this similar to teachers? If we learn more about the worlds beyond our classrooms – including the worlds of our students, their families, and communities – might we become better teachers, but might we also learn some uncomfortable truths and encounter some difficult obstacles?

Reflective Break
1. Can you identify a gap in your own knowledge, a gap that is making it difficult for you become an even better teacher?
2. How could you try to close that gap? Could others help you?
3. How are we teachers similar to the people with the elephant, or like the frogs in the well? What can we do to overcome our lack of knowledge and lack of awareness of alternative perspectives?

Another long-told tale of the dangers of incomplete observation comes from the Greek philosopher Plato (Lewin & Ergas, 2018). Plato's story of 'The Cave' urges us to question whether our beliefs flow from well-grounded knowledge. Psychologists Fishbein & Ajzen (1975) posited that our beliefs exert a fundamental influence on our actions. Relating this insight to education, Brownlee (2001) and Burns (1992) found that, indeed, teachers' beliefs strongly impact what we do in classrooms.

In Plato's story [for an elaborated, animated version, see: https://www.studiobinder.com/blog/platos-allegory-of-the-cave], a group of people are imprisoned their entire lives in a cave. Out of the prisoners' sight, a fire burns, and other people hold up puppets and other objects, but the prisoners see only the shadows cast by these puppets and other objects, and they believe the shadows are real. One day, a prisoner goes free and realizes that a very different world exists beyond the cave, but when the escapee returns and tells the others, they do not believe this very different account of reality. Instead, they prefer to go on believing in the reality of the shadows created by others.

The parable raises the question of what might happen when we teachers learn more about reality. Would that new knowledge cause us to question our beliefs, or would we stubbornly hold on to the beliefs that have guided our teaching for so many years, not just guiding how we teach but, before that, guiding how we ourselves learned and were taught? Lodhi (2017) posits that the moral of 'The Cave' is that we must continually push ourselves to learn and then reshape our lives based on this new evidence, because once we have seen the world differently, we can never unsee what we have seen. Others may be able to fool us into a false view of reality, but can we fool ourselves?

Reflective Break
1. What was a time that you learned something new about your students, the communities where they live, or about some of the other teachers and other staff at your school?
2. Did you change anything based on that new knowledge?

The above three parables challenge us teachers to use reflection to seek a fuller knowledge of our world and to be brave enough to perhaps make changes to our teaching based on what we encounter as we reflect. To gain a better understanding of our students and the larger context in which they and we live, we need to acknowledge the extent of our ignorance, to be curious to learn more, and to be open to learning from anyone and anything that might aid our understanding. Another term for exercising such curiosity is to boggle, which, to paraphrase the *Cambridge Dictionary* (Cambridge University Press, 2021), is defined as to show happiness, surprise, doubt, and wonder when faced with a situation. Young children tend to boggle more than adults, especially adults such as teachers, who may worry we will lose face by admitting our ignorance. Perhaps surprisingly, Kushnir & Koenig (2017) found that students tended to have more faith in adults who sometimes admitted ignorance, rather than those who falsely claimed superhero omniscience. Furthermore, Shulman and other leaders in education (Shulman & Sherin, 2004) urged teachers to admit our ignorance and to seek to overcome it by collaborating with colleagues in Communities of Learners. Of course, we can count students among our colleagues.

One more story illustrates the benefits of acknowledging our weaknesses. *The empty pot* (Nunn et al., 2015) tells the story of an emperor approaching the end of his life. He had no heirs, so he gathered together all the children in the kingdom and gave each a seed, telling them that whoever was able to grow the best plant from that seed would be the next emperor. One of the children, Cheng, was from a humble background and had substantial experience and skill at growing plants.

However, Cheng could not get his seed to grow, despite all the growing strategies he used. Months later, when the emperor once again summoned the children to the palace, they all came with pots abundant with healthy, blossoming plants, all of them except Cheng. His pot was empty. Much to Cheng's surprise, when the emperor saw his empty pot, he smiled and said, 'You will be the next emperor, because you are the only honest one. You see, all the seeds I distributed had been cooked; none of them could grow.' Just like the students in Kushnir & Koenig's (2017) research, the emperor appreciated Cheng's willingness to admit his (temporary) inadequacies.

Reflective Break

1. Novice teachers are often full of curiosity. How can veteran teachers maintain their enjoyment of boggling?
2. Would your students respond to your admission of ignorance in the same positive way as the students in Kushnir & Koenig's study?

ADVANTAGES OF TEACHER–TEACHER COOPERATION

Farrell & Jacobs (2016) recommended that teachers consider that cooperation with peers can gain them the same advantages that their students gain from cooperation with their own peers. The advantages that teachers gain from peer collaboration include:

a. Lightening their workload, as sometimes 'many hands make light work,' e.g., creating new teaching materials or planning an event together.
b. Bringing to bear different strengths, e.g., one teacher is skilled at design while another can phrase ideas in captivating ways or spot typos.
c. Exerting more power, as one teacher with an idea for change exerts less influence than eight teachers all advocating the same idea.
d. Offering different perspectives and information, e.g., when helping a student with difficulties, different teachers will likely have had different experiences with that student or with students having a similar profile.
e. Providing a sounding board for frustrations as well as for breakthroughs and victories; as a Native American proverb states, 'Happiness was born a twin – to experience joy, we must share it.'
f. Experiencing the advantages of cooperation; when we teachers see the benefits of working with our own peers, that inspires us to push harder to facilitate our students experiencing the same benefits with their peers.

An important point about the pluses of teacher–teacher cooperation should be highlighted: the advantages lie in not just the cognitive realm but also in the affective domain. It seems paradoxical, but teaching can be a lonely profession. How can we be lonely when so much of our day is spent surrounded by people? Except that those people are our students, not our peers. Even if we teach adults, we are separated from our students by a power hierarchy, just as school principals and vice-principals are separated from teachers (Dor-Haim, 2021). Of course, we can spend time with colleagues in many non-academic ways, such as gathering for a meal, going together for exercise, or organizing and attending parties for birthdays or public holidays. We can also collaborate as part of our teaching, such as occasionally merging classes, taking an online course together, or attending the same webinar. All these ideas add a vital social element to our teaching lives.

Reflective Break
1. Of all the advantages of teacher–teacher collaboration mentioned above, which one have you experienced the most?
2. Of all the advantages of teacher–teacher collaboration mentioned above, which one have you experienced the least or not at all?

Farrell's Definition of Reflective Practice

While the above comprise useful ways to enjoy teacher–teacher interaction, the purpose of this chapter lies in engaging with peers to promote teacher reflection. Farrell (2015, p. 123) defined teacher reflective practice as 'A cognitive process accompanied by a set of attitudes in which teachers systematically collect data about their practice, and, while engaging in dialogue with others, use the data to make informed decisions about their practice both inside and outside the classroom.'

Given that the title of the present book is *Cooperative Learning through a Reflective Lens*, it seems only fitting to discuss how peer interaction among teachers can enhance teachers' reflective practice. Cooperative learning refers mostly to peer interaction among students, but such interaction between teachers, indeed between any individuals, can be beneficial and can be facilitated by ideas from the cooperative learning literature.

Please note that cooperation plays a useful or even necessary role in at least three key points in Farrell's above definition of teacher reflective practice. First, systematic data collection greatly benefits from multiple pairs of eyes, ears, and hands. Colleagues' eyes can observe what the teacher and students are doing, as well as observing their faces and body language while doing. The ears can listen in on the discussion of a group on one side of the room while the teacher listens in on the interaction of a group on the other side. The other teachers' hands can hold a video camera or sound recording equipment, as well as holding a clipboard with a checklist of points to observe.

Reflective Break

1. Have you ever collected data on your own teaching, such as recording your voice to see whether you use fillers, e.g., 'you know?', 'um,' 'right?', and 'ah.'
2. Have you ever collaborated with colleagues to collect data on them or their students, such as recording how often students use their first language in class instead of the target language, and for what purposes they seemed to be using their target language?

A second place in Farrell's (2015) definition of teacher reflective practice where fellow teachers could be of immense assistance lies in 'engaging in dialogue.' After all, who better to serve as dialogue partners than those who have such great familiarity with the reflecting teachers' contexts. Third, but definitely not least, peers facilitate teacher reflective practice in the step in which the data collected are analyzed toward the goal of making informed decisions and taking informed actions based on those decisions. For instance, peers can play devil's advocates to suggest possible flaws in their colleague's thinking; as brainstormers they can propose alternative interpretations of the data; as planners, fellow teachers can discuss implementation steps; and as cheerleaders they can encourage perseverance.

COOPERATIVE LEARNING PRINCIPLES AND TEACHER REFLECTION GROUPS

Chapter 2 explained eight cooperative learning principles and suggested how they could be implemented in student groups. Here, those principles are reviewed and ideas proposed for their implementation in the context of groups of language teachers engaged in reflective practice.

Reflective Break

1. In what kinds of settings do you work with fellow teachers?
2. Is this collaboration usually of mutual benefit?

Positive Interdependence

Positive interdependence is the principle which seeks to supply the glue to hold groups together, as well as the concern that encourages groupmates to look out for and support each other. Farrell (2014) underscored that teacher reflection groups provide teachers with a safe space where they need not fear being judged, because people are there to support each other in their quest to experience the blossoming of their full potential as teachers and as persons as a whole. To put positive interdependence in statistical terms, it is the feeling among group members that their outcomes are positively correlated, i.e., what helps one helps all, and what hurts one hurts all. Chapter 2 described eight ways to facilitate the feeling of positive interdependence among group members, including:

a. The group has a common **Goal** (or goals). Everyone understands that goal and works to achieve it. In a group of language teachers doing reflective practice, a key goal is to better understand their classrooms, to share their new knowledge, and to trial ways to implement what they have learned.

b. Each member has or obtains **Resources** that are unique to that individual, such as information and equipment, and these resources need to be shared for the group to achieve its goal(s). Examples of resources would be knowledge of how to use a video camera and to edit the resulting footage, a new article about reflective practice in language teaching, knowledge of one of the first languages of your school's students, or a food processor for making healthy, plant-based snacks for your group meetings.

c. Each member of the language teachers' group for reflective practice has one or more **Roles**, and these roles often rotate. Possible roles might be those of the recorder, who notes the main points discussed and any decisions taken; the data director, who helps the group save, organize, and analyze the data they have all collected; or the insight seeker, who asks advice from various people whose insights could aid the group. Of course, the person designated a given role is not the only one who can perform or help with that role.

d. Groups need to feel that they are moving forward toward their goals, even if their achievements are small steps. Thus, **Celebration/Reward** positive interdependence merits attention. For instance, Seligman (2012) listed five elements necessary for positivity in individuals' and groups' existence. The acronym PERMA expresses these five elements: positive emotion, engagement (i.e., people feel keen about what they are doing), relationships (i.e., they feel kindly toward the people with whom they engage), meaning (i.e., they believe what they are doing is valuable), and achievement (i.e., they experience some success in reaching their valuable goals). Celebrations can be as simple as shouting 'Hurray!'

Another way to celebrate involves a specific application of the cooperative learning technique Circle of Writers – All at Once. Here are the *general steps* in the technique.

1. Everyone in a group of 3 or 4 has a piece of paper or a device for electronic writing.
2. Each person takes a turn to write and then passes the paper to the left.
3. After receiving a partner's paper or electronic text, people continue what the previous person has written before passing on the paper again.
4. When each paper returns to the person who started it, they write an ending (in the case of a story) or add more information (in the case of non-fiction). Later, they can share what was written with the entire group.

For a celebration after a group has made progress toward achievement of their goals, the Group Thank You Note can be used. This is a *specific application* of Circle of Writers – All at Once. It works as follows.

1. Everyone begins with a piece of paper. They write their name at the top and pass the paper to their left.
2. Upon receiving a partner's paper, they check the name at the top of the paper and, then, at the *bottom* of the paper, they write something specific about the actions taken by that person to assist the group in its progress toward its goal. By 'specific' is meant something such as 'Ambaree is very knowledgeable about teacher reflection and kindly connected us to articles and books on the topic,' not 'Ambaree is very knowledgeable.' After writing their praise, they fold over the bottom of the page, so that others cannot read what they have written, and then pass the paper to their left.
3. This process of writing, folding, and passing continues until the paper returns to the person whose name is written at the top of each paper. That person then unfolds the paper and reads and enjoys the peer praise.

The Group Thank You Note rewards people for their contributions to the group, encourages them to continue such meritorious contributions, and perhaps leads others to emulate their groupmates' praiseworthy actions. Achor (2018) explained ways to maximize both the quantity and the quality of praise in a variety of contexts including education and the workplace. His many suggestions included democratizing praise, i.e., praise can be not only top-down, e.g., teachers to students, but also bottom-up; avoiding comparison praise, i.e., rather than saying someone is better than someone else, simply highlight what one person does well; praising not just the outcome but also the process *to* the outcome; providing multiple means of praising, e.g., making 'praiser' one of the roles in the group, or allocating time during or at the end of a session to praise others; and finding meaning in every task, i.e., by reminding ourselves of the importance of what we are doing in education, any praise we give/receive for promoting education becomes that much more substantial.

> **Reflective Break**
> 1. What kind of celebrations does your school, department, etc. have? Do most people seem to enjoy them? Any suggestions for improving the celebrations?
> 2. Have you ever participated in anything like the Group Thank You Note? If so, was it successful? Regardless of whether you tried the activity, can you think of any tweaks that might improve it?

Individual Accountability

A second cooperative learning principle that can boost the performance of groups of reflective language teachers is individual accountability. While positive interdependence provokes groupmates to support each other, individual accountability asks groupmates to apply appropriate pressure on each other to do their fair share in the group. As to what constitutes 'appropriate' pressure, a teacher once told us about a time when the pressure went too far. A student came seeking this teacher's urgent assistance as he had not done his agreed upon fair share for his group's presentation that day, and, as a result, his groupmates were going to beat him up after school.

Teachers are very unlikely to beat each other up for not doing their duty to the group, but the point remains: peers need to appropriately pressure each other to contribute to the group's achievement of their goals. And, one must remember that individual accountability involves people doing their *fair* share, not necessarily their *equal* share. For instance, a teacher at the beginning of their career, who has just moved to the area where the school is located, likely has less to contribute to their reflective practice group than a teacher with thirty years' experience who was born and raised in the area where the school is located and has been doing reflection for five years. No worries. The novice teacher can learn and, in the future, mentor others, just as the more senior teachers in their current group are now mentoring this beginning teacher.

This appropriate pressure on teacher peers has much in common with the scaffolding that teachers and peers use with students (Wood, Bruner, & Ross, 1976).

The central concept of scaffolding involves supplying and then gradually removing support. The provision of support goes from the more to the less capable, but everyone needs support; everyone needs to learn. Thus, everyone can scaffold for everyone else, and everyone should feel individually accountable to their group. Below are five ideas for scaffolding in groups of reflective language teachers.

a. Set a good example for peers. Noticing details from peers' examples can often be the best way of learning, better than listening to lectures on how to be skilled at teacher reflective practice.

b. Establish reasonable expectations for each group member. As the saying goes, 'One size does not fit all.'

c. Appreciate that 's*** happens.' We can only control so much in our lives. Thus, we need to be forgiving when the unexpected arises in the lives of others and to inform team members when it occurs in our own lives.

d. Identify people from beyond the group who can help. For example, 'critical friends' (Costa & Kallick, 1993) are people we trust to give us honest, straightforward, but at the same time supportive, evaluations of our ideas and work. As a Russian proverb puts it, 'An enemy will agree, but a friend will argue.' Nobel Prize-winning scientists Watson and Crick highlighted the crucial role of disagreement in the process by which they discovered the structure of DNA (Watson, 1968). To paraphrase their process, whenever one of them developed an idea and presented it to the other, their research partner, in a collegial manner, would seek to find all manner of flaws in that idea. Other types of helpful people beyond the group could be those with skills in statistics, IT, or students' languages and cultures.

e. Remember Celebration/Reward positive interdependence and the Group Thank You Note activity (earlier in this chapter). Indeed, Achor (2018) urged that we not miss opportunities to praise and to celebrate. He cited Oprah Winfrey, who, to paraphrase, advised that the more we celebrate, the more we will have to celebrate.

Reflective Break

1. What have you or others tried when teacher colleagues did not do their fair share?
2. Have you ever been the one who was accused, rightly or wrongly, of not doing their fair share? How was the situation resolved, or was it ever resolved?

Equal Opportunity to Participate

Readers will recall from Chapter 2 that the cooperative learning principle of equal opportunity to participate calls on groups to attend to the frequent problem of some members feeling excluded from the group process. Perhaps, they feel as though they have not 'earned' the right to speak. We, the authors of this book, witness this in groups in which we participate. Sometimes, we are the experts who have earned the right to speak and to be listened to. In such cases, we need to be careful not to dominate the groups we are in. For example, when someone asks us a question, wanting to hear our 'expert' opinion, instead of answering straight away, we may ask them or another group member to offer their opinion or to recount their experiences on the topic. Contrariwise, in other groups to which we belong we sometimes feel as though we have little to contribute, thus we had best keep quiet for fear of wasting the group's time or even being ridiculed. In those cases, we try to ask good questions, to repeat back our emerging understanding, and to check if others in the group are, like us, also struggling.

Several ideas may prove useful in promoting equal opportunity to participate. One, distributed leadership (Torres, 2019), means that everyone in a group should consider themselves, and be considered by others, as a leader. In fact, a myriad ways to lead exist, as long as people look for them and are willing to take them on and do the work needed, which sometimes includes learning new skills to do the work, e.g., learning to use a new software. For instance, someone can lead by doing such non-intellectual tasks as keeping track of time, reminding people of the next meeting and of the tasks they promised to accomplish in preparation for that meeting, or securing a meeting room for that meeting with the necessary equipment. Somewhat similar to distributed leadership might be the idea of 'Leading from the 11th chair' (Achor, 2018). The 11th chair refers to an orchestra, where the first chair for a particular instrument, e.g., the violin, goes to the violinist perceived to be the best. If the orchestra has 11 violinists, the 11th chair is seen to be the weakest of the orchestra's violinists. Achor's point is that leadership should not be left to those who might be (at least for now) the best at various tasks. If we put too much pressure on those who currently display top abilities, these people may well burn out (Kelly & Adams, 2018), and the others will have fewer opportunities to develop.

When those members of a group of reflecting language teachers who may (for now) be less skilled offer their thoughts, we need to look for the good in what everyone says (Ron, Dreyfus, & Hershkowitz, 2010). Constructivist theory tells us that knowledge construction is an ongoing experience. Thus, we should think about the future. Everyone needs to develop, and everyone needs to be so kind as to give all others the space, i.e., opportunity, to do that developing.

Mantasiah & Yusri (2018) called this the *Pay It Forward* method in which people share kindness with others, who in turn share kindness with still others. (We like to share this video with our students – https://www.youtube.com/watch?v=nwAY-pLVyeFU&ab_channel=LifeVestInside – as it wordlessly, except for the lyrics of the song playing in the background, shows the spirit of Pay It Forward.) Paying It Forward can occur among strangers (Horita et al., 2016), as well as, in the case of groups of reflective language teachers, among people who know each other. The point is that by showing kindness in the form of encouraging fuller participation by group members who may be less skilled, or more hesitant, their fellow group members are paying forward kindness which could benefit the entire group, future groups of reflective language teachers, and all those teachers' students.

Reflective Break

1. Have you ever been one of the members in a group of teachers or any other kind of group in which you were a potentially dominant member? Did you do anything to encourage participation by the other members?
2. Have you ever been in a position similar to that of the 11th chair? Were you able to find a way to lead from that position?

Maximum Peer Interactions

As you may recall from Chapter 2, the cooperative learning principle of maximum peer interactions has two focuses. One focus calls for maximizing the number of peer interactions, and the other focus of this cooperative learning principle centers on the quality of interactions among group members. How does this principle play out when language teachers form groups for reflective practice? Here are some ideas.

To maximize the *number* of peer interactions among their group members, teachers need to consider both face-to-face (F2F) and electronic meetings. F2F meetings can occur as regular meetings, e.g., meeting around a table, as well as when group members observe each other's classes or go together to collect data, such as visiting students' homes or other places where teachers can better understand their students' lives (Caspe, 2003). As to meeting via electronic devices, a growing number of options are available. We just need to ensure that everyone is comfortable with the options we choose, e.g., that they are comfortable with using the various features of WhatsApp or other communication software. Comfort involves not only skill in using a particular software, but also comfort with the privacy protections in use (Hay Newman, 2021).

Maximizing the *quality* of peer interactions can have different meanings in groups of language teachers who collaborate for reflective practice. One aspect of quality interactions ties in with Farrell's (2019) emphasis on collecting data and referring to those data. Yes, intuition can have value (Sipman et al., 2019); yet, our reflections also need to incorporate the data that we and others have collected. Another sign of quality in peer interactions among teachers involves reference to theory. Yes, many people, including teachers, view theories as impractical, ivory-tower, snobbish wastes of time. However, Kurt Lewin, whose work was foundational to Social Interdependence Theory from which has flowed positive interdependence and cooperative learning, not to mention other very practical ideas for promoting education and social harmony, such as Action Research (Schmuck, 2006), has a famous quote: 'Nothing is as practical as a good theory' (Lewin, 1959, p. 169). Furthermore, it is not only university professors who have theories; psychologists tell us that many of our actions in life flow from our own personal theories of the world (Hsien, 2018; Männikkö & Husu, 2019).

However, we need not rely on our own theories. By referring to the thinking of scholars before us – and, yes, we reflective teachers are scholars, too! – we are doing what Isaac Newton did; we are 'standing on the shoulders of giants' (Newton, 1675/2021). In our current century, another famous scientist, Stephen Hawking (2002), employed the same metaphor in a book about physicists and astronomers from whom he had learned. Of course, giants need not be famous; our parents, our teachers from our childhood, our colleagues, and even our students can provide us with invaluable insights into not only how to teach but also how to live. Quality peer interactions among reflective teachers should be seeded with these insights. We will return later in this chapter to the topic of maximizing peer interactions when we look at the cooperative learning principle of teaching cooperative skills.

Reflective Break

1. What are two of your favorite forms of electronic communication, such as WhatsApp or Telegram? Have you recently learned any tricks to maximize their use?
2. Who are some giants upon whose shoulders you stand? They might or might not be in Education, and they might or might not be famous.

Heterogeneous Grouping

Who should be the members of our group of reflective language teachers? Many factors need to be considered. The cooperative learning principle of heterogeneous grouping offers a way. The principle tells us that heterogeneity among group members can bring benefits, in a way similar to what horticulturalists call 'hybrid vigor' (Shen et al., 2017), also known as heterosis, i.e., that interbreeding of plants from different backgrounds results in heartier offspring. With teachers from different backgrounds, a similar hope exists, that the ideas which spring from the reflections of such groups will be stronger so as to better overcome the difficulties we face, along with our students, fellow teachers, and other education stakeholders. At the same time, do not underestimate the heterogeneity that can exist even when members of a language teachers' reflection group seem the same, e.g., all veteran female teachers.

An example of the benefits of heterogeneous grouping can be seen in the case of the three authors of this book. Two are female. Also, two were born and raised in Indonesia and one in the US, although he has been living in Singapore for about 30 years. We have different religions, come from different ethnic groups, have taught in a wide variety of levels of institutions from elementary to university, from private to public and non-profit sectors, from tutoring one student at a time to teaching classes of 100+, from teaching in classrooms with only the basics to teaching in state-of-the-art classrooms, and from formal to informal and nonformal education contexts. Among our commonalities are a strong belief in cooperative learning and a great faith in and enjoyment of education.

Group members can vary in so many ways, but however they vary, they bring with them their varied knowledge, experience, perspectives, skills, and personalities. For instance, what about a teacher from another subject area joining a reflection group of language teachers, a first language teacher in a group of second language teachers, a veteran teacher with three novice teachers, or a special needs teacher amongst a group of teachers who have only one or two special needs students mainstreamed into their classes. Via the affordances of technology, it might even be possible to have a group member from another school, such as an elementary school teacher in a group of intermediate school teachers, with the elementary school teacher reminding their colleagues about what students experience prior to entering intermediate school.

Getting Comfortable with New Group Members

Initially, teachers may feel uncomfortable interacting with peers who are different from themselves. Students often experience similar discomfort in heterogeneous groups. As noted in Chapter 2, icebreaker activities offer one means of building trust. Reflection at its best delves into areas that may spark unease and even embarrassment. Thus, building and maintaining trust becomes essential (Lopez-Fresno & Savolainen, 2014). Toward this end, Hughes & Bourner (2005) suggested beginning meetings with each person taking a turn to 'check in,' i.e., to share what is on their mind, which often does not directly link with the topic of the meeting. Check-ins might involve many different emotions, including happiness, concern, sadness, and surprise. Although check-ins in might seem to be off-topic distractions, they can enhance empathy and support among group members. Similarly, we should allow and even encourage groups of our students to spend a bit of time on chit-chat before getting down to business.

Everyone taking a few deep breaths can be another way to start meetings. Studies with participants ranging from preschool children to business leaders have found that benefits accrue when a little deep breathing and other forms of relaxation take place. For instance, results of a study done with business meetings by researchers at Singapore Management University suggested that improvements could take place, such as more successful negotiations, enhanced work engagement, and more ethical decision-making (Masters-Waage, Peters, & Reb, 2021). Just as with check-ins, a few deep breaths can clear our minds in preparation for productive meetings.

The Lifespan of Groups

For a big-picture view of the lifespan of groups, Luckman & Jensen (1977) offered a five-stage model: forming, storming, norming, performing, and adjourning, although this model may not fit the experience of every group. Table 6.1 presents each of the five stages in the life of a group; these are not the stages in a single group meeting. Note: stages can be of very different lengths of time.

Table 6.1. Five stages in the life of a group

Stage	Role	Example activity
Forming	Getting acquainted.	Everyone shares brief information about their background as teachers and people.
Storming	Negotiating the group's mission and work style.	Taking turns (to promote equal opportunity to participate) so that everyone's voice is heard and everyone's views are explained. Lack of clear communication can result in hidden conflicts emerging later.
Norming	Reaching agreements on how the group will operate, what they will do, and how they will do it, even if agreements are partial and tentative.	Making a plan for what to do next and the various roles that each person will play in enacting that plan. Working of cooperative skills. (See the relevant section later in this chapter.)
Performing	We hope this is by far the longest stage. The group moves forward together to implement its plan.	Carrying out and sometimes tweaking the plan. Checking that everyone is comfortable with their roles.
Adjourning	Wrapping up the group's work, reflecting on what was learned, sharing learnings with others, and considering what the future holds.	Having a short celebration of the group's achievements. Preparing short 'thank you' messages for each other.

Reflective Break

1. Who might be the members of your group of reflective language teachers? In what different ways is that group heterogeneous? Who might be a wild-card choice to boost the group's heterogeneity even further?
2. In past groups, of any type, that you have been in, did you do anything for the norming stage? If not, do you wish you had? If you did something in the norming stage, what was it?

Group Autonomy

Group autonomy constitutes the cooperative learning principle that urges students to rely on each other as their first option for help, rather than looking immediately to outside experts for support. How does group autonomy relate to groups of reflective language teachers? Too often, education functions in a very top-down way. Not only does information and decision-making flow from teachers to students but also from school administrators and university professors to teachers (Fullan, 1994). Indeed, the larger paradigm in many societies calls for citizens to follow their leaders, rather than having faith in their own abilities to understand and decide (Farrell & Jacobs, 2020). As noted in Chapter 1, cooperative learning links with Dewey's (1897) view that education should model democracy.

Thus, group autonomy in the case of groups of language teachers involves teachers using reflection and the power of groups to boost their confidence in their ability to figure out for themselves what paths to take in their teaching. Of course, autonomy does not mean isolation, and teachers need to be bold in seeking out wisdom from wherever it might be found. As Holec (1981) noted in the case of learner autonomy, autonomy is about people controlling what they do; it is not about going it alone to gather information or to implement decisions. When we teachers exercise more autonomy, perhaps we do more to encourage our students to also exercise more autonomy. Plus, when we share our reflection with students or involve them in it, 'we role model autonomy for our students' (Power & Wilson, 2019; Szűcs, 2018).

Reflective Break

1. Are the administrators where you teach supportive of reflection among teachers? If so, what kind of support do they provide? If not, what kind of support would you like them to provide?
2. Do you tend to put more faith in what you and your colleagues think on a topic, or more faith in what is said in journals and textbooks on Education?

Teaching Cooperative Skills

Group functioning can be problematic not only for students who collaborate with their peers but also for language teachers when working together in groups. Thus, the cooperative learning principle of teaching cooperative skills needs to apply not only when with our students' groups but also with our own. Furthermore, this links with the cooperative learning principle of maximum peer interactions because high quality interactions necessarily involve fluent use of cooperative skills. Yes, teachers likely have better skills than students, and we may be more inclined to interact politely than will many students. Nonetheless, we teachers too often have room for improvement (Sylvia & Saroja, 2019).

How can groups of language teachers improve our use of cooperative skills in reflective practice groups? This can be a question for reflection among teachers, starting with what cooperative skills we already use frequently and well, moving to those cooperative skills in which we and those with whom we collaborate might benefit from improvement, and moving on to how to improve on the skills found to be in need of enhancement. We might even find that enhancing our cooperative skills via our interactions with our fellow reflective language teachers pays dividends when we interact with people in other areas of our lives (Eisler & Frederiksen, 2012).

Learning Cooperative Skills

Teachers, students, families, etc. can use a 6-Step procedure (Johnson & Johnson, 1989) for enhancing understanding and deployment of cooperative skills. This same procedure can also be useful in bringing other skills to the stage of automatic use. To demonstrate the six steps, we will employ the cooperative skill of Praising Others. Praising might seem to be a simple skill; yet, our own experience with our use of this cooperative skill is that we let pass far too many opportunities for praising others, not to mention praising ourselves. (Note that with this 6-Step procedure only one skill is learned at a time.)

Step 1 – Why use this skill?

Beliefs come first. To use a cooperative skill, first we must believe it has benefits. Therefore, in the case of the cooperative skill of Praising Others, teachers (and anyone else) must believe this skill will enhance their groups and their lives generally. For example, praising others can create a more pleasant atmosphere and encourage others to repeat those actions which have led them to be praised. Also, when we praise others, they may be more likely to do the same for us or others. Another means of convincing people of the benefits of praising would be for group members to share stories from their own lives, from friends or family, and from fictional characters to illustrate the advantages of praise.

Step 2 – What does the skill look and sound like?

Once people believe in the importance of a particular cooperative skill for facilitating promotive peer interactions, i.e., the Why, the next step involves understanding what the skill looks and sounds like, i.e., the How. 'Looks like' refers to the non-verbal aspects of a skill, such as gestures and facial expressions, whereas 'sounds like' refers to the words used. This is Step 2 of the 6-Step procedure for integrating cooperative skills into our daily routines.

Reflective groups of language teachers will be able to call on their lived experience as well as their language knowledge to generate many instances of the How of a cooperative skill. Indeed, cooperative skills fit with language functions. Teachers' knowledge can be supplemented by the practice of noticing during daily interaction or when consuming media such as films. This is similar to the way in which students use noticing to enhance their grasp of grammar and other language features (Ellis, 2005).

Teachers can combine the results of all this data gathering to construct a Looks Like – Sounds Like table for the skill they are currently focusing on, with the Looks Like column listing non-verbal instances of the skill and the Sounds Like column listing words and phrases for enacting the skill (see Table 6.2 for an example). However, it must be kept in mind that how a skill is enacted may vary in different cultures and for people with different personalities.

Table 6.2. Cooperative skill of 'praising others': Looks Like – Sounds Like

Looks Like	Sounds Like
Making eye contact	'Exactly what we needed. Thanks so much.'
Smiling	'You're the best!'
Using a praise emoticon	'You saved the day.'
Clapping	Praise is best accompanied by some explanation of what people did and what made it so praiseworthy.

Step 3 – Practicing the skill

To reach the goal of automatic/natural use of a cooperative skill, we often have to begin by using the skill in a conscious/artificial way. This is what takes place in Step 3 of the 6-Step procedure for mastering cooperative skills. It resembles the process of going from unconscious incompetence all the way to unconscious competence, explained in Chapter 7, with Step 3 involving the development of conscious competence. Again, please remember that we are learning only one cooperative skill at a time. Of course, teachers, with our greater language proficiency and often greater maturity and level of professionalism (except when we teach adults), will likely incorporate skills into our active repertoires – or maybe some skills are already there – faster than our students. To work on practicing the skill, perhaps we can play a game in which we try to outdo each other in our praise of our groupmates. It may seem comical to use the skill in such an artificial manner, but it is all part of the process of 'getting to natural.'

Step 4 – Using the skill during other learning activities

In Step 4 of increasing teachers' use of cooperative skills, teachers employ the designated skill during their normal peer interactions, such as at face-to-face meetings and in electronic communication with the other members of their language teacher reflective practice group. To monitor group members' progress toward automatic skill use, teachers can do either self-assessment or peer assessment. This assessment can be as simple as making a check mark each time someone praises a groupmate, or it could also involve recording the Looks Like and Sounds Like when group members praise each other. Furthermore, doing this assessment keeps skill use on people's minds.

Step 5 – Discussing use of the skill

The data collected via the self and peer monitoring of the designated cooperative skill during Step 4 can be used in Step 5, when the groups reflect on their progress toward automatic use of the skill. A Reflective Break can take place during a group meeting or after a meeting has concluded. Part of the Reflective Break should include a plan, if needed, for improving on the group members' use of the skill.

Step 6 – Keeping the skill on people's minds

We seldom reach automatic use of a given cooperative skill in just one try. Instead, we need to persevere. Ways to encourage ourselves include:

a. Using the skill with family members and friends
b. Teaching the skill to our students and using it with them
c. Thinking about the skill in other languages we speak and using it in those languages
d. Repeating now and then the data collection in Step 4 and the discussion in Step 5.

To follow-up on point b above, when we facilitate our students' development and use of cooperative skills (see Chapter 2 and Chapter 4), if we can tell our students that we and our colleagues are also seeking to enhance our own cooperative skill use, it now becomes a case of 'Do as I do, not only as I say.'

To wrap up this section on how the cooperative learning principle of teaching cooperative skills applies to reflective groups of language teachers, it bears noting that cooperative skills come into play not only in oral communication but also in written and video communication. As to written communication, Francis (1995) suggested the value of dialog journaling among teachers. Journals provide a vessel for group members to share such matters as their feelings, their aha moments (Nieto, 2013), and their frustrations. As language teachers will know from their experience of responding to their students' dialog journals (Linares, 2019), optimal responses are those that encourage more dialoging, greater trust, and deeper thinking. Video communication, too, requires thought as to how people are portrayed, not just the words they say or are said about them. For example, when group members appear in videos that will be shown to others, will those in the video consider the images to be flattering or at least not unflattering?

Reflective Break
1. What is one cooperative skill in which you feel you are fairly adept?
2. What is one cooperative skill in which you might wish to improve? How could you facilitate your improvement?

Cooperation as a Value

The cooperative learning principle of cooperation as a value, the eighth and final principle, circles back to the first of our list of principles: positive interdependence. Positive interdependence encourages us to see our outcomes as positively correlated with the outcomes of others, so that we are motivated to help each other because by helping each other we, every bit as much, help ourselves. Positive interdependence and the other six cooperative learning principles listed here before cooperation as a value center on small learning groups. The 'each other' referred to are usually assumed to be the others in our small group. In contrast, the principle of cooperation as a value reaches out to others beyond our small groups. In the case of language teacher reflection groups, this outreach can include other teachers in our schools, other institutions, etc., as well as teachers, other educators, and indeed everyone elsewhere in the place we live, elsewhere in our country, or around the world.

Farrell (2019) advised teachers that data collection for reflection should not be confined to classrooms nor should reflection be confined to matters of students' educational attainment, important as that is. Rather, to understand what happens in classrooms, we have to look more broadly at the many factors outside classrooms that impact students. Furthermore, it seems inevitable that a look at education-impacting factors beyond classrooms will find both the praiseworthy and inspiring, as well as those factors in need of change. Some of these major factors involve students' families, e.g., their income levels (Machebe, Ezegbe, & Onuoha, 2017) and their parenting styles (Ugwuanyi, Okeke, & Njeze, 2020). Bourdieu (1972), Coleman (1988), and Putnam (2000) all discussed how children's success in academics and in life depends to a large extent on the cultural capital that they earn by virtue of growing up in particular communities. (Of course, definitions of 'success' vary.) Sandel (2020) highlighted social and economic factors when he questioned the validity of labeling technologically developed countries such as the US as meritocracies, i.e., places where success is mainly determined by effort. Furthermore, Farrell (2015) and Henri Holec (cited in Yuliani & Lengkanawati, 2017) emphasized, like Dewey (1897), that education must be more than the aggrandizement of individual students, and should, instead, look at the welfare of the larger whole, as does the cooperative learning principle of cooperation as a value. This emphasis on teachers spreading our reflecting wings beyond our classrooms also calls on us, based on our reflections, to *take action* beyond classrooms (Crookes, 2013; Jacobs & Crookes, 2022).

Are we just school employees who should confine ourselves to our designated duties, or do we have a right, even a duty, to act on matters outside our classrooms, especially on matters that impact our students' school performance and lives, now and in the future? For example, action needs to be taken if support for low-income students does not include adequate resources to provide these students sufficient quantity and quality of food to support their physical and cognitive growth. Similarly, too often, an absent parent does not provide their children with the financial support they are obligated to provide, yet enforcement measures remain inadequate (Rios-Salas, 2017). Pressuring governments to upgrade enforcement might be another way teachers can improve the situation in their schools. One teacher (Lie, a co-author of this book, 2022) has over the years written to the media on behalf of what she saw as important changes in education policy. Now, with social media, we teachers have many more ways to make our voices heard. Jablon (in press) used social media to encourage people in his neighborhood to join a book club to discuss books relevant to issues at his intermediate school.

For too long, language teaching has been seen to be exclusively about language. For instance, a friend of ours in Malaysia, Meng Huat Chau, taught English at secondary school level for about ten years, and now he teaches current and future teachers of English and other languages at university level. His department is called Applied Linguistics. That would be similar to saying that mathematics teachers are teaching Applied Mathematics. Yes, they are teaching Applied Mathematics, but they and we language teachers are also teaching so much else: Applied Psychology (see Chapter 1), Applied Sociology, Applied Philosophy, Applied Neurobiology, etc. That does not even include areas within language teaching such as Languages for Specific Purposes and Content-Based Language Teaching. So much lies beyond and enters into our classrooms! Of course, we need not be experts in a hundred different areas; the point instead is to take an interest.

We can involve our students in joining us to reach out beyond our/their classrooms. For example, this joint student–teacher action frequently occurs when we facilitate student participation in service learning projects (Lake & Adinolfi, 2017). Service learning involves the combination of students doing service to others and also learning content and skills relevant to their school curriculum. In language curricula, this learning often occurs via the keeping of reflective journals (Lypka, 2018), and teachers can reflect in concert with their students. One especially noteworthy service learning project was done by Liss (2022) and her students. Over multiple years, various of Liss's primary school classes worked to overcome prejudice in the school and in the world generally. The capstone on many years of effort by many classes of students was to collect 1.5 million bandages from all over the world to commemorate the 1.5 million children who died in the holocaust, with the bandages being a symbol of healing (https://www.kcra.com/article/sacramento-students-teach-community-about-anne-frank/29098168#).

As we are language teachers, we will be especially drawn to language issues. While the prominence of such issues varies widely given our different teaching contexts, some of the issues include matters of subtractive bilingualism, the role of first/heritage languages in second language learning, what variant(s) of languages should be learned, e.g., only prestige native speaker varieties or should one take a Global Englishes approach (Rose & Galloway, 2017), and how much, if any, language support should be provided for migrants from other countries. Given our positions as language teachers, our voices on these issues may attract more listeners. Thus, we should not hesitate to air our views after careful consideration in consultation with our reflection group colleagues. Of course, in various locations, we teachers have more or less freedom to publicly voice our views (Sadlier, 2016).

Another area in which the world beyond education institutions impacts what happens inside these institutions involves a question close to the heart of the authors of this book on cooperative learning: Is cooperating with other people the smart choice? Similar questions ask: (a) Are humans basically good, bad, or does it depend on the people around them or their genes? (b) Does cooperation make us weak? (c) Is democracy a form of rule by the ignorant and irreverent? (d) Can we believe in the science on the many cognitive and emotional benefits of cooperation, or is that and much other science a ruse (Lieberman, 2013; Tabibnia & Lieberman, 2007)? How we and others answer these questions has huge implications for how we teach. Thus, we and our colleagues might wish to use reflection to consider the questions; and then again, reflection can guide us in how we attempt to share our reflections with others.

> **Reflective Break**
> 1. If you have visited some of your students' families, what is something you would like to learn, and how could you try to learn it? Or maybe you could take a more open-ended approach by just having a friendly chat, observing, and seeing what learning emerges?
> 2. Are you a member of some kind of teachers' association, union, etc.? Does that organization ever take positions or actions on socio-economic issues or language policy issues? Do you have other ideas about how teachers as a united force can influence society for the better?
> 3. As a student or a teacher, have you ever been involved in service learning?

ANOTHER BOOK AND A CONCLUSION TO THIS CHAPTER

Readers will be aware that this book is one in a series on reflective practice in language teaching, edited by Tom Farrell, whom we have cited multiple times in the pages of this volume. We would like to take an opportunity to briefly recommend another book in this series, a book that looks very promising as a source of ideas for how we teachers can collaborate with peers to reflect on our use of cooperative learning. The book, by Hansun Waring and Sarah Creider, is titled *Micro-Reflection on Classroom Communication: A FAB Framework*. It focuses on classroom communication as captured on video and then analyzed by teachers and students to gain insight into the past and future of students' language learning and how teachers can facilitate it. A useful term from the book is 'micro-reflection,' i.e., examining both the big picture of what happens, as well as the small moves that contribute to this big picture.

Coming back to the present book and this chapter on teacher collaboration, at the heart of reflective practice is an unquenchable curiosity and a deep empathy for our students and others. At the heart of cooperative learning is a faith that working with others enhances our efforts and an excitement about getting to know others and how we can complete each other. Language teacher reflection on practice promises that when teachers cooperate, we can reach up toward the sky. This chapter has highlighted the benefits of teacher–teacher cooperation, and explored how cooperative learning principles can facilitate not just student–student cooperation but also mutual assistance among teachers.

Chapter 7

Putting It All Together: Cooperative Learning and Teacher Reflection in Language Lessons

INTRODUCTION

Here we bring together ideas from this book's previous six chapters in the form of five lessons, with each lesson followed by commentary by the book's authors and reflection opportunities for you, the readers of this book. We hope you will reflect on such matters as the links between the lessons themselves and the cooperative learning principles; how you might use some of the cooperative learning techniques in the lessons in your own language teaching; and what variations to the lessons you might like to try.

These lessons can be adapted for use with a range of language skills, age groups, proficiency levels, and cooperative learning techniques. The eight cooperative learning principles are used as the foundation for planning the lessons. However, this does not imply that every lesson plan must follow those given below as some kind of model. Instead, the hope is that:

a. The eight principles and teachers' other knowledge of cooperative learning serve as tools in a toolbox and teachers and their students can access that toolbox when they feel a need.

b. As teachers and students become more experienced with cooperative learning, they will develop unconscious competence (Bradley, 1997) in its use. Unconscious competence involves the ability to do something well without conscious thought. This is the fourth step in a process beginning with unconscious incompetence, in which people do not even know that the ability exists. As an example, someone who has never played or watched badminton might be unconsciously incompetent in hitting a drop shot. Once they become aware of drop shots, they are consciously incompetent, i.e., they know about drop shots but they do not know how to hit them.

The third step, conscious competence, lasts while they learn drop shots, practice hitting them, and become able to hit them in a game if they focus on doing so. Finally, they reach unconscious competence when they do drop shots naturally, as naturally as putting one foot in front of the other when walking down a street. Reflection can facilitate the journey to unconscious competence.

c.   Cooperative learning lesson planning can actually be very easy, once teachers and students are familiar with a small (and then increasingly large) variety of cooperative learning techniques. We can take our pre-existing content, e.g., in a textbook, student book, or workbook, or content we have developed ourselves previously and then add a cooperative learning technique, and voila, we have a cooperative learning lesson. The following examples are from Ling, Smith, & Peng (2016) a students' book for studying English in the 3rd grade of elementary school. One task asks students in pairs to each make a list of fruits, share their list with their partner, and then see which pair has the longest list. Maybe we could use Write-Pair-Square to help students make, compare, and grow their lists. Another twosome task asks one student to name the parts of trees and flowers, e.g., trunk and petals, and then their partner will spell the words. Maybe we could use Circle of Speakers for this, with students taking turns to name and spell words. Perhaps to add thinking skills, students could also talk about the functions of each part, and whether the part has an equivalent in the human body. Then, in the last step in Circle of Speakers, whoever's number is randomly called by the teacher can talk about their pair's discussion of one of the words for the parts of trees and flowers.

Reflective Break

1. Have you experienced the process of going from unconscious incompetence to unconscious competence?
2. Does the cooperative learning lesson planning formula of cooperative learning technique + already prepared content = cooperative learning lesson seem doable to you?

LESSON ONE – EXTENSIVE READING

Extensive reading involves students in reading large quantities of material at a level of difficulty roughly equal to or perhaps even below students' current reading level

(Extensive Reading Foundation, 2021). The two main ways that students do extensive reading are:

a.   Everyone in a class reads the same book. This requires a class set of the book, i.e., enough hard copies for everyone, or sufficient access to electronic copies of the book and/or audio books.

b.   Everyone reads a different book. In order that the books are at an appropriate difficulty level, students often read books known as graded readers (Teaching English, n.d.), i.e., books either specially written or adapted to be at an easier level than books written for adults who are proficient in the language of the books. Graded readers are graded into different levels, such as Level 3, to make it easier for students to find books that match their current level. For example, X-Reading (xreading.com) offers online access to a wide variety of graded readers.

An important point in designing extensive reading lessons involves what students do after they finish a book (Day & Bamford, 2002). Post-reading activities can be motivating if they provide students with opportunities to think about and discuss what they have read.

However, too often post-reading tasks, e.g., book reports, can be so onerous as to be demotivating, i.e., to discourage students from reading more. Indeed, sometimes the best post-reading task might be to just read another book (Robb, 2018). One potentially motivating task for students before, during, and after they read a book could be for them to share with peers as to why they chose the book, whether the book is enjoyable (and why or why not), and who (if anyone) might enjoy the book.

The Lesson Plan

Students form groups of four divided into pairs. The groups all have the same goal: to increase the amount of extensive reading their class does and their enjoyment of that reading. To achieve that goal each person is charged with creating a brief online advertisement containing text and one or more visuals for a book they enjoyed. Their partner acts as their editor, who is listed at the end of each advertisement. The other pair in the foursome act as advisors, e.g., on IT matters. The class develops a rubric to guide advertisement construction and editing. Table 7.1 (adopted from Jacobs & Chau, 2021) shows one possible rubric. When the advertisements are ready, the other pair view them and comment.

Table 7.1. Rubric for assessing advertisements for fiction books

Characteristic	Exceeds expectations	Meets expectations	Approaches expectations
Plot summary	The book's plot is clearly summarized in no more than 75 words.	A summary is provided, but a key element is missing or may be unclear.	The summary is too short or is copied.
Details about the book that assist others in locating it to read themselves	Title, author(s), year of publication, publisher, place where it was bought, borrowed, or viewed are provided.	One piece of information is missing.	More than one piece of information is missing.
Types of readers who might enjoy the book	Ages, interests, favoured types of reading materials, reading level are provided.	Some of the reader information is missing.	Much of the reader information is missing.
Reasons to read the book	Persuasive reasons are given to attract others to read this particular book.	Reasons lack persuasiveness and elaboration.	Only one reason is given and it is unelaborated.
Visual	Visual is attractive and clear.	Visual is okay as to attractiveness and clarity.	Visual lacks either attractiveness or clarity or both.

Commentary

a. *Positive interdependence* – The group has a common goal: to create advertisements that will increase their class's quantity and enjoyment of extensive reading. Everyone has a unique resource, as they are going to create their own advertisement about a different book they have read. They all play the roles of creator, editor, and advisor.

b. *Individual accountability* – Everyone needs to do their fair share by creating an advertisement and helping with partners' advertisements.

c. *Equal opportunity to participate* – Everyone has a chance to make their own advertisement and to play the other roles. Working in a small group of only two, with possible assistance from another pair, makes it less likely that anyone will be left out of their group.

d. *Maximum peer interactions* – Working in pairs increases the quantity of peer interactions, and the varied aspects of the task up the quality of the interactions. For example, students need to summarize the plot of their book, and they need to do perspective-taking as they consider who else might like the book they read.

e. *Heterogeneous grouping* – Types of heterogeneity that might be useful with this task include reading and writing skill, IT skill, and different backgrounds to help each other understand who might like their book, e.g., some people enjoy books about cooking, whereas others only enjoy books about food, or some enjoy books about how to sing, whereas others only enjoy listening and prefer books about famous singers.

f. *Group autonomy* – Students have their partner/editor as the first option for help, not to mention the other pair in their group, before they need to ask their teacher for help.

g. *Teaching cooperative skills* – Many cooperative skills can be useful in any one lesson. One particularly useful skill in this lesson might be offering specific praise. For instance, when editors use the template to give their partner feedback, they should provide ample praise which specifically highlights what exactly was done well or was a step in the direction of doing it well.

h. *Cooperation as a value* – In this lesson, the goal lies not only with increasing the amount of extensive reading that group members do, but also the reading of all class members, including maybe the teacher as well. Plus, the class could brainstorm ways to share their book suggestions with people throughout their school and beyond. A fairly new trend is that of book trailers, similar to the long-established movie trailers (Han, Choi, & Oh, 2016). The class could also consider donations to schemes for people without access to books.

Variations

a. Some children may not yet be writing or may not have the computer skills to create an advertisement. They can create a hard-copy advertisement instead or draw a poster.

b. Instead of choosing a book they enjoyed and discussing why others might enjoy it, students can create an advertisement for a book they did not enjoy and talk about others who also might not enjoy the book; or they can talk about who might enjoy it and why, despite the fact that the creator of the advertisement did not enjoy it.

   c.   The class could find a way to encourage the entire class to view all the advertisements and collect data on whether the advertisements impacted people's reading choices.

   d.   While students are working on their advertisements, the class can use the cooperative learning technique Friendly Spy. The steps are:

Step 1 – Group members have numbers, such as 1, 2, 3, or 4.

Step 2 – A number is chosen at random. The group member with that number becomes the Spy who visits other groups to see how they are going about the task in which the class is engaged. The spy observes, asks questions, and can give advice.

Step 3 – The Spy returns and shares ideas gained from other groups.

Friendly Spy provides one more source of support that students can turn to before checking with the teacher, thereby promoting the cooperative learning principle of group autonomy.

   e.   Students alone or in groups can create their own books, including anthologies, for peers to read (Ivone, Jacobs, & Santosa, 2020).

Reflective Break

1. Do your students do extensive reading? If so, how successful is it? Do you have ideas for how extensive reading can be more fruitful?

2. Do you feel that rubrics, such as the one in this lesson, can improve peer feedback?

3. In this lesson, would it be worthwhile for teachers to stay away from their students for a while to see how they do on their own before teachers start to observe and perhaps intervene? Should teachers create their own advertisements?

LESSON TWO – DEBATE

Debates offer an activity that allows students to practice their speaking and listening skills at the same time that they do complex thinking. Debate topics focus on controversies; controversies exist whenever people hold differing opinions about matters which they all believe are important. Some teachers may wish to stay away from controversies, as they can raise strong emotions and result in prolonged bad feelings, as well as resulting in interference from people outside the classroom. However, debates can also bring benefits. These include: (a) more and deeper thinking, as students dig deep to find and develop effective arguments in favor of their positions (Craik & Lockhart, 1972); (b) heightened motivation, as the controversies push students to do their best (Dewey, 1916); and (c) more perspectives, as students encounter a variety of points of view on an issue (Piaget, 1975).

In a typical debate, students select or are assigned to a position on the issue to be debated (students seldom choose the issue), and they remain faithful to that position throughout the debate. Furthermore, the debate is an adversarial activity, with one team winning and the other(s) losing. The goal is to win; the goal is not a better understanding of the issue or an attempt to resolve any problems at the root of the issue. For example, in a debate about whether to tax unhealthy foods, such as sugary beverages or processed meat, no effort is made after the debate to take action – whatever action people on different sides of the issue might support – to improve people's diets.

The Lesson Plan

As the traditional debate promotes a feeling of negative interdependence (see Chapter 1), Johnson & Johnson (1995) developed an alternative which they called the Academic Controversy technique, which has been elaborated on by Green & Klug (1990), Hammrich & Blouch (1998), Johnson, Johnson, & Smith (1998), and Overby et al. (1996). Of course, the technique can be varied. Plus, the time needed for the steps will also vary depending on the curriculum time available, the depth of the research students do, and the modes of presentation students use when debating, e.g., video or PowerPoint. To save class time, students can do preparation at home, and/or at school but after class.

Step 1 – Students form foursomes of two pairs each. Each twosome is assigned one of two possible positions on a controversial topic, such as: Should governments subsidize the prices of healthy foods to encourage consumption? For example, one twosome in each foursome might argue for subsidizing healthier food, while the other pair argues against.

Students must argue for their assigned view even if their real view differs. Each pair has time to work together, but separate from the other pair in their foursome, to prepare a presentation in favor of their assigned position. After they have developed various talking points, they divide them so that each person will have approximately the same amount of presentation time.

Step 2 – Each member of each pair takes a turn to present their assigned view, while the other twosome keep track of time, listen, and take notes, but do not speak.

Step 3 – Each person takes a turn to rebut points made in Step 2 by the other side. After one round of turn taking, they can continue to rebut and to respond to the rebuttal points.

Step 4 – This is the step in which Academic Controversy starts to differentiate itself from traditional competitive debates. The twosomes exchange positions. The pair who had been assigned to speak in favor of the proposition, e.g., in favor of subsidizing the prices of healthy food, are now opposed, and vice versa. Step 4 is the same as Step 1, except with the new positions.

Step 5 is the same as Step 2, and Step 6 is the same as Step 3.

Step 7 shows another difference between Academic Controversy and traditional debates. Now, the students work alone; they are no longer part of a duo, and they no longer have an assigned position. Instead, they individually formulate and represent their real view on the issue, and the group seeks to reach a consensus. Their real view could be one of the two assigned views or a third view. For instance, on the topic in the example – subsidizing the prices of healthy food, maybe someone would argue that this could only be done for food for children in order to encourage them to develop healthy eating habits which, it is hoped, they would continue on their own as they grow older. It is fine if the group do not reach a consensus, as long as they try. Finally, a randomly selected member of each group presents their consensus or, when no consensus has emerged, the different views of their group members.

Commentary

a. *Positive interdependence* – The common goal is to learn more about the topic. In the example used in this lesson, the topic involves how to practice healthy eating and how to encourage others to do so. Everyone has the same varied roles: researcher, presenter, timekeeper, listener, rebutter. Also, they have resource positive interdependence, as they seek to develop unique information to share in the cooperative debate.

b. *Individual accountability* – Everyone needs to do their fair share in the foursome, e.g., in Steps 2 and 5, each person has to present the points which they developed with their partner.

c. *Equal opportunity to participate* – Everyone has a chance to present ideas, e.g., in Steps 3 and 6, everyone takes turns to rebut points made by the other twosome in their group of four.

d. *Maximum peer interactions* – Academic Controversy maximizes the quantity of peer interactions by keeping group size to either two or four. The quality of peer interactions increases compared to traditional debate because students need to represent at least two and possibly three different opinions (the third opinion being their own personal view if it differs from either of the two assigned views).

e. *Heterogeneous grouping* – Being in a group with different backgrounds makes it more likely students will hear different perspectives and learn about the reasons people hold different views. Encountering disparate opinions in a cooperative environment without winners and losers encourages students to be accepting of opinions not the same as theirs.

f. *Group autonomy* – Teachers can recommend resources, but students also have their partners to help them understand the various sides of an issue.

g. *Teaching cooperative skills* – Disagreeing politely can be a vital skill if we want debates to generate more light (of knowledge) and less heat (of argument).

h. *Cooperation as a value* – Recall that groups are not seeking to defeat others; they all want to learn more. Thus, the enemy is not other people. Instead, the enemy in this case is ill-health or, more generally, lack of knowledge and lack of putting into action the knowledge we do have. Students can take what they learn during the Academic Controversy debate, and perhaps, in Step 7, consider what they can do – small steps are great – in humanity's battle against this enemy.

Variations

In our experience of using Academic Controversy, sometimes foursomes find Steps 4, 5, and 6 a bit boring. They complain, 'We're just going to say the same things that the other pair said when they represented the position that we are now going to present.' In response, we challenge them to present some new arguments, and we tell them that they may benefit from 'putting themselves in the shoes' of people with different opinions. However, if students insist, D'Eon & Proctor (2001) have developed an option. In this option, one pair change places with a pair from an adjoining foursome, so that pairs present to and debate with new people.

Reflective Break

1. When you were a student, did you ever participate in or observe a debate? What do you remember of it?
2. What might be some topics for your students to debate? Might any topics be 'too hot to handle'?
3. Do your students have sufficient cooperative skills to debate in a cooperative manner?
4. How might your class link an Academic Controversy topic with the cooperative learning principle of cooperation as a value?

LESSON 3 – READING NON-FICTION

In Lesson 1, we did a cooperative learning lesson that focused on reading of fiction texts. In this lesson, we focus on reading of non-fiction texts. The cooperative learning technique we will use was renamed by us as SUMMER, and it was designed by cognitive psychologists based on their knowledge of how people learn (Hythecker, Dansereau, & Rocklin, 1988). This knowledge can be found in Information Processing Theory, which is linked to Cognitive Psychology (see Chapter 1).

Information Processing Theory (Sampson et al., 2020) uses a three-part metaphor for what happens in the brain as we learn. The first part is the Sensory Register. It uses our five senses to collect information, and we, thankfully, lose the large majority of that huge amount of information entering our brains via our senses because we do not feel the information is useful. Next in the three-part model comes the Working Memory, which is where we process (work on) information that we select from the Sensory Register. To process this selected information, we need the third part of the apparatus by which we learn, the Long-Term Memory. This where we store the new knowledge we learn along with the knowledge we have had in our minds for a long time (that is why it is called 'long-term'). The Long-Term Memory has the knowledge we use to process information in the Working Memory. For example, if our ears hear someone speaking to us, we check our Long-Term Memory for knowledge. If the person speaks to us in Spanish, and we have no Spanish in our Long-Term Memory, we probably will rapidly lose that information. However, if we do know Spanish, maybe we will remember the information because understanding is vital to memory.

Thus, knowledge goes from Part 3, the Long-Term Memory, to Part 2, the Working Memory to help us understand. But the big question is, how do we learn by getting knowledge from Part 2, the Working Memory, to Part 3, the Long-Term Memory? This happens in two ways. One is for us to use that information repeatedly, e.g., we seldom learn new vocabulary by encountering it only one time; we need to see, hear, and use it repeatedly. Extensive reading (see Lesson 1) and extensive listening (Ivone & Renandya, 2019) provide interesting and meaningful ways for this to happen. The point here is that rote memorizing – just saying a word again and again – is not the best type of repetition. The best type involves meaningful repetition, e.g., encountering the word multiple times in meaningful contexts.

The second strategy for securely transferring information from the Working Memory to the Long-Term Memory involves connecting it to information that already resides in the Long-Term Memory. This strategy works because we do not store information as isolated pieces of information, rather we store it in networks. For example, we might store information on mangoes in one network with other information on fruit, and in another network of foods that are good to eat with peanut butter, and (if you are language nerds like us) in yet another network of words that form plurals by adding 'es.' Elaborations can be used to form networks, because elaborations prompt use of deep thinking, and deep thinking helps us place new information into networks in our Long-Term Memory. Next, we will see how SUMMER facilitates learning by both strategies: repeated meaningful use and elaboration.

The Lesson Plan

The lesson plan follows the six steps in SUMMER. Note that the first and sixth steps, the S and the R in SUMMER, take place only once, whereas the other four steps take place multiple times. First, we need a text for reading, such as an article from a newspaper or a website, that, just like with texts for extensive reading, is at the students' current reading level or perhaps slightly below that level. This text should be clearly divided into four or more sections. Sometimes, the headings already in a text can serve as the section dividers. Other times, it may be possible to identify logical breaks in the text to use as section dividers. Of course, those breaks probably should be neither too close together nor too far apart.

Step 1 – **S**et the mood. Students form pairs. Ideally, these dyads, aka pairs, are mixed in terms of their current reading level. Before the groups of two begin reading, it could be useful to 'set the mood' for collaboration, i.e., establish a relaxed, yet purposeful mood in the group. To do this, the two students might have some casual chat, e.g., asking about what each other did or will do on the weekend, or a question about their families. (No, chit-chat is not necessarily a waste of time.) Then, they need to make sure that each understands the SUMMER process, although it may take a couple times for students to become unconsciously competent at doing SUMMER. Also, sometimes when students do a cooperative learning technique wrongly, they are actually inventing a perfectly acceptable variation. Therefore, we keep an open mind about whether students are doing a technique 'correctly' or not.

Step 2 – **U**nderstand by reading silently. The two students each have the same text that has been divided into sections. This could be material found by students or found or written by the teacher or others, or a portion of a textbook. The material has been divided into sections. Each of the dyad silently reads the same section of the text.

Step 3 – **Mention the key ideas.** Without looking back at the text, one member of the pair will mention, i.e., state, the key ideas, the main points in the section. The reason that they do not look at the text is that looking at the text might tempt them to read from the text, whereas they want to be only summarizing the section of the text, not trying to paraphrase or read it. Summaries should be much shorter than paraphrases.

Step 4 – **Monitor the summary.** While one partner summarizes the section without looking at the text, the other partner looks at the text in order to monitor the summary: is it too short or too long, and does it contain any inaccuracies? Students may need to practice summarizing and monitoring summaries. Frequently, student summaries are too long. Of course, what to put in a summary depends in part on why people are reading the text.

Step 5 – **Elaborate.** In Steps 3 and 4, students identified the main ideas in the section; now, they take turns to present elaborations on those ideas. Elaborating can take many forms, including:

- connecting to what students studied previously;
- associating with students' lives;
- adding information to what is already in the section of the text;
- agreeing or disagreeing with what the authors have stated;
- giving emotional reactions to the information in the section, including surprise, happiness, or sadness;
- suggesting ways to apply key ideas in the section;
- asking comprehension questions or I-want-to-know-more questions.

Of course, not all types of elaboration need to be used for every section of the text. The pair repeats the U, M, M, and E for each section of the text. As they do so, they rotate who does the first and second M – mention the main ideas and monitor the summary.

Step 6 – **Review the entire text.** After going through all the sections of the text via the U, M, M, and E, students are ready to do a summary of the main ideas in the whole text, the R. They take turns to contribute to this super summary.

Commentary

   a. *Positive interdependence* – SUMMER provides a good example of encouraging role positive interdependence. Everyone has roles to play, and they are rotating roles with the two Ms – Mention the main ideas and Monitor the summary. In contrast, what we want to avoid is students only doing the role they are best at. When that happens, students' development is hampered. The group's goal in SUMMER is to understand the text they read and to improve their overall reading skills.

b.   *Individual accountability* – The E, Elaborate, recurring step in SUMMER provides one place where everyone is expected to do their fair share, as the two take turns to elaborate on the main ideas in the section they just read. Elaborating may be difficult. Thus, partners can give each other clues. Giving clues, but not doing for others, is another cooperative skill.

c.   *Equal opportunity to participate* – What happens when the higher achiever in the twosome tries to do all the steps? For example, when the pair do the U, Understand, recurring step in SUMMER, and one person finishes reading faster, do they wait for their partner? Do they offer to help their partner with comprehension problems? Here, teachers play a major role. First, teachers need to choose texts carefully. Also, texts can be abridged, just like the graded readers in extensive reading, or pre-teaching of concepts and vocabulary can be done (by the way, some graded readers also do this). Second, teachers can facilitate students' development of such cooperative skills as (1) waiting patiently and (2) asking people if they would like help. These two skills greatly benefit peer interactions in heterogeneous groups.

d.   *Maximum peer interactions* – As mentioned previously, groups of two promote maximum quantity of peer interactions. For instance, in a class of 60 students learning in pairs, potentially 30 peer interactions take place at the same time. Of course, it should also be stated that groups of three, with 20 peer interactions, and groups of four with 15 are also excellent. As to maximum quality of peer interaction, SUMMER mobilizes two of the premier thinking skills: summarizing in the first M, Mention the main ideas, and in the R, Review the entire text, steps; and elaborating in the E, Elaborate, step.

e.   *Heterogeneous grouping* – A key point in Constructivist, aka Social Constructivist Theory emphasizes that everyone constructs their own understanding. Thus, the content and the architecture of everyone's Long-Term Memory is necessarily different. As a result, a fascinating aspect of the dialoguing that occurs as twosomes go through the dyadic SUMMER scripts arises from the differences in the partners' summaries and especially their elaborations. Furthermore, as mentioned in the commentary on the cooperative learning principle of equal opportunity to participate, heterogeneous grouping according to reading proficiency means that instead of there being only one teacher available to assist students with reading and processing the text, they now have their partners to also help them.

f.   *Group autonomy* – Following on from the discussion under the cooperative learning principle of heterogeneous grouping, when students form dyads with different current levels of reading skill, they have somewhere else to turn, other than to the teacher, for help. In fact, the slogan cited in Chapter 2, of 3 +1 B4 T, encourages students to also consult members of other groups before asking for teacher assistance.

g.   *Teaching cooperative skills* – Three cooperative skills have already been mentioned in this Commentary about SUMMER: giving clues without giving away answers, waiting patiently, and asking people if they would like help. However, as stated in the Chapter 2 discussion on teaching cooperative skills, it may be best to teach only one cooperative skill at a time and to work on the skill for a while, until students approach automatic use of that skill.

h.   *Cooperation as a value* – Cross-age tutoring involves older students sharing the skills they have learned with younger students as their tutees. The skills needed for SUMMER, both the cognitive skills in the SUMMER script as well as the cooperative skills needed to productively and harmoniously interact with peers, would benefit tutees. Additionally, a cornerstone of cooperative learning rests on the insight that by teaching others, we learn more and more thoroughly. Many cross-age tutoring programs limit participation as tutors to high-achieving students, but Watts et al. (2019) found that lower-achieving students can also effectively participate in such programs.

Variations

We make two variations to SUMMER when we use it, although, no doubt, many other variations can be made. One variation encourages interaction between two pairs as to their section summaries, elaborations, and reviews. As stated previously, there are no right answers in SUMMER, and students can benefit by seeing peers' responses. Also, bringing in another pair can help with comprehension. A second variation involves focused elaborations to fit a point in the curriculum. For instance, if the class has chosen to spend their 'SUMMER vacations' reading a text about growing food at home, the students could focus their elaborations on how to apply ideas in the text for starting or improving on their family's home gardening projects, even if those projects are as small as growing herbs or sprouts in pots on the windowsill in their kitchen.

Another variation on SUMMER that students and teachers might like to try would be to encourage students to use the SUMMER script even when they read alone. Hythecker et al. (1988) found that not only did students have higher comprehension scores immediately and three weeks after using SUMMER with a partner, but also when they used SUMMER on their own. Indeed, explaining to students about Information Processing Theory can help students study smarter. Knowing about the Sensory Register might persuade students to focus their senses on what they believe to be important to learn. Then, understanding about Working Memory might lead students away from rote memorizing and toward meaningful learning. Plus, understanding how Long-Term Memory works encourages students to connect what they are trying to learn to what they already know.

Reflective Break
1. Do you ever have time to increase student comprehension of reading texts by creating easier versions of the texts or by pre-teaching important vocabulary?
2. What are times out of school where your students summarize or elaborate? For example, when students tell peers about a film or a video they watched, the students are summarizing. When students ask peers for more details about a vehicle accident they saw, they are requesting elaboration.
3. This lesson mentioned three cooperative skills: giving clues without giving away answers, waiting patiently, and asking people if they would like help. At which of those three cooperative skills are your students best?

LESSON 4 – LEARNING GRAMMAR

Providing reasons, as Webb et al. (2009; cited in van Leeuwen & Janssen, 2019) found in their research, appears to boost the learning of both the givers and the receivers of the reasons. At a workshop on cooperative learning attended by one of the authors of the current book, David and Roger Johnson, two very well-known experts on cooperative learning and education generally, told the following story to emphasize the importance of sharing reasons, not just answers.

A psychologist at a mental hospital had been working with three patients for about a year, and they had made a lot a progress. So, she was planning to release them from the hospital and allow them to return home to their families.

However, she wanted to make one more check to be sure the patients were really ready to be released. So, she called the three of them into her office, and she asked them, 'Please tell me – what is 3 times 3?' The first patient said, 'Sure, I know. 3 times 3 is Thursday.'

The psychologist couldn't believe it. She'd worked so hard with this patient, and now this! What had gone wrong?

But, undaunted, she turned to the second patient and said, 'You know what 3 times 3 is, don't you?' 'Of course,' the patient replied, '3 times 3 is mangoes.' Well, the psychologist threw up her hands in frustration. She was ready to tear up her diplomas, quit her comfortable, well-paid job, and set up a stall selling mangoes and mango juice.

In desperation, she faced the third patient. With a pleading voice, she asked, 'Please, please, you know, I'm sure you do, what 3 times 3 is.' The reply came without a moment's hesitation: '3 times 3 is 9.'

The psychologist let out a huge sigh of relief. At least she wasn't a total failure; one patient could be released.

Then, the psychologist had an idea. She'd get the third patient to explain to the other two how 3 times 3 equals 9, they'd understand, they could all be released, she'd be a success.

However, when she asked the third patient to explain his answer, he said, '3 times 3 = 9 because Thursday times mangoes = 9.'

Reasons can be part of every cooperative learning technique. Indeed, asking for and giving explanations are two prominent cooperative skills. However, the cooperative learning technique used in the present lesson, Everyone Can Explain, makes explicit the need for explanations. Furthermore, while all cooperative learning techniques are generic – useful with any subject matter and age of student – Everyone Can Explain seems to be particularly flexible and robust.

The Lesson Plan

Learning grammar constitutes a key focus of many language learning programs, as well as a major focus of language assessment instruments. A spectrum of ways of learning grammar exists, with explicit grammar instruction using worksheets and decontextualized sentences on one end of the spectrum and implicit learning and contextualized language on the other end (Richards & Rodgers, 2014). Generally, cooperative learning seems more congenial to a contextualized approach to grammar, as the conversations students have with one another in their groups provide contextualized language. That said, cooperative learning, including giving reasons, can also fit with activities closer to the decontextualized end of the spectrum.

Cloze activities have long been used to teach as well as to assess grammar, vocabulary, and other aspects of language (Kılıçkaya, 2018). In cloze, we begin with a whole text, such as a 300-word text. Then, words are removed from the text and replaced with blanks. Sometimes, those blanks include multiple-choice options for choosing words to go into the blanks. The students' task is to read the new version of the text with the blanks one time in order to grasp the overall meaning of the text, and then to read it again and put a word in each blank, either the original word or a reasonably appropriate substitute. The two main ways for creators of cloze passages to decide which words to remove are Nth word deletion, e.g., to remove every 11th word, or rational deletion, i.e., either to remove words for which sufficient clues exist to enable students to make informed guesses or to remove words in line with a particular pedagogic focus. For example, in this lesson, there is a short cloze passage created by rational deletion, removing only possessive determiners, such as *my* or *her*.

Table 7.2 and a review of possessive determiners facilitates student collaboration and success in the lesson.

Table 7.2. Possessive determiners

Personal pronoun	Possessive determiner
I	My
You	Your
It	Its
She	Her
He	His
We	Our
They	Their

To make this into a cooperative learning activity, students can use the Everyone Can Explain technique which works as follows.

Step 1 – Students form groups of two, three, or four members. Everyone in the group has a number, e.g., in a group of three, one member is #1, another is #2, and the third member is #3.

Step 2 – Students have a task, in this case to do a cloze exercise. They first work alone and then compare answers, trying to reach agreement on both the answers and the explanations for the answers. No worries if they cannot agree on answers and/or explanations (perhaps multiple reasonable answers and explanations exist).

Step 3 – Groups make sure that everyone can give and explain their group's answers. They might want to rehearse their responses, so the groupmates may coach each other.

Step 4 – A number is chosen, and the person in each group with that number may be asked to share their group's answers and explanations with the others. In the case of this lesson, Everyone Can Explain is used with the brief rational deletion cloze passage below.

Acupuncture
One day, Sumitra met her friend Hui Min at a rock climbing wall. Sumitra said, 'Hi, Hui Min. (1)______back hurts. What should I do?' 'Hi, Sumitra,' Hui Min responded. 'Sorry to hear about (2)______ back. When (3)______mother's back hurts she goes for acupuncture at a clinic near (4)______home. Usually, (5)______back feels better after that.'

Commentary

a. *Positive interdependence* – Each group has the goal of developing good answers and reasonable explanations for those answers. A key understanding is that when the group member whose number is called presents, they are not presenting their individual response; they are presenting their group's response. Thus, they sink or swim together. Whether the response from the group member receives positive or negative feedback, the entire group, not just the presenter, owns that feedback.

b. *Individual accountability* – In group activities not informed by cooperative learning principles, what too often happens is that (1) the group works on a task, (2) the teacher calls a group, and (3) the highest-achieving member of the group responds on behalf of the group. This does not support individual accountability. For example, in a group of four members, the three members who are not the highest-achieving member know that they will not have to be ready to give and explain their group's answers, because if their group is selected, their star will reply. At the same time, the star knows that they do not have to help the rest of the group be ready, because if their group is selected, they (the star) will answer. Thus, the group loses the magic of cooperative learning, in which students engage in dynamic discussion. Fortunately, in Everyone Can Explain, chances increase that individual accountability will be felt by all and that dynamic discussion will inspire the magic of learning to manifest.

c. *Equal opportunity to participate* – Because the group does not know who will be selected as their representative, and because, as explained above regarding positive interdependence, the group sinks or swims together, it becomes more likely, we hope, that everyone will be included in the interactions in the group.

d. *Maximum peer interactions* – In Steps 2 and 3 of Everyone Can Explain, as groups prepare their responses to the designated task, the quantity of peer interactions is high. In Step 4, when the class uses the variation Everyone Can Explain Mobile, explained in the Variations subsection below, the maximum quantity of peer interactions continues to take place. As to the quality of peer interactions, this is maximized by the explanations that need to be provided to accompany the answers. As demonstrated in the story by David and Roger Johnson, it is wholly insufficient for students to know that 3 times 3 equals 9 if their explanation of their correct answer is that 'Thursday times mangoes equals 9.'

e. *Heterogeneous grouping* – Groups mixed according to past achievement are more likely to successfully do academic tasks with more peer interactions taking place, as lower achievers ask questions, try their best, and improve over successive attempts, while higher achievers learn by teaching peers. Tomlinson (1999, p. 12) explained the rationale for differentiated instruction, also known as personalized instruction.

> [It is based on] the twin values of equity and excellence. Our schools can achieve both of these competing values only to the degree that they can establish heterogeneous communities of learning (attending to issues of equity) built solidly on high-quality curriculum and instruction that strive to maximize the capacity of each learner (attending to issues of excellence).

In differentiated instruction, students do different tasks, tasks which suit their current proficiency level. Cooperative learning does not seem to fit with differentiated instruction, as the entire heterogeneous group does the same task. However, given the peer tutoring that goes on in cooperative learning groups, members do have different tasks, e.g., the higher achievers tutor the lower achievers.

f. *Group autonomy* – In Everyone Can Explain, the groups work alone to develop answers and explanations, although teachers and other groups are available for consultation.

g. *Teaching cooperative skills* – Among the many cooperative skills of value when students do Everyone Can Explain would be reminding group members about time limits. A class may use time limits to encourage groups to get down to the task, although a bit of time, but not too much, spent on chit-chat (see the SUMMER cooperative learning technique above) and joking around can improve the working environment. Also, it should be kept in mind that sometimes the group that finishes a task the last is actually the group that did the task best because they had the most discussion and were willing to try one way and then change to another. Thus, even if group members use the cooperative skill of reminding each other about time limits, groups may finish at different times.

The question that arises when groups finish at different times is: What should the other groups do while waiting for the groups that have yet to finish? First, perhaps the groups that have finished might want to revisit the task and see if they can improve their work. Second, it might be necessary to say that time is up, and groups have to stop even though they have yet to conclude their work. A third option is to have a 'sponge activity,' e.g., an activity that 'soaks up' extra time, similar to the way that a sponge soaks up extra water around a sink. For example, some language teachers have a collection of word or logic puzzles for waiting groups to do. Other times, students can design their own sponge activity, work on their homework, or enjoy their extensive reading book.

h.   *Cooperation as a value* – In the spirit of helping people beyond their own group, students could think of ways to improve the activity that they just finished, in this case, the cloze activity they did via Everyone Can Explain. They could share this with the teacher, and the next time one of the teacher's classes does this activity, they could consider the modification suggested. This offers a great way to encourage students to reflect on what does or does not aid their learning.

Variations

One variation of Everyone Can Explain which highlights the cooperative learning principle of maximum peer interactions (quantity) is Everyone Can Explain Mobile, which has nothing to do with mobile phones, although mobile phones could be used in another variation of the technique. In Everyone Can Explain Mobile, in Step 4 of Everyone Can Explain, the group member whose number has been called at random does not stand and share their group's answers and explanations with the entire class. Instead, they go mobile, i.e., they change places with someone from an adjoining group who has the same number. When they arrive at the other group, they share their original group's answers and explanations with the new group who respond, and a dialogue ensues. After some time, all the mobile students return to their home groups and report on the response their ideas received.

With Everyone Can Explain Mobile, instead of only one person at a time speaking, as in Everyone Can Explain (the student whose group was chosen), one person per group speaks, either the mobile student or one of the students in the group they visit. Both arrangements have advantages. With Everyone Can Explain Mobile, the quantity of peer interactions increases. On the other hand, with the regular Everyone Can Explain, the whole class hears one set of answers and explanations at a time, and whole-class discussion takes place. Perhaps, different versions of Everyone Can Explain can be used at different times.

Reflective Break

1. Can you think of other ways to use cooperative learning in the teaching of grammar?
2. Have you ever seen the phenomenon in which one student always answers for their group?
3. What was your reaction to the Johnsons' story about 3 times 3? Have you ever seen a gap between students having a good answer but a bad explanation for that answer?

LESSON 5 – PROJECT-BASED LESSONS

Group projects are extended tasks that students do with peers. They tend to last for days or even weeks, rather than for a shorter time, e.g., some cooperative learning tasks last for one class period, for 20 minutes, or even for 5 minutes. In group projects, students usually create something, such as a solution to a problem, a new idea, a report, or a presentation. Also, group projects are often multimodal, for example, including skits, videos, and songs in addition to standard writing and presenting.

Like most everything else, group projects have both pros and cons. The cons include that group activities can take a great deal of time, which means students have less time for other activities. Also, group projects are more complicated than short activities that finish in 15 minutes or in one class period. Also, because of their complexity, group projects can be more difficult for students to coordinate. Furthermore, as a good deal of the work on group projects takes place outside of class, it can be difficult for teachers to monitor what students do when working alone or when interacting with peers at someone's home, on a bench at school, online, etc., thereby complicating assessment.

At the same time, group projects can have positive aspects. These include being more similar to the kinds of tasks that people work on outside of school. Plus, students can focus on a topic in a more long-term way. In contrast, in school, the tendency is to change topics many times a day. Students spending more time on topics of interest can enhance their intrinsic motivation. The extra time also provides students more time to get to know their groupmates and, we hope, develop more positive views of them, not to mention raising students' self-esteem as they look back on what they have produced at the culmination of the project. Working on the project can provide opportunities for students to make choices on such matters as what to study, how to study it, how to present their results, and what their opinions should be on the topics they study. Last, but not least, projects call for deeper thinking, as students have time to dive deep into topics.

Many frameworks have been developed to guide students as they do projects. One of the best-known of these frameworks is Problem-Based Learning (PBL), originally developed for students at medical schools. For example, rather than listening to lectures about the workings of the kidney, students begin learning about kidneys by attempting to solve a problem faced by a patient who has a kidney disease. Thus, the learning becomes more practical, more real-life. Although PBL does not carry a label as a cooperative learning technique, students work in groups in PBL, and certainly ideas from cooperative learning facilitate the effectiveness of the groups.

One framework for projects that does carry an explicit 'cooperative learning' label is Group Investigation (Sharan & Sharan, 1992, 1999). It might be of interest to learn a little about the developers of Group Investigation, as Yael Sharan and Shlomo Sharan have long been in the forefront of cooperative learning. They were part of a small group of teachers and researchers who in 1979 formed the International Association for the Study of Cooperation in Education (IASCE), an organization which for about 40 years played a leading role in research into cooperative learning and professional development based on this. The Sharans based their Group Investigation most centrally on the ideas of John Dewey (Chapter 1), including such ideas as active learning, democratic functioning, learning that serves society rather than only the interests of the learners, and connecting the classroom to the world beyond. This can be clearly seen in the following lesson plan.

The Lesson Plan

Here are the steps in a Group Investigation lesson plan.

Step 1 – The class and teacher agree on a multifaceted problem that the students feel is important. Multifaceted problems have room for different investigations by various groups within the class. Such problems are also known as 'fuzzy problems,' i.e., complex problems that do not have only one reasonable answer. Students spend time to better understand the problem. While doing that, they construct related questions they might like to investigate. Groups form within the class based on the questions about which students have expressed interest. Thus, the class becomes a group of groups.

Step 2 – Each group plans the what, how, who, and when of their investigation. This includes the questions to investigate, the resources to be used, which group members will investigate what, and by when they will report back to the group. For example, they might want to construct a roster of who will do what by when. However, as the investigation moves forward and the members of the group better understand the questions involved and the resources for understanding those questions, they might need to revise their plan.

Step 3 – Groups implement their plan. Part of this involves each student evaluating the information they find, recording it, and organizing it to be ready to report back to their group. The group reviews and analyzes their members' findings. Do they need more information? Can they develop tentative ideas for addressing their self-assigned questions? Have other questions arisen?

Step 4 – Groups prepare to present to the class, deciding on what information to present as well as how best to present it in the clearest, most persuasive manner possible. Presentations should emphasize main ideas, rather than repeating every detail the groups learned in their investigations. Also, time limits should be closely observed, including time for questions and comments. Everyone in the group should have a speaking part in the group's presentation. Presentations should not be like teacher-centered lectures. Instead, the rest of the class should be active, e.g., doing group work and offering feedback. Finally, rehearsals can improve the quality of the presentations, as well as seeing if the group will stay within the time limit and whether the technology, if any is used, is likely to work.

Step 5 – Groups present. Peer, teacher, and self-evaluations are done on the presentations using a rubric constructed by the class. Based on the data and recommendations of the various groups, the class discusses the overall problem chosen in Step 1 and considers what they might do on their own and by reaching out to others to ameliorate the problem.

Step 6 – Evaluation and reflection. In addition to the presentation assessments using the class-constructed rubric, the class can construct a test of students' comprehension of main ideas in the presentations. Alternatively, other forms of assessment might be used, including essays related to the problems. Or, as suggested in Chapter 4, sometimes perhaps no graded assessments are needed. Individually, in groups, and as a class, students and teachers reflect on their experience. Questions to consider include: How did it feel to dive deep into a problem? What was learned about how to do a project in a group? Were any new research tools and skills discovered? Is it better to investigate alone or with others?

Commentary

a. *Positive interdependence* – Of the eight ways of promoting positive interdependence described in Chapter 2, resource positive interdependence features prominently in Group Investigation. Also, goal interdependence deserves mention, as the class is investigating and proposing solutions to address an important real-world problem. Thus, many people can benefit from the ideas and actions that the class generates based on their research and analysis.

b. *Individual accountability* – In Step 1 of Group Investigation, each student develops their own questions related to the problem selected by the class. This is much different from the situation in teacher-centered learning in which what students work on is dictated by teachers and educational institutions, not necessarily by the students' own interests and choices. In Step 2, each group compiles a roster of what each member will investigate and by when they need to report back to the group on what they have learned.

c. *Equal opportunity to participate* – Step 4 is one of the many points within Group Investigation designed to give everyone in all the groups a chance to take an active part in what their group does. In Step 4, groups plan their presentation, and each group's presentation must include a speaking part for all group members. Furthermore, groups rehearse their presentations, so that partners offer feedback to improve each member's presentation.

d. *Maximum peer interactions* – As to the quantity of peer interactions, with group size kept to four or less, many peer interactions can take place. Quality of peer interactions is where Group Investigation really shines. Students' minds receive a great workout in all the steps, doing all sorts of complex thinking, including in Steps 5 and 6 where they need to evaluate the work done and reflect on their experience as investigators and analysts, as well as synthesizers of a plan to deal with the problem their class selected in Step 1.

e. *Heterogeneous grouping* – Many variables can be used in forming heterogeneous groups. The multiple intelligences profile (see Chapter 1) can be one such variable. Cohen & Lotan (2014) advocate that cooperative learning groups work on what they call 'multiple ability tasks,' i.e., tasks that involve a range of intelligences. For example, as part of their investigations, students can interview people, thus using and developing their interpersonal intelligence. Additionally, logical/mathematical intelligence plays an important role when groups use statistics in their analyses and presentations.

f.   *Group autonomy* – Group Investigation provides a blend of whole-class, group-based, and individual activity. One way of using the 3 + 1 B4 T (ask your three groupmates plus one other group before asking the teacher) strategy would be for groups to consult with another group investigating a related aspect of the problem, in order to compare notes on both the information sources they find as well as the solutions they propose. Furthermore, many organizations – public, private, for-profit, not-for-profit – address the kinds of fuzzy problems tackled by students doing Group Investigation, problems such as climate change and pandemics. These organizations can provide useful alternatives to consulting teachers.

g.   *Teaching cooperative skills* – Let us talk about a simple, but too often neglected cooperative skill: thanking others. As a language skill, saying 'thank you' is so simple, compared to more complicated skills such as disagreeing politely; and thanking others is a skill that we have so many opportunities to use. For instance, the authors of this book would like to pause here and thank all of you for reading all the way to Chapter 7. We appreciate it sooooooo much!

h.   *Cooperation as a value* – Dewey, a key inspiration for Group Investigation, stated: 'The acquisition of skills is not an end in itself. They are things to be put to use, and that use is their contribution to a common and shared life' (cited in Archambault, 1964, p. 11). Yes, a large body of research suggests that cooperative learning boosts student achievement, enabling them to go to 'better' schools, get higher-paying, higher-status jobs, but is that the main goal? (Please remember goal positive interdependence.) Cooperation as a value does not ask students to forget about their own needs or those of their family members, but it does emphasize that we are positively interdependent with our fellow homo sapiens, not to mention with the world's other animal species.

Variations

In Step 5 of Group Investigation, whole-class discussion takes place about what, based on their investigation and cogitation, the class might do to address the problem they chose in Step 1. Such whole-class discussion has great value. Perhaps it could be supplemented by discussion in twosomes, in order to give students more chances to share their views. This also fits with the quantity aspect of the cooperative learning principle of maximum peer interactions.

One cooperative learning technique for facilitating such dialogues with members of different groups is 7S (Jacobs & Zainal Abiden, 2017). The technique works as follows.

Step 1 – Stand. Everyone stands up.

Step 2 – Slide. If students have separate chairs and desks, they slide their chairs under their desks to create more space for future steps in 7S.

Step 3 – Stretch. As students have probably been sitting for a while, it might be useful for them to stretch a bit upon standing.

Step 4 – Sip. Students sip from their water bottles. Students' bodies and especially brains need hydration (Hecht et al., 2017).

Step 5 – Stir. Students mix around the room. They do this separately, not with their groupmates.

Step 6 – Stop. When someone gives a signal, students stop stirring and form a pair with the person from another group who is standing nearest to them.

Step 7 – Speak. Students share on the selected topic with their new partner. In the case of Group Investigation, the topic could be solutions to the problem selected by the class or reflections on the investigation experience.

Notes: (a) if the classroom is very crowded, it might be necessary to orchestrate student movement, e.g., numbering the seats, and have half of the class change seats; (b) in Round 2 of 7S, students may only do steps 1, 5, 6, and 7, and this time, they share their first partner's thoughts with their second partner.

At several points in this book, we have stated that cooperative learning techniques *can* be modified, keeping in mind cooperative learning principles. Maybe we should modify that statement and say instead: cooperative learning principles *should* be modified, keeping in mind cooperative learning principles and *using students' and teachers' observations and insights*. 7S offers an example. It started as 4S: Stand, Stir, Stop, Speak. One of us had already used 4S a number of times, when ideas came to us for modifications. First, our classrooms often had separate tables and chairs, and sometimes, after standing, students did not push their chairs all the way under their tables. As a result, students had less space to Stir. To correct for this, we added a fifth S, Slide (i.e., slide your chair under your table). Then, we observed that after standing, some students stretched, and some drank from their water bottles. This brought to mind what we had been reading about the benefits of standing versus prolonged sitting (Vallance et al., 2018) and the benefits of drinking water (Drozdowska et al., 2020). Thus, we added a sixth and seventh S, Stand and Sip. No doubt, students and teachers in other classrooms will modify 7S in who knows how many other ways.

Chapter 3 talks about how students and teachers can experiment with moving around and adding/subtracting components of cooperative learning techniques.

All sorts of fun permutations come to mind, especially with kids, e.g., when students do the Stir step, instead of using a normal walk as they go about the room mixing with classmates from different groups, students can do animal walks, such as crab walks or penguin waddles (Robson, 2017). Furthermore, rather than everyone moving around the same way, e.g., using frog hops, students can bust out whatever individual moves occur to them. Maybe even teens and adults can release their inner child for a few moments.

Reflective Break

1. Does your school encourage you to facilitate group projects among your students? What are your views on group projects?
2. Are your students ready to exercise the level of independence needed for a group project? If not, how can you prepare them?
3. What can teachers do while students work on their projects?

CONCLUSION

There have been at least three purposes to this chapter. First, we wanted to put more cooperative learning techniques into your teacher toolkits. Of course, there is no need to use different cooperative learning techniques every day or every week. Student interest can be aroused more by the content and skills being learned, the peer interaction, and the learning materials. However, seeing the diversity among cooperative learning techniques may inspire you to reflect on more ways to use cooperative learning and more ways to vary it. Second, by discussing how cooperative learning principles sync with cooperative learning techniques, we hope you have more to reflect on as you observe students doing cooperative learning. Are the principles we teachers seek to promote actually being lived in our students' groups, e.g., do students act as though they feel positively interdependent with each other? Third, we hope you will look at situations you are in or observe outside of education and ask yourself about the presence or absence of cooperative learning principles. For instance, what is being done to promote equal opportunity to participate, and would this situation benefit from heterogeneous grouping?

Conclusion

Hurray for Cooperative Learning through a Reflective Lens

Collectively, the authors of this book have written at least seven other books on cooperative learning, and this is the one we have enjoyed writing the most. What makes this book special is, first of all, 'We're not getting older, we're getting better!' Thus, although we probably have forgotten some useful ideas here and there, the sum total of our accumulated knowledge has grown. For this growth, we need to thank our students, fellow teachers, and others in education and related fields, as well as the power of the ideas underlying cooperative learning.

A second reason – actually, the main reason – we enjoyed doing this book was all the Reflective Breaks that are liberally sprinkled throughout the book. We hope you enjoyed reflecting on some of the short questions and tasks, and that you will find occasion to return to some of them in the future, as well as creating many of your own reflection tasks for yourself, your students, and your colleagues, as reflection continues to be a must-have part of how you teach and live. For ourselves, we just can't survive without regular doses of Vitamin R (reflection). Also, please do not think of us as harsh taskmasters for giving you so many reflections to do. We did all of them ourselves too.

Special thanks go to our Series Editor, Professor Tom Farrell. This book is part of Equinox's *Reflective Practice in Language Education* series, and Tom wrote the initial book in the series, *Reflective Practice in ELT*. He is a master of the reflective break, of empowering teachers to see the world through a reflective lens. In fact, one of his best-selling books is subtitled *80 reflective breaks for busy teachers* (Farrell, 2004). We have learned from Tom, and we hope that, if you are not doing so already, that you will soon be encouraging your students and everyone else with whom you collaborate to join you on reflective breaks.

To quickly recap this book, the Introduction reminds us of how important cooperation is in so many facets of our lives. Chapter 1 supplies background on cooperative learning, including history, roots in cultural traditions, supporting theories from general education and second language education, and the impressive and ongoing research support that cooperative learning enjoys. Chapter 2 dives deep into principles that underlie cooperative learning, and most deeply into the principle of positive interdependence, the principle most central to growing a we-sink-or-swim-together feeling among group members. Chapter 3 serves up what we hope is a large helping of practical advice on how student and teachers can implement cooperative learning. This practical angle continues in Chapter 4 which grapples with some of the sticky issues that arise in assessing students when they cooperate.

Chapter 5 takes a philosophical turn, linking cooperative learning and reflective teaching in the context of the student-centered paradigm in language teaching. Chapter 6 asks and tries to answer the logical next two questions: Since teachers are encouraging students to cooperate, shouldn't teachers also cooperate with each other? How can teachers reflect together on how they facilitate student–student cooperation? Finally, Chapter 7 presents and annotates five language learning lessons in which students cooperate with their peers, assisted by their teachers. In all the chapters, Reflective Breaks are always right around the corner,

Every concluding chapter needs its own conclusion. To end this chapter and this book, we, the authors, want to urge you to make cooperation and reflection foundations upon which you build your teaching and your life. Cooperation brings strength and kindness, and reflection brings insight and wisdom. Now, more than ever, teachers and everyone else can never have enough of those qualities.

References

Abualhaija, N. (2019). Using constructivism and student-centered learning approaches in nursing education. *International Journal of Nursing and Health Care Research*, 5(7), 1–6.

Achor, S. (2018). *Big potential: How transforming the pursuit of success raises our achievement, happiness, and well-being.* Currency.

Al Amin, M., & Greenwood, J. (2018). The UN sustainable development goals and teacher development for effective English teaching in Bangladesh: A gap that needs bridging. *Journal of Teacher Education for Sustainability*, 20(2), 118–138. https://files.eric.ed.gov/fulltext/EJ1218224.pdf. https://doi.org/10.2478/jtes-2018-0019

Al Ghozali, M. I., Barnawi, B., & Pratama, F. A. (2019). Fish Bowl method in learning talking skills. *Action Research Journal Indonesia (ARJI)*, 1(2), 87–98.

Al-Bataineh, A. T., Brenwall, L., Stalter, K., & York, J. (2019). Student growth through goal setting. *International Journal of Learning and Teaching*, 11(4), 147–161. https://doi.org/10.18844/ijlt.v11i4.4329

Ali, H., & Shah, A. H. (2018). Role of extrovert and introvert personality factors in second language acquisition in UOS, Pakistan. *Modern Journal of Language Teaching Methods*, 8(6), 111–119.

Aliyyah, R. R., Widyasari, W., Rasmitadila, R., Ulfah, S. W., Humaira, M. A., & Mulyadi, D. (2020, February). Outstanding teachers' competition: Between strategies and challenges. In *3rd International Conference on Research of Educational Administration and Management (ICREAM 2019)* (pp. 153–157). Atlantis Press. https://doi.org/10.2991/assehr.k.200130.160

All About Philosophy. (2020). *The blind men and the elephant.* https://www.allaboutphilosophy.org/blind-men and-the-elephant.htm

Allport, G. W. (1954). *The nature of prejudice.* Addison-Wesley.

Allred, J. B., & Cena, M. E. (2020). Reading motivation in high school: Instructional shifts in student choice and class time. *Journal of Adolescent & Adult Literacy*, 64(1), 27–35. https://doi.org/10.1002/jaal.1058

Archambault, R. (1964). *John Dewey on education: Selected writings.* The Modern Library.

Aronson, E. (1978). *The jigsaw classroom.* Sage.

Aronson, E. (2021). *The jigsaw classroom*. https://www.jigsaw.org/

Aronson, E., & Bridgeman, D. (1979). Jigsaw groups and the desegregated classroom: In pursuit of common goals. *Personality and Social Psychology Bulletin*, 5(4), 438–446. https://doi.org/10.1177/014616727900500405

Arunsirot, N. (2021). A study of cooperative learning approach in EFL classroom. *Journal of Education Naresuan University*, 23(2), 13–28.

Au, O. T. S. (2020, August). Mini-lectures interleaved with exercises found beneficial in online learning. In *2020 International Symposium on Educational Technology (ISET)* (pp. 138–141). https://doi.org/10.1109/ISET49818.2020.00038

Auerbach, E. R., & Burgess, D. (1985). The hidden curriculum of survival ESL. *TESOL Quarterly*, 19(3), 475–495. https://doi.org/10.2307/3586274

Austin Community College. (2015). *Do I grade on a curve?* https://www.austincc.edu/sziser/Biol%202404/Grading%20on%20a%20Curve.pdf

Bailenson, J. N. (2021). Nonverbal overload: A theoretical argument for the causes of Zoom fatigue. *Technology, Mind, and Behavior*, 2(1). https://doi.org/10.1037/tmb0000030

Baker, T., & Clark, J. (2010). Cooperative learning – a double-edged sword: A cooperative learning model for use with diverse student groups. *Intercultural Education*, 21(3), 257–268. https://doi.org/10.1080/14675981003760440

Bandura, A., Ross, D., & Ross, S. A. (1963). Vicarious reinforcement and imitative learning. *The Journal of Abnormal and Social Psychology*, 67(6), 601–607. https://doi.org/10.1037/h0045550

Barr, R. B., & Tagg, J. (1995, November/December). From teaching to learning – A new paradigm for under-graduate education. *Change*, 13–25.

Bazzi, S., Fiszbein, M., & Gebresilasse, M. (2021). 'Rugged individualism' and collective (in)action during the COVID-19 pandemic. *Journal of Public Economics*, 195, 104357. https://doi.org/10.1016/j.jpubeco.2020.104357

Bell, A. (1823/2019). *Mutual tuition and moral discipline: Or, manual of instructions from conducting schools through the agency of the scholars themselves, for the use of schools and families*. Forgotten Books.

Benson, P. (1997). Concepts of autonomy in language learning. In R. Pemberton, E. S. L. Li, W. W. F. Or, & H. D. Pierson (Eds.), *Taking control: Autonomy in language learning* (pp. 27–34). Hong Kong University Press.

Benson, P. (2007). Autonomy in language teaching and learning. *Language Teaching*, 40, 21–40. https://www.pucsp.br/inpla/benson_artigo.pdf

Benson, P. (2013). Learner autonomy. *TESOL Quarterly*, 47(4), 839–843. https://doi.org/10.1002/tesq.134

Bereiter, C., & Bird, M. (1985). Use of thinking aloud in identification and teaching of reading comprehension strategies. *Cognition and Instruction*, 2(2), 131–156. https://doi.org/10.1207/s1532690xci0202_2

Binfet, J. T. (2015). Not-so random acts of kindness: A guide to intentional kindness in the classroom. *International Journal of Emotional Education*, 7(2), 49–62. https://files.eric.ed.gov/fulltext/EJ1088155.pdf

Bloom, B. S., Engelhart, M. D., Furst, E. J., Hill, W. H., & Krathwohl, D. R. (1956). *Taxonomy of educational objectives. Vol. 1: Cognitive domain.* McKay.

Bloomfield, R. J. (2017). *What counts and what gets counted* (2nd ed.). Cornell University. https://papers.ssrn.com/sol3/papers.cfm?abstract_id=2899141. https://doi.org/10.2139/ssrn.2899141

Bossert, S. T. (1988–1989). Cooperative activities in the classroom. *Review of Research in Education, 15,* 225–252. https://doi.org/10.2307/1167365

Bourdieu, P. (1972). *Outline of a theory of practice.* Cambridge University Press.

Boyd, M. P., Jarmark, C. J., & Edmiston, B. (2018). Building bridges: Coauthoring a class handshake, building a classroom community. *Pedagogies: An International Journal, 13*(4), 330–352. https://doi.org/10.1080/1554480X.2018.1437731

Bradley, F. (1997). From unconscious incompetence to unconscious competence. *Adults Learning (England), 9*(2), 20–21.

Bregman, R. (2020a). *Humankind: A hopeful history.* Bloomsbury.

Bregman, R. (2020b, May 20). The real Lord of the Flies: What happened when six boys were shipwrecked for 15 months. https://www.theguardian.com/books/2020/may/09/the-real-lord-of-the-flies-what-happened-when-six-boys-were-shipwrecked-for-15-months

Brody, C. (2009). Cooperative learning and collaborative learning: Is there a difference? *IASCE Newsletter, 28*(1), 7–9. https://jasce.jp/iasce/www.iasce.net/home/IASCE-NL/28(1)2009.pdf

Brown, A. L., & Palincsar, A. S. (2018). *Guided, cooperative learning and individual knowledge acquisition.* In L. B. Resnick (Ed.), *Knowing, learning, and instruction* (pp. 393–451). Routledge. https://doi.org/10.4324/9781315044408-13

Brownlee, J. (2001). Knowing and learning in teacher education: A theoretical framework of core and peripheral epistemic beliefs. *Asia-Pacific Journal of Teacher Education and Development, 4*(1), 131–155.

Bruffee, K. A. (1993). *Collaborative learning: Higher education, interdependence and the authority of knowledge.* Johns Hopkins University Press.

Bruner, J. S. (1973). *Beyond the information given: Studies in the psychology of knowing.* W. W. Norton.

Bruton, A., & Samuda, V. (1980). Learner and teacher roles in the treatment of oral error in group work. *RELC Journal, 11*(2), 49–63. https://doi.org/10.1177/003368828001100204

Burnard, P. (1999). Carl Rogers and postmodernism: Challenges in nursing and health sciences. *Nursing & Health Sciences, 1*(4), 241–247.

Burns, A. (1992). Teacher beliefs and their influence on classroom practice. *Prospect, 7*(3), 56–66.

Burns, E. C., Martin, A. J., & Collie, R. J. (2019). Understanding the role of personal best (PB) goal setting in students' declining engagement: A latent growth model. *Journal of Educational Psychology, 111*(4), 557–572. https://doi.org/10.1016/j.cedpsych.2018.02.001

Cain, S. (2012). *Quiet: The power of introverts in a world that can't stop talking.* Crown. https://doi.org/10.1037/e549532012-001

Cain, S., Mone, G., & Moroz, E. (2016). *Quiet power: The secret strengths of introverts.* Penguin.

Cambridge University Press. (2021). Boggle. In *Cambridge Dictionary.* https://dictionary.cambridge.org/dictionary/hinese/boggle

Caspe, M. S. (2003). How teachers come to understand families. *School Community Journal, 13*(1), 115–131. https://www.adi.org/journal/ss03/caspe%20115-132.pdf

Chamot, A. U., & O'Malley, J. M. (1994). *The CALLA handbook: Implementing the cognitive academic language learning approach.* Addison-Wesley.

Chau, M. H., & Jacobs, G. M. (2021). Applied Linguistics, language guidelines, and inclusive practices: The case for the use of who with nonhuman animals. *International Journal of Applied Linguistics.* https://doi.org/10.1111/ijal.12357

Cho, E. H., & Larke, P. J. (2010). Repair strategies usage of primary elementary ESL students: Implications for ESL teachers. *TESL-EJ, 14*(3). http://www.tesl-ej.org/pdf/ej55/a4.pdf

Christison, M. A., & Kennedy, D. (1999). *Multiple intelligences: Theory and practice in adult ESL.* ERIC Digest. ED441350. https://eric.ed.gov/?id=ED441350

Cohen, E. G. (1994). Restructuring the classroom: Conditions for productive small groups. *Review of Educational Research, 64*(1), 1–35. http://files.eric.ed.gov/fulltext/ED363952.pdf. https://doi.org/10.3102/00346543064001001

Cohen, E., & Lotan, R. (2014). *Designing group work: Strategies for the classroom* (3rd ed.). Teachers College Press.

Coleman, J. S. (1988). Social capital in the creation of human capital. *American Journal of Sociology, 94,* S95–S120. https://doi.org/10.1086/228943

Collins, T. A., Drevon, D. D., Brown, A. M., Villarreal, J. N., Newman, C. L., & Endres, B. (2020). Say something nice: A meta-analytic review of peer reporting interventions. *Journal of School Psychology, 83,* 89–103. https://doi.org/10.1016/j.jsp.2020.10.002

Costa, A. L., & Kallick, B. (1993). Through the lens of a critical friend. *Educational Leadership, 51,* 49–51.

Craik, F. I., & Lockhart, R. S. (1972). Levels of processing: A framework for memory research. *Journal of Verbal Learning and Verbal Behavior, 11*(6), 671–684. https://doi.org/10.1016/S0022-5371(72)80001-X

Crookes, G. V. (2013). *Critical ELT in action: Foundations, promises, praxis.* Routledge. https://doi.org/10.4324/9780203844250

Csikszentmihalyi, M. (1990). *Flow: The psychology of optimal experience.* Harper Perennial.

D'Eon, M., & Proctor, P. (2001). An innovative modification to Structured Controversy. *Innovations in Education and Teaching International, 38*(3), 251–256. https://doi.org/10.1080/14703290110051398

Day, R. R., & Bamford, J. (2002). Top ten principles for extensive reading. *Reading in a Foreign Language, 14*(2). https://scholarspace.manoa.hawaii.edu/bitstream/10125/66761/1/14_2_10125_66761_day.pdf

Debate.org. (2019). *Are humans innately selfish?* https://www.debate.org/opinions/are-humans-innately-selfish

Deutsch, M. (1949). A theory of cooperation and competition. *Human Relations*, 2, 129–152. https://doi.org/10.1177/001872674900200204

Dewey, J. (1897). *My pedagogic creed*. E. L. Kellogg & Company.

Dewey, J. (1916). *Democracy and education: An introduction to the philosophy of education* (1966 ed.). Free Press.

Dixson, D. D., & Worrell, F. C. (2016). Formative and summative assessment in the classroom. *Theory into Practice*, 55(2), 153–159. https://doi.org/10.1080/00405841.2016.1148989

Dor-Haim, P. (2021). Expressions of loneliness: Different perspectives of loneliness among school deputy principals. *Educational Management Administration & Leadership*, 52, 1–17. https://doi.org/10.1177/17411432211021425

Dörnyei, Z. (2014). *The psychology of the language learner: Individual differences in second language acquisition*. Routledge. https://doi.org/10.4324/9781410613349

Drozdowska, A., Falkenstein, M., Jendrusch, G., Platen, P., Luecke, T., Kersting, M., & Jansen, K. (2020). Water consumption during a school day and children's short-term cognitive performance: The CogniDROP randomized intervention trial. *Nutrients*, *12*(5). https://doi.org/10.3390/nu12051297

Dyrendahl, H. P. (2012). Volunteer work: A Q-methodological study of volunteers' subjective experience of working at a crisis helpline. Master's thesis, Norwegian University of Science and Technology.

Eisler, R. M., & Frederiksen, L. W. (2012). *Perfecting social skills: A guide to interpersonal behavior development* (Vol. 56). Springer Science & Business Media.

Ellis, R. (2005). Principles of instructed language learning. *Asian EFL Journal*, *7*(3), 9–24. https://doi.org/10.1016/j.system.2004.12.006

Evans, N., & Levinson, S. (2009). The myth of language universals: Language diversity and its importance for cognitive science. *Behavioral and Brain Sciences*, *32*, 429–492. https://doi.org/10.1017/S0140525X0999094X

Extensive Reading Foundation. (2011). *Guide to extensive reading*. http://erfoundation.org/ERF_Guide. Pdf

Extensive Reading Foundation. (2021). *What is ER?* https://erfoundation.org/wordpress/what_is

Extensive Reading Foundation. (n.d.). *Graded readers*. https://erfoundation.org/wordpress/graded-readers/

Farrell, T. S. C. (2004). *Reflective practice in action: 80 reflective breaks for busy teachers*. Sage.

Farrell, T. S. C. (2014). *Reflective practice in ESL teacher development groups: From practices to principles*. Palgrave Macmillan. https://doi.org/10.1057/9781137317193

Farrell, T. S. C. (2015). *Promoting teacher reflection in second language education: A framework for TESOL professionals*. Routledge. https://doi.org/10.4324/9781315775401

Farrell, T. S. C. (2019). *Reflective practice in ELT*. Equinox. https://doi.org/10.4324/9781315659824-5

Farrell, T. S. C., & Jacobs, G. M. (2016). Practicing what we preach: Teacher reflection groups on cooperative learning. *TESL-EJ, 19*(4), 1–9. http://www.tesl-ej.org/pdf/ej76/a5.pdf

Farrell, T. S. C., & Jacobs, G. M. (2020). *Essentials for successful English language teaching* (2nd ed.). Bloomsbury.

Fishbein, A. R., Fritz, J. B., Idsardi, W. J., & Wilkinson, G. S. (2020). What can animal communication teach us about human language? *Philosophical Transactions of the Royal Society B.* https://doi.org/10.1098/rstb.2019.0042

Fishbein, M., & Ajzen, I. (1975). *Belief, attitude, intention and behavior.* Addison-Wesley.

Forrest, A. (2019, February 5). Democracy undergoing 'alarming' decline around the world, study finds. *Independent.* https://www.independent.co.uk/news/world/democracy-freedom-house-annual-report-civil-liberties-authoritarian-donald-trump-us-a8763196.html

Francis, D. (1995). The reflective journal: A window to preservice teachers' knowledge. *Teaching and Teacher Education, 11,* 229–241. https://doi.org/10.1016/0742-051X(94)00031-Z

Frankl, V. (1946). *Man's search for meaning.* Beacon Press.

Freire, P. (2000). *Pedagogy of the oppressed.* Continuum Press. (Originally published 1970.)

Fullan, M. (1994). Coordinating top-down and bottom-up strategies for educational reform. In R. J. Anson (Ed.), *Systemic reform: Perspectives on personalizing education* (pp. 7–24). https://files.eric.ed.gov/fulltext/ED376557.pdf#page=12

Fushino, K. (2010). Causal relationships between communication confidence, beliefs about group work, and willingness to communicate in foreign language group work. *TESOL Quarterly, 44*(4), 700–724. https://doi.org/10.5054/tq.2010.235993

Fushino, K., & Jacobs, G. M. (2017). Promoting equal opportunity to participate in language learning. *Cooperation and Education, 13,* 27–40.

Gagné, N., & Parks, S. (2013). Cooperative learning tasks in a Grade 6 intensive ESL class: Role of scaffolding. *Language Teaching Research, 17*(2), 188–209.

Gardihewa, P. N. (2021). The impacts of cooperative learning on demoting communication anxiety with special reference to engineering undergraduates. *Sri Lanka Journal of Social Sciences and Humanities, 1*(1). http://repo.lib.sab.ac.lk:8080/xmlui/handle/123456789/1689. https://doi.org/10.4038/sljssh.v1i1.26

Gardner, H. (1987). *The mind's new science: A history of the cognitive revolution.* Basic Books.

Gardner, H. (1993). *Multiple intelligences: The theory and practice.* Basic Books.

Ghosh, A. (2021). Promoting student discourse in a linguistically diverse community-of-learners classroom. *InterActions: UCLA Journal of Education and Information Studies, 17*(1). https://doi.org/10.5070/D417150291

Gilbride, K. A. (2020). The use of group tests to promote collaboration and learning: Do they work? *McGill Journal of Education, 55*(1), 237–257. https://doi.org/10.7202/1075728ar

Gozali, I., Lie, A., & Tamah, S.M. (2021). HOTS questioning ability and HOTS perception of language teachers in Indonesia. *Indonesian Journal of Applied Linguistics, 11*(1), 60–71. https://ejournal.upi.edu/index.php/IJAL/article/view/34583/15029. https://doi.org/10.17509/ijal.v11i1.34583

Grossman, P., Smagorinsky, P., & Valencia, S. W. (1999). Appropriating tools for teaching English: A theoretical framework for research on learning to teach. *American Journal of Education*, *108*(1), 1–29. https://doi.org/10.1086/444230

Green, C. S., & Klug, H. G. (1990). Teaching critical thinking and writing through debates: An experimental evaluation. *Teaching Sociology*, *18*, 462–411. https://doi.org/10.2307/1317631

Green, T., Hoffmann, M., Donovan, L., & Phuntsog, N. (2017). Cultural communication characteristics and student connectedness in an online environment: Perceptions and preferences of online graduate students. *International Journal of E-Learning and Distance Education*, *32*(2). http://www.ijede.ca/index.php/jde/article/view/1033/1664

Hammrich, P. L., & Blouch, K. K. (1998). A cooperative controversy lesson designed to reveal students' conceptions of the 'Nature of Science'. *The American Biology Teacher*, *60*(1), 50–51. https://doi.org/10.2307/4450412

Han, Y. O., Choi, Y. H., & Oh, D. S. (2016). A study on the effectiveness of book trailers as an element of reading motivation for teenagers. *Journal of the Korean Society for Library and Science*, *50*(1), 5–23. https://doi.org/10.4275/KSLIS.2016.50.1.005

Harjanto, I., Lie, A. & Wijaya, J. (2019). Home, school, and community factors on Indonesian secondary students' self-identity changes. *Indonesian Journal of Applied Linguistics*, *9*(2). https://doi.org/10.17509/ijal.v9i2.20232

Harmer, J. (2015). *The practice of English language teaching*. Pearson.

Harvey, F. (2020, March 22). Poor water infrastructure is greater risk than coronavirus, says UN. *The Guardian*. https://www.theguardian.com/environment/2020/mar/22/water-saving-an-important-but-ignored-weapon-in-solving-climate-crisis-says-un

Hatch, E. M. (1978). *Second language acquisition: A book of readings*. Newbury House Publishers.

Hawking, S. (2002). *On the shoulders of giants: The great works of physics and astronomy*. Running Press.

Hay Newman, L. (2021, May 15). WhatsApp's new privacy policy just kicked in: Here's what you need to know. *Wired*. https://www.wired.com/story/whatsapp-privacy-policy-facebook-data-sharing/

Hecht, A. A., Grumbach, J. M., Hampton, K. E., Hecht, K., Braff-Guajardo, E., Brindis, C. D., ... & Patel, A. I. (2017). Validation of a survey to examine drinking-water access, practices and policies in schools. *Public Health Nutrition*, *20*(17), 3068–3074. https://doi.org/10.1017/S1368980017002312

Henson, K. T. (2003). Foundations for learner-centered education: A knowledge base. *Education*, *124*(1), 5–16.

Holec, H. (1981). *Autonomy and foreign language learning*. Pergamon.

Horita, Y., Takezawa, M., Kinjo, T., Nakawake, Y., & Masuda, N. (2016). Transient nature of cooperation by pay-it-forward reciprocity. *Scientific Reports*, *6*(1), 1–11. https://doi.org/10.1038/srep19471

Hsien, I. W. M. (2018). The espoused and enacted personal practical theories of early childhood teachers' inclusive classrooms. Doctoral dissertation, University of

Melbourne. https://rest.neptune-prod.its.unimelb.edu.au/server/api/core/bitstreams/
e6b027d4-5e92-53dd-9d7a-69b6b06a6040/content

Huber, G. L., Sorrentino, R. M., Davidson, M. A., Epplier, R., & Roth, J. W. (1992).
Uncertainty orientation and cooperative learning: Individual differences within and
across cultures. *Learning and Individual Differences, 4*(1), 1–24.
https://doi.org/10.1016/1041-6080(92)90013-5

Hughes, G. (Ed.). (2017). *Ipsative assessment and personal learning gain: Exploring international case studies*. Springer. https://doi.org/10.1057/978-1-137-56502-0

Hughes, M., & Bourner, T. (2005). Action learning set meetings: Getting started by 'checking in'. *Action Learning: Research and Practice, 2*(1), 89–95.
https://doi.org/10.1080/14767330500041681

Hythecker, V. I., Dansereau, D. F., & Rocklin, T. R. (1988). An analysis of the processes
influencing the structured dyadic learning environment. *Educational Psychologist, 23*(1), 23–37. https://doi.org/10.1207/s15326985ep2301_2

Irwin, B. R., Speechley, M., Wilk, P., Clark, A. F., & Gilliland, J. A. (2019). Promoting
healthy beverage consumption habits among elementary school children: Results of the
Healthy Kids Community Challenge 'Water Does Wonders' interventions in London,
Ontario. *Canadian Journal of Public Health*, 1–12.
https://doi.org/10.17269/s41997-019-00262-9

Ivone, F. M., Jacobs, G. M., & Santosa, M. H. (2020). Information and communication
technology to help students create their own books the dialogic way. *Beyond Words, 8*(2), 78–91. http://journal.wima.ac.id/index.php/BW/article/view/2545.
https://doi.org/10.33508/bw.v8i2.2545

Ivone, F. M., & Renandya, W. A. (2019). Extensive listening and viewing in ELT. *TEFLIN
Journal, 30*(2), 237–256. https://doi.org/10.15639/teflinjournal.v30i2/237-256

Jablon, J. (in press). *To Kill a Mockingbird* is a racist book. In G. M. Jacobs & G. V. Crookes
(Eds.), *Becoming community-engaged editors*. Springer.

Jackson, J. (2013). The transformation of 'a frog in the well': A path to a more intercultural,
global mindset. In C. Kinginger (Ed.), *Social and cultural aspects of language learning
in study abroad* (pp. 179–204). John Benjamins. https://doi.org/10.1075/lllt.37.08jac

Jacobs, G. M. (1989). Miscorrection in peer feedback in writing class. *RELC Journal, 20*(1), 68–76. https://doi.org/10.1177/003368828902000105

Jacobs, G. M. (2013, April 25). How Chinese culture can convince Singapore staff to be
team players. *Singapore Business Review*. http://sbr.com.sg/hr-education/commentary/
how-chinese-culture-can-convince-singapore-staff-be-team-players

Jacobs, G. M. (2015). Collaborative learning or cooperative learning? The name is not
important; flexibility is. *Beyond Words, 3*(1), 32–52. http://journal.wima.ac.id/index.
php/BW/article/view/676

Jacobs, G. M. (2017). Introverts and cooperative learning. *IASCE Newsletter, 36*(1), 7–8.
https://files.eric.ed.gov/fulltext/ED573549.pdf

Jacobs, G. M. (2019). *Cooperative games for language teaching*. National Institute of
Education, Singapore.
https://www.academia.edu/40321619/Cooperative_Games_for_Language_Teaching

Jacobs, G. M., & Chau, M. H. (2021). Two approaches for promoting student centered language learning: Cooperative learning and positive psychology. *Beyond Words*, *9*(1). http://journal.wima.ac.id/index.php/BW/article/view/3042. https://doi.org/10.33508/bw.v9i1.3042

Jacobs, G. M., & Crookes, G. V. (Eds.). (2022). *Becoming community-engaged educators*. Springer.

Jacobs, G. M., & Farrell, T. S. C. (2001). Paradigm shift: Understanding and implementing change in second language education. *TESL-EJ*, *5*(1). http://www.cc.kyoto-su.ac.jp/information/tesl-ej/ej17/toc.html

Jacobs, G. M., & Greliche, N. (2017). Convincing students that their groupmates' success can increase, not diminish, their own success. *Insight: A Journal of Scholarly Teaching*, *12*, 145–157. https://doi.org/10.46504/12201709ja

Jacobs, G. M., Power, M. A., & Loh, W. I. (2002). *Teachers handbook for cooperative learning*. Corwin.

Jacobs, G. M. & Renandya, W. A. (2016). Student-centred learning in ELT. In W. A. Renandya & H. P. Widodo (Eds.), *English language teaching today: Linking theory and practice* (pp. 13–23). Springer Nature. https://doi.org/10.1007/978-3-319-38834-2_2

Jacobs, G. M., Renandya, W. A., & Power, M. A. (2016). *Simple, powerful strategies for student centered learning*. Springer. https://doi.org/10.1007/978-3-319-25712-9

Jacobs, G. M., & Zainal Abiden, K. (2017). Standing up for cooperative learning: Alternatives to students usually sitting. *IASCE Newsletter*, *36*(2), 10–12. https://www.researchgate.net/publication/319008157_Standing_Up_For_Cooperative_Learning_Alternatives_to_Students_Usually_Sitting

John, P., & Woll, N. (2020). Using grammar checkers in an ESL context: An investigation of automatic corrective feedback. *Calico Journal*, *37*(2), 169–192. https://doi.org/10.1558/cj.36523

Johnson, D. W., Johnson, D., Johnson, R. T., & Johnson, R. L. (2004). *Assessing students in groups: Promoting group responsibility and individual accountability*. Corwin.

Johnson, D. W., & Johnson, F. (1989). *Joining together: Group theory and group skills* (11th ed. 2013). Pearson Education.

Johnson, D. W., & Johnson, R. T. (1995). *Creative controversy: Intellectual challenge in the classroom* (3rd ed.). Interaction Book Company.

Johnson, D. W., & Johnson, R. T. (2009). An educational psychology success story: Social interdependence theory and cooperative learning. *Educational Researcher*, *38*(5), 365–379. https://doi.org/10.3102/0013189X09339057

Johnson, D. W., Johnson, R. T., & Holubec, E. J. (1994). *The nuts and bolts of cooperative learning*. Interaction Book Company.

Johnson, D. W., Johnson, R. T., & Smith, K. A. (1998). Cooperative learning returns to college: What evidence is there that it works? *Change: The Magazine of Higher Learning*, *30*, 26–35. https://doi.org/10.1080/00091389809602629

Johnson, D. W., Johnson, R. T., & Stanne, M. B. (2000). *Cooperative learning methods: A meta-analysis*. Cooperative Learning Center, University of Minnesota.

Kader, N. A. (2013). An analysis of classroom interaction in cooperative learning: New insights for secondary school English teachers. *Educational Quest, 4*(2), 137–141. https://doi.org/10.5958/j.2230-7311.4.2.010

Karlsson, J., van den Broek, P., Helder, A., Hickendorff, M., Koornneef, A., & van Leijenhorst, L. (2018). Profiles of young readers: Evidence from thinking aloud while reading narrative and expository texts. *Learning and Individual Differences, 67,* 105–116. https://doi.org/10.1016/j.lindif.2018.08.001

Karmina, S., Dyson, B., Watson, S. J., Penelope, W., & Philpot, R. (2021). Teacher implementation of cooperative learning in Indonesia: A multiple case study. *Education Sciences, 11*(5), 218. https://doi.org/10.3390/educsci11050218

Kearney, P. (1993). *Cooperative learning techniques.* Artemis Publishing.

Kelly, L. A., & Adams, J. M. (2018). Nurse leader burnout: How to find your joy. *Nurse Leader, 16*(1), 24–28. https://doi.org/10.1016/j.mnl.2017.10.006

Kılıçkaya, F. (2018). Recycling English vocabulary through rational/selected deletion cloze, c-test and cloze elide. In M. Krawiec & R. Pritchard (Eds.), *Seize the day: New perspectives on foreign language learning and teaching* (pp. 133–154). https://eric.ed.gov/?id=ED588887

Kilpatrick, W. H. (1918, September). The project method. *Teachers College Record, 19,* 319–334.

Kim, L. S. (1995, January). Creative games for the language class. *English Teaching Forum, 33*(1), 35–36.

Klein, C., Diaz Granados, D., Salas, E., Le, H., Burke, C. S., Lyons, R., & Goodwin, G. F. (2009). Does team building work? *Small Group Research, 40*(2), 181–222. https://doi.org/10.1177/1046496408328821

Kohn, A. (1992). *No contest: The case against competition* (2nd ed.). Houghton Mifflin.

Kramsch, C. J. (1998). *Language and culture.* Oxford University Press.

Krashen, S. (1982). *Principles and practice in second language learning and acquisition.* Pergamon.

Krashen, S. D., & Terrell, T. (1983). *The natural approach: Language acquisition in the classroom.* Pergamon.

Kristof, N. (2021, January 2). Starving children don't cry. *New York Times.* https://www.nytimes.com/2021/01/02/opinion/Sunday/2020-worst-year-famine.html

Kuhn, T. S. (1970). *The structure of scientific revolutions* (2nd ed.). University of Chicago Press.

Kulkarni, C. E., Bernstein, M. S., & Klemmer, S. R. (2015, March). Peer Studio: Rapid peer feedback emphasizes revision and improves performance. In *Proceedings of the Second (2015) ACM Conference on Learning @ scale* (pp. 75–84). https://doi.org/10.1145/2724660.2724670

Kumaravadivelu, B. (2003). *Beyond method: Macrostrategies for language teaching.* Yale University Press.

Kushnir, T., & Koenig, M. A. (2017). What I don't know won't hurt you: The relation between professed ignorance and later knowledge claims. *Developmental Psychology, 53*(5), 826–835. https://doi.org/10.1037/dev0000294

Lake, V. E., & Adinolfi, S. D. (2017). Preschool: Young children take action: Service learning with preschoolers. *YC Young Children*, *72*(2), 80–84.

Lamb, S., Pagán-Ortiz, M., & Bonilla, S. (2021). How to provide sexual education: Lessons from a pandemic on masculinity, individualism, and the neoliberal agenda. *International Journal of Environmental Research and Public Health*, *18*(8), 4144. https://doi.org/10.3390/ijerph18084144

Lansing, J. S. (1987). Balinese 'Water Temples' and the management of irrigation. *American Anthropologist*, *89*(2), 326–341. https://doi.org/10.1525/aa.1987.89.2.02a00030

Lantolf, J. P. (Ed.), *Sociocultural theory and second language learning*. Oxford University Press.

Latip-Panggaga, S. (2021). Cooperative learning strategy: Its effects on enhancing the vocabulary and reading compression skills of MSU-ILS grade six pupils. *International Journal of Linguistics, Literature and Translation*, *4*(4), 55–69. https://doi.org/10.32996/ijllt.2021.4.4.7

Lee, W. R. (1979). *Language teaching games and contests*. Oxford University Press.

Lemmetty, S., & Collin, K. (2020). Self-directed learning as a practice of workplace learning: Interpretative repertoires of self-directed learning in ICT work. *Vocations and Learning*, *13*(1), 47–70. https://doi.org/10.1007/s12186-019-09228-x

Letek, M. (2020). Alexander Fleming, The discoverer of the antibiotic effects of penicillin. *Frontiers for Young Minds*. https://doi.org/10.3389/frym.2019.00159

Lewin, D., & Ergas, O. (2018). Eastern philosophies of education: Buddhist, Hindu, Daoist, and Confucian readings of Plato's cave. In P. Smeyers (Ed.), *International handbook of philosophy of education* (pp. 479–497). Springer. https://doi.org/10.1007/978-3-319-72761-5_40

Lewin, K. (1951). *Field theory in social science: Selected theoretical papers*. Harper & Row.

Lewis, M. (2017). *The Undoing Project: A friendship that changed the world*. Penguin.

Lie, A. (2002). *Cooperative learning*. Grasindo.

Lie, A. (2022). Tackling poverty. In G. M. Jacobs & G. V. Crookes (Eds.), *Becoming community-engaged educators* (pp. 7–16). Springer.

Lie, A., Chau, M. H., Jacobs, G., Zhu, C. H., & Winarlim, H. (under review). The downside of merit: A study of Indonesian English teachers' views on the role of effort in success.

Lieberman, M. D. (2010). Social cognitive neuroscience. In S. T. Fiske, D. T. Gilbert, & G. Lindzey (Eds.), *Handbook of social psychology* (pp. 143–193). John Wiley & Sons, Inc. https://doi.org/10.1002/9780470561119.socpsy001005

Lieberman, M. D. (2013). *The social brain and its superpowers* [video]. TED Conferences. https://www.youtube.com/watch?v=NNhk3owF7RQ&ab_channel=TEDxTalks

Linares, R. E. (2019). Meaningful writing opportunities: Write-alouds and dialogue journaling with newcomer and English learner high schoolers. *Journal of Adolescent & Adult Literacy*, *62*(5), 521–530. https://doi.org/10.1002/jaal.932

Ling, J., Smith, A., & Peng, C. L. (2016). *My pals are here! (3A, Pupil's book)*. Marshall Cavendish Education.

Liss, L. (2022). Promoting religious tolerance. In G. M. Jacobs & G. V. Crookes (Eds.), *Becoming community-engaged educators* (pp. 37–46). Springer.

Lodhi, A. (2017, June 22). Education and Plato's allegory of The Cave. *Medium*. https://medium.com/indian-thoughts/education-and-platos-allegory-of-the-cave-bf7471260c50

Long, M. H. (1981). Input, interaction, and second language acquisition. In H. Winitz (Ed.), *Native language and foreign language acquisition* (Vol. 379, pp. 259–278). Annals of the New York Academy of Sciences. https://doi.org/10.1111/j.1749-6632.1981.tb42014.x

Long, M. H. (1983). Linguistic and conversational adjustments to non-native speakers. *Studies in Second Language Acquisition*, *5*(2), 177–193. https://doi.org/10.1017/S0272263100004848

Long, M. H. (2017). *Problems in second language acquisition*. Routledge.

Lopez-Fresno, P., & Savolainen, T. (2014). Working meetings: A tool for building or destroying trust in knowledge creation and sharing. *Electronic Journal of Knowledge Management*, *12*(2), 137–143. https://academic-publishing.org/index.php/ejkm/article/view/1020/983

Lypka, A. (2018). Infusing participatory digital service-learning to deepen community-engaged professional excellence: Triumphs and challenges. *The Reading Matrix: An International Online Journal*, *8*(2), 77–93. https://readingmatrix.com/files/19-mh2w200n.pdf

Machebe, C. H., Ezegbe, B. N., & Onuoha, J. (2017). The impact of parental level of income on students' academic performance in high school in Japan. *Universal Journal of Educational Research*, *5*(9), 1614–1620. https://eric.ed.gov/?id=EJ1170144. https://doi.org/10.13189/ujer.2017.050919

Mancilla, R. L., Polat, N., & Akcay, A. O. (2017). An investigation of native and nonnative English speakers' levels of written syntactic complexity in asynchronous online discussions. *Applied Linguistics*, *38*(1), 112–134. https://doi.org/10.1093/applin/amv012

Männikkö, I., & Husu, J. (2019). Examining teachers' adaptive expertise through personal practical theories. *Teaching and Teacher Education*, *77*, 126–137. https://doi.org/10.1016/j.tate.2018.09.016

Mantasiah, R., & Yusri, Y. (2018, June). Pay it forward model in foreign language learning to increase student's self efficacy and academic motivation. *Journal of Physics: Conference Series*, *1028*, 1–4. https://iopscience.iop.org/article/10.1088/1742-6596/1028/1/012178/pdf. https://doi.org/10.1088/1742-6596/1028/1/012178

Marcus, E. (2021, April 8). A guide to neopronouns. *New York Times*. https://www.nytimes.com/2021/04/08/style/neopronouns-nonbinary-explainer.html

Marzano, R. J. (2001). *Designing a new taxonomy of educational objectives: Experts in assessment*. Corwin Press.

Maslow, A. H. (1970). *Motivation and personality* (2nd ed.). Harper & Row.

Masters-Waage, T. C., Peters, E. K., & Reb, J. (2021). *Helping organisations excel, one breath at a time: A meditation toolkit for business leaders*. Singapore Management University. https://ink.library.smu.edu.sg/cgi/viewcontent.cgi?article=1145&context=ami

McCafferty, S. G. (2016). Dynamic Systems Theory and Sociocultural Theory: Some connections and distinctions. *Language and Sociocultural Theory, 3*(1), 83–88. https://doi.org/10.1558/lst.v3i1.30476

McGroarty, M. (1989). The benefits of cooperative learning arrangements in second language instruction. *NABE Journal, 13*(2), 127–143. https://doi.org/10.1080/08855072.1989.10668555

McSweeney, K. (2012). *Assessment for learning: From theory to practice.* A research report.

McSweeney, K. (2014). Assessment practices and their impact on home economics education in Ireland. Thesis, The University of Stirling Faculty of Education. https://dspace.stir.ac.uk/bitstream/1893/21804/1/Thesis%20Kathryn%20McSweeney.pdf

Moskowitz, G. (1978). *Caring and sharing in the foreign language class: A sourcebook of humanistic techniques.* Newbury House.

Murniati, C. T. (2008). A critique of traditional pedagogical methods in the teaching of English language skills. *CELT, 8*(1), 59–75.

Murphey, T., & Jacobs, G. M. (2000). Encouraging critical collaborative autonomy. *JALT Journal, 22,* 220–244. https://doi.org/10.37546/JALTJJ22.2-1

Murphy, P. (Ed.). (1999). *Learners, learning, and assessment.* Open University.

National Geographic Society Education Program. (1987). *The world in a candy bar.* https://scholarworks.iupui.edu/bitstream/handle/1805/3076/Worldinacandybar.pdf

Newman, F., & Holzman, L. (1993). *Lev Vygotsky: Revolutionary scientist.* Routledge.

Newton, I. (1675/2021). *Isaac Newton letter to Robert Hooke, 1675.* https://discover.hsp.org/Record/dc-9792/Description#tabnav

Nieto, S. (2013). Language, literacy, and culture: Aha! moments in personal and sociopolitical understanding. *Journal of Language and Literacy Education, 9*(1), 8–20. https://files.eric.ed.gov/fulltext/EJ1008170.pdf

Novariana, S. (2021). Improving students' writing ability through diary writing at the eighth grade of Mts Istiqlal Kubuhitu Lampung at the second semester in the academic year of 2019/2020. Doctoral dissertation, UIN Raden Intan Lampung.

Nugroho, A. R., & Wiyatmi, W. (2019, April). The effectiveness of the acrostic technique toward the poetry writing class for Grade VIII students of SMP Negeri 5 Wates. In *International Conference on Interdisciplinary Language, Literature and Education (ICILLE 2018)* (pp. 32–35). Atlantis Press. https://doi.org/10.2991/icille-18.2019.7

Nunn, D., Rissman, R., Smith, S., & Kammer, G. (2015). *The empty pot.* Capstone.

Oppenheim, C. E. (2012). Nelson Mandela and the power of Ubuntu. *Religions, 3*(2), 369–388. https://doi.org/10.3390/rel3020369

Orlick, T. (2006). *Cooperative games and sports: Joyful activities for everyone.* Human Kinetics.

Overby, L. Y., Colon, G., Espinoza, D., Kinnunen, D., Shapiro, D., & Learman, J. (1996). Structured academic controversies in the professional Physical Education classroom. *Journal of Physical Education, Recreation, and Dance, 67*(8), 30–34. https://doi.org/10.1080/07303084.1996.10604834

Palmer, P. J. (1998). *The courage to teach: Exploring the inner landscape of a teacher's life.* Jossey-Bass.

Palmer, P. J. (2004). *A hidden wholeness: The journey toward an undivided life*. Jossey-Bass.

Palonsky, S. B. (1986). *900 shows a year: A look at teaching from the teacher's side of the desk*. Random House.

Panitz, T. (1999). *Collaborative versus cooperative learning: A comparison of the two concepts which will help us understand the underlying nature of interactive learning*. https://files.eric.ed.gov/fulltext/ED448443.pdf

Pecore, J. L. (2015). From Kilpatrick's project method to project-based learning. In M. Y. Eryaman & B. C. Bruce (Eds.), *International handbook of progressive education* (pp. 155–171). Peter Lang.

Pennings, H. J., Brekelmans, M., Sadler, P., Claessens, L. C., van der Want, A. C., & van Tartwijk, J. (2018). Interpersonal adaptation in teacher-student interaction. *Learning and Instruction*, *55*, 41–57. https://doi.org/10.1016/j.learninstruc.2017.09.005

Piaget, J. (1970). *Science of education and the psychology of the child*. Orion Press.

Piaget, J. (1975). *Equilibration of cognitive structures*. University of Chicago Press.

Pica, T., & Doughty, C. (1985). The role of group work in classroom second language acquisition. *Studies in Second Language Acquisition*, 233–248. https://doi.org/10.1017/S0272263100005398

Pica, T., Kang, H. S., & Sauro, S. (2006). Information gap tasks: Their multiple roles and contributions to interaction research methodology. *Studies in Second Language Acquisition*, 301–338. https://doi.org/10.1017/S027226310606013X

Porreca, K. L. (1984). Sexism in current ESL textbooks. *TESOL Quarterly*, *18*(4), 705–724. https://doi.org/10.2307/3586584

Porter, P. A. (1983). Variations in the conversations of adult learners of English as a function of the proficiency level of the participants. Doctoral dissertation, Stanford University.

Power, A., & Wilson, A. (2019). Mentor, coach, teacher, role model: What's in a name? *British Journal of Midwifery*, *27*(3), 184–187. https://doi.org/10.12968/bjom.2019.27.3.184

Procházka, J., Ovcari, M., & Durinik, M. (2020). Sandwich feedback: The empirical evidence of its effectiveness. *Learning and Motivation*, *71*, 101649. https://doi.org/10.1016/j.lmot.2020.101649

Putnam, R. D. (2000). *Bowling alone: The collapse and revival of American community*. Simon & Schuster. https://doi.org/10.1145/358916.361990

Quote Investigator. (2010). *Not everything that counts can be counted*. https://quoteinvestigator.com/2010/05/26/everything-counts-einstein/

Rakab, M. B. (2021). The use of L1 metalanguage in L2 classrooms: The case for Arabic. *Journal of English Language Teaching and Applied Linguistics*, *3*(7), 60–69. https://doi.org/10.32996/jeltal.2021.3.7.5

Renandya, W. A., Ivone, F. M., & Hidayati, M. (2021). Extensive reading: Top ten implementation issues. *JACET Journal*, *65*, 11–21. https://willyrenandya.com/extensive-reading-top-ten-implementation-issues

Reynolds, M. (2021). Pokémon Go medals list, all platinum medals and catch bonus explained. *Eurogamer*. https://www.eurogamer.net/articles/pokemon-go-catch-bonus-medals-list-platinum-medals-7002

Richards, J. C., & Rodgers, T. S. (1986). *Approaches and methods in language teaching*. Cambridge University Press.

Richards, J. C., & Rodgers, T. S. (2014). *Approaches and methods in language teaching* (3rd ed.). Cambridge University Press.

Rios-Salas, V. (2017). *The role of formal child support in children's academic achievement*. Institute for Research on Poverty, University of Wisconsin-Madison. https://www.irp. wisc.edu/wp/wp-content/uploads/2019/10/CS-2016-2018-T9A.pdf

Rivers, W. P. (1976). *Speaking in many tongues: Essays in foreign language teaching* (2nd ed.). Newbury House.

Robb, T. (2018). An introduction to online sites for extensive reading. *TESL-EJ, 22*(1), 1–16. https://tesl-ej.org/~teslejor/pdf/ej85/int.pdf

Robinson, P. (Ed.). (2002). *Individual differences and instructed language learning*. Benjamins. https://doi.org/10.1075/lllt.2

Robson, D. (2017, November 7). 12 animals walks to help calm kids and get them moving. https://www.cbc.ca/parents/learning/view/12-animals-walks-for-kids-to-get-moving

Rodriguez, V. (2012). The teaching brain and the end of the empty vessel. *Mind, Brain, and Education, 6*(4), 177–185. https://doi.org/10.1111/j.1751-228X.2012.01155.x [12]

Rogers, C. R. (1979). The foundations of the person-centered approach. *Education, 100*(2), 98–107.

Rogers, C. R. (1983). *Freedom to learn for the 80s*. Merrill Publishing.

Rogoff, B., Matusov, E., & White, C. (1996). Models of teaching and learning: Participation in a community of learners. In D. R. Olsen & N. Torrance (Eds.), *The handbook of education and human development* (pp. 388–414). Wiley.

Ron, G., Dreyfus, T., & Hershkowitz, R. (2010). Partially correct constructs illuminate students' inconsistent answers. *Educational Studies in Mathematics, 75*(1), 65–87. https://doi.org/10.1007/s10649-010-9241-x

Rose, H., & Galloway, N. (2017). Debating standard language ideology in the classroom: Using the 'Speak Good English Movement' to raise awareness of global Englishes. *RELC Journal, 48*(3), 294–301. https://doi.org/10.1177/0033688216684281

Rose, T. (2016, January 16). When the U.S. Airforce discovered the flaw of averages. *Toronto Star*. https://www.thestar.com/news/insight/2016/01/16/when-us-air-force-discovered-the-flaw-of-averages.html

Roy, S., & Clark, D. (2019). Digital badges, do they live up to the hype? *British Journal of Educational Technology, 50*(5), 2619–2636. https://doi.org/10.1111/bjet.12709

Russell, J. A. E. (2014, January 12). Career coach: The power of using people's names. *Washington Post*. https://www.washingtonpost.com/business/capitalbusiness/career-coach-the-power-of-using-a-name/2014/01/10/8ca03da0-787e-11e3-8963-b4b654bcc9b2_story.html

Sadlier, S. T. (2016). La Parte Chusca of a pedagogical here and now: Oaxacan teachers' heteroglossic joking about state repression and educational reform. *Journal of Latinos and Education, 15*(4), 320–332. https://doi.org/10.1080/15348431.2015.1134534

Sadriyeva, G. S. K. (2021). Language learning strategy use: Do extroversion and introversion impact learners' preferences. *Academic Research in Educational*

Sciences, *2*(3). https://cyberleninka.ru/article/n/language-learning-strategy-use-do-extroversion-and-introversion-impact-learners-lls-preferences/viewer

Sampson, J. P., Osborn, D. S., Bullock-Yowell, E., Lenz, J. G., Peterson, G. W., Reardon, R. C., ... & Saunders, D. E. (2020). *Introduction to cognitive information processing theory, research, and practice.* Florida State University. https://doi.org/10.33009/fsu.1593091156

Sandel, M. J. (2020). *The tyranny of merit: What's become of the common good?* Farrer, Straus, and Giraux.

Schippers, M. C., Morisano, D., Locke, E. A., Scheepers, A. W., Latham, G. P., & de Jong, E. M. (2020). Writing about personal goals and plans regardless of goal type boosts academic performance. *Contemporary Educational Psychology, 60,* 101823. https://doi.org/10.1016/j.cedpsych.2019.101823

Schmuck, R. A. (2006). *Practical action research for change.* Corwin Press.

Seligman, M. E. (2012). *Flourish: A visionary new understanding of happiness and well-being.* Simon and Schuster.

Seligman, M. E., & Csikszentmihalyi, M. (2000). Positive psychology: An introduction. *American Psychologist, 55*(1), 5–14. https://doi.org/10.1037/0003-066X.55.1.5

Sever, R. (2016). Preparing for a future of diversity: A conceptual framework for planning and evaluating multicultural educational colleges. *Malta Review for Educational Research, 10*(1), 23–49.

Sharan, S. (1980). Cooperative learning in small groups: Recent methods and effects on achievement, attitudes and ethnic relations. *Review of Educational Research, 50,* 241–271. https://doi.org/10.3102/00346543050002241

Sharan, S. (Ed.). (1999). *Handbook of cooperative learning methods.* Greenwood.

Sharan, Y., & Sharan, S. (1992). *Expanding cooperative learning through group investigation.* Teachers College Press.

Sharan, Y., & Sharan, S. (1999). Group investigation in the cooperative classroom. In S. Sharan (Ed.), *Handbook of cooperative learning methods* (pp. 97–114). Greenwood.

Shen, Y., Sun, S., Hua, S., Shen, E., Ye, C. Y., Cai, D., ... & Fan, L. (2017). Analysis of transcriptional and epigenetic changes in hybrid vigor of allopolyploid *Brassica napus* uncovers key roles for small RNA s. *The Plant Journal, 91*(5), 874–893. https://doi.org/10.1111/tpj.13605

Shor, I. (1992). *Empowering education: Critical teaching for social change.* University of Chicago Press. https://doi.org/10.7208/chicago/9780226147864.001.0001

Shulman, L. S., & Sherin, M. G. (2004). Fostering communities of teachers as learners: Disciplinary perspectives. *Journal of Curriculum Studies, 36*(2), 135–140. https://doi.org/10.1080/0022027032000135049

Simon, B. (1999). Why no pedagogy in England? In J. Leach & B. Moon (Eds.), *Learners and pedagogy* (pp. 10–24). Sage Publications.

Sipman, G., Thölke, J., Martens, R., & McKenney, S. (2019). The role of intuition in pedagogical tact: Educator views. *British Educational Research Journal, 45*(6), 1186–1202. https://doi.org/10.1002/berj.3557

Siu, E. (2021). *The next 40,000 hours.* New Degree Press.

Skinner, B. F. (1953). *Science and human behavior*. Simon & Schuster.

Slavin, R. E. (1995). *Cooperative learning: Theory, research, and practice* (2nd ed.). Prentice Hall.

Slavin, R. E. (2011). Instruction based on cooperative learning. In R. E. Mayer & P. A. Alexander (Eds.), *Handbook of research on learning and instruction* (pp. 358–374). Routledge. https://doi.org/10.4324/9780203839089-26

Sloan, S. (1992). *The complete ESL/EFL cooperative & communicative activity book: Learner directed activities for the classroom*. National Textbook Company.

Smagorinsky, P. (1996). Multiple intelligences, multiple means of composing: An alternative way of thinking about learning. *NASSP Bulletin, 80*(583), 11–17.

Smidt, E., Chau, M. H., Rinehimer, E., & Leever, P. (2021). Exploring engagement of users of Global Englishes in a community of inquiry. *System*. https://doi.org/10.1016/j.system.2021.102477

Standage, M., Cumming, S. P., & Gillison, F. B. (2013). A cluster randomized controlled trial of the best you can be intervention: Effects on the psychological and physical well-being of school children. *BMC Public Health, 13*(1), 1–10. https://doi.org/10.1186/1471-2458-13-666

Stenger, M. (2014). 5 research-based tips for providing students with feedback. *Edutopia*. https://www.edutopia.org/blog/tips-providing-students-meaningful-feedback-marianne-stenger

Sutherland, A. (2019, October 17). What Shamu taught me about a happy marriage. *New York Times*. https://www.nytimes.com/2019/10/11/style/modern-love-what-shamu-taught-me-happy-marriage.html

Swain, M. (1993). The output hypothesis: Just speaking and writing aren't enough. *The Canadian Modern Language Review, 50*, 158–164. https://doi.org/10.3138/cmlr.50.1.158

Swain, M. (2000). The output hypothesis and beyond: Mediating acquisition through collaborative dialogue. In J. P. Lantolf (Ed.), *Sociocultural theory and second language learning* (pp. 97–114). Oxford University Press.

Swann, C., Rosenbaum, S., Lawrence, A., Vella, S. A., McEwan, D., & Ekkekakis, P. (2021). Updating goal-setting theory in physical activity promotion: A critical conceptual review. *Health Psychology Review, 15*(1), 34–50. https://doi.org/10.1080/17437199.2019.1706616

Sylvia, M. A. V., & Saroja, D. M. M. (2019). Social competence of prospective teachers: An imperative skill for effective teaching. *International Educational Scientific Research Journal, 5*(9), 110–114.

Szűcs, I. Z. (2018). Teacher trainers' self-reflection and self-evaluation. *Acta Educationis Generalis, 8*(2), 9–23. https://doi.org/10.2478/atd-2018-0008

Tabibnia, G., & Lieberman, M. D. (2007). Fairness and cooperation are rewarding: Evidence from social cognitive neuroscience. *Annals of the New York Academy of Sciences, 1118*(1), 90–101. https://doi.org/10.1196/annals.1412.001

Tamah, S. M. (2017). *Pernak-pernik kerja kelompok berbasis pembelajaran kooperatif* [*The nuts and bolts of cooperative learning oriented group work*]. Widya Mandala Catholic University Surabaya.

Tamah, S. M. (2020). Making formative tests more genuine. *The International Journal of Interdisciplinary Educational Studies, 15*(2), 73–81. https://doi.org/10.18848/2327-011X/CGP/v15i02/73-81

Tamah, S. M., & Prijambodo, L. (2014). *Metode asesmen berbasis pembelajaran kooperatif* [*Assessment in cooperative learning: A research report*]. Widya Mandala Catholic University Surabaya. http://repository.wima.ac.id/4496/

Tamah, S. M., & Prijambodo, L. (2015). *Model asesmen pembelajaran kooperatif: Strategi menjawab tantangan* [*Models of cooperative learning assessment: Strategies to respond to challenges*]. Revka Petra Media. http://repository.wima.ac.id/4138/

Tamah, S. M., & Wirjawan, J. V. (2018). *Kerja kelompok ber-struktur++: Pelaksanaan dan asesmennya. Laporan Penelitian Tahun ke-1* [*Structured++ group work: Its implementation and assessment. Year 1 research report*]. Widya Mandala Catholic University Surabaya. http://repository.wima.ac.id/16634/

Tamah, S. M., & Wirjawan, J. V. (2019). Assessment-oriented formative test. *International Journal of Innovation and Learning, 26*(1), 66–81. https://doi.org/10.1504/IJIL.2019.100521

Tarone, E. (1980). Communication strategies, foreigner talk, and repair in interlanguage. *Language Learning, 30*(2), 417–428. https://doi.org/10.1111/j.1467-1770.1980.tb00326.x

Teaching English. (n.d.). *Using graded readers*. https://www.teachingenglish.org.uk/article/using-graded-readers

Tomlinson, C. A. (1999). Mapping a route toward differentiated instruction. *Educational Leadership, 57*, 12–17. https://education.illinoisstate.edu/downloads/linc/linccurriculummodule/Tomlinson.pdf

Torres, D. G. (2019). Distributed leadership, professional collaboration, and teachers' job satisfaction in US schools. *Teaching and Teacher Education, 79*, 111–123. https://doi.org/10.1016/j.tate.2018.12.001

Ugwuanyi, C. S., Okeke, C. I., & Njeze, K. C. (2020). Parenting style and parental support on learners' academic achievement. *Journal of Sociology and Social Anthropology, 11*(3–4): 198–205. https://doi.org/10.31901/24566764.2020/11.3-4.352

UNICEF. (2018). *Malnutrition rates remain alarming: Stunting is declining too slowly while wasting still impacts the lives of far too many young children*. http://data.unicef.org/topic/nutrition/malnutrition/#

Vallance, J. K., Gardiner, P. A., Lynch, B. M., D'Silva, A., Boyle, T., Taylor, L. M., ... & Owen, N. (2018). Evaluating the evidence on sitting, smoking, and health: Is sitting really the new smoking? *American Journal of Public Health, 108*(11), 1478–1482. https://doi.org/10.2105/AJPH.2018.304649

van Leeuwen, A., & Janssen, J. (2019). A systematic review of teacher guidance during collaborative learning in primary and secondary education. *Educational Research Review, 27*, 71–89. https://doi.org/10.1016/j.edurev.2019.02.001

Vygotsky, L. S. (1978). *Mind in society*. Edited by M. Cole, V. John-Steiner, S. Scribner, & E. Souberman. Harvard University Press.

Vygotsky, L. S. (1981). The genesis of higher mental functions. In J. V. Wertsch (Ed.), *The concept of activity in Soviet psychology* (pp. 144–188). M. E. Sharpe.

Wang, J., Engelhard Jr, G., Raczynski, K., Song, T., & Wolfe, E. W. (2017). Evaluating rater accuracy and perception for integrated writing assessments using a mixed-methods approach. *Assessing Writing, 33*, 36–47. https://doi.org/10.1016/j.asw.2017.03.003

Wang, W. (2017). Using rubrics in student self-assessment: Student perceptions in the English as a foreign language writing context. *Assessment & Evaluation in Higher Education, 42*(8), 1280–1292. https://doi.org/10.1080/02602938.2016.1261993

Watson, J. D. (1968). *The Double Helix: A personal account of the discovery of the structure of DNA*. Atheneum. https://doi.org/10.1063/1.3035117

Watts, G. W., Bryant, D. P., & Carroll, M. L. (2019). Students with emotional–behavioral disorders as cross-age tutors: A synthesis of the literature. *Behavioral Disorders, 44*(3), 131–147. https://doi.org/10.1177/0198742918771914

Webb, N. M., Franke, M. L., De, T., Chan, A. G., Freund, D., Shein, P., & Melkonian, D. K. (2009). 'Explain to your partner': Teachers' instructional practices and students' dialogue in small groups. *Cambridge Journal of Education, 39*(1), 49–70. https://doi.org/10.1080/03057640802701986

Wertsch, J. V. (Ed.). (1986). *Culture, communication, and cognition: Vygotskian perspectives*. Cambridge University Press.

Wiggins, G. (1998). *Educative assessment. Designing assessments to inform and improve student performance*. Jossey-Bass.

Wiggins, G., & McTighe, J. (2005). *Understanding by design* (Expanded 2nd ed.). Association for Supervision & Curriculum Development.

Wittrock, M. C. (1974). Learning as a generative process. *Educational Psychologist, 11*(2), 87–95. https://doi.org/10.1080/00461527409529129

Wood, D. J., Bruner, J. S., & Ross, G. (1976). The role of tutoring in problem solving. *Journal of Child Psychiatry and Psychology, 17*(2), 89–100. https://doi.org/10.1111/j.1469-7610.1976.tb00381.x

World Health Organization. (2019, June 14). *Sanitation*. https://www.who.int/news-room/fact-sheets/detail/sanitation

Wright, A., Betteridge, D., & Buckby, M. (2005). *Games for language learning* (3rd ed.). Cambridge University Press. https://doi.org/10.1017/CBO9780511667145

Xiao, Y., & Hu, J. (2019). Assessment of optimal pedagogical factors for Canadian ESL learners' reading literacy through artificial intelligence algorithms. *International Journal of English Linguistics, 9*(4), 1–14. https://doi.org/10.5539/ijel.v9n4p1

Yashima, T. (2002). Willingness to communicate in a second language: The Japanese EFL context. *The Modern Language Journal, 86*(1), 54–66. https://doi.org/10.1111/1540-4781.00136

Yuliani, Y., & Lengkanawati, N. S. (2017). Project-based learning in promoting learner autonomy in an EFL classroom. *Indonesian Journal of Applied Linguistics, 7*(2), 285–293. https://doi.org/10.17509/ijal.v7i2.8131

Zainuddin, Z., Chu, S. K. W., Shujahat, M., & Perera, C. J. (2020). The impact of gamification on learning and instruction: A systematic review of empirical evidence. *Educational Research Review, 30.* https://doi.org/10.1016/j.edurev.2020.100326

Zarrinabadi, N., Lou, N. M., & Darvishnezhad, Z. (2021). To praise or not to praise? Examining the effects of ability vs. effort praise on speaking anxiety and willingness to communicate in EFL classrooms. *Innovation in Language Learning and Teaching,* 1–14. https://doi.org/10.1080/17501229.2021.1938079

Zhang, S., & Xiong, Y. (2020). Language learning beyond content: An exploratory study of higher-order thinking and digital literacy via digital book trailers in an ESL reading classroom. In B. Hokanson, G. Clinton, A. Tawfik, A. Grincewicz, & M. Schmidt (Eds.), *Educational technology beyond content* (pp. 57–69). Springer. https://doi.org/10.1007/978-3-030-37254-5_5

Zhou, L., & Li, C. (2020). Can student self-directed learning improve their academic performance? Experimental evidence from the instruction of protocol-guided learning in China's elementary and middle schools. *Science Insights Education Frontiers, 5*(1). https://ssrn.com/abstract=3549428. https://doi.org/10.15354/sief.20.ar016

Zipp, J. F. (2007). Learning by exams: The impact of two-stage cooperative tests. *Teaching Sociology, 35*(1), 62–76. https://doi.org/10.1177/0092055X0703500105

scaffolding 8, 74
seating arrangements
    circle class 63
      horseshoe class 64
      small group 65
      standard rows 61
      student-centered 65
self-esteem 10, 28, 178
Social Cognitivism 6
Social Interdependence Theory 13, 40, 146
social nature 108
social psychology 13
Sociocultural Theory 6, 8, 15, 19, 53
STAD 38, 40, 92, 100, 101, 102
SUMMER 166, 167, 168, 169, 170, 171, 175

Talking Tokens 45, 46
target language use 68
tasks 46, 96
teacher reflection groups 139
teachers as co-learners 114
team spirit 71
team-building 52, 72
Twenty Questions 74

UBUNTU 109

Write-Pair-Square 22, 45, 62, 66, 67
Write-Pair-Switch 62, 63, 68

Zone of Proximal Development 8

Authors

Abualhaija, N. 106
Achor, S. 141, 143, 144
Adams, J. M. 144
Adinolfi, S. D. 155
Ajzen, I. 135
Akcay, A. O. 46
Al Amin, M. 57
Al Ghozali, M. I. 77
Al-Bataineh, A. T. 69
Ali, H. 23
Aliyyah, R. R. 73
All About Philosophy 135
Allport, G. W. 33, 52
Allred, J. B. 92
Archambault, R. 181
Aronson, E. 33, 35, 47, 118
Arunsirot, N. 29
Au, O. T. S. 48
Auerbach, E. R. 18
Austin Community College 88

Bailenson, J. N. 38
Baker, T. 47
Bamford, J. 159
Bandura, A. 12
Barnawi, B. 77
Barr, R. B. 106
Bazzi, S. 7
Bell, A. 5
Benson, P. 24, 107
Bereiter, C. 97
Bernstein, M. S. 86
Betteridge, D. 72
Binfet, J. T. 89
Bird, M. 97
Bloom, B. S. 16, 17, 49, 50, 99
Bloomfield, R. J. 90
Blouch, K. K. 163
Bonilla, S. 7
Bossert, S. T. 28
Bourdieu, P. 154

CPSIA information can be obtained
at www.ICGtesting.com
Printed in the USA
BVHW010106071222
653533BV00003B/14